Frontier Military Series
XIII

THE "BRAVE PEACOCK"
Lieutenant General Nelson A. Miles at the apogee of his career.
Courtesy, Library of Congress

Nelson A. Miles

A Documentary Biography
of His Military Career
1861 - 1903

edited by
BRIAN C. POHANKA

in collaboration with
JOHN M. CARROLL

Foreword by
ROBERT M. UTLEY

THE ARTHUR H. CLARK COMPANY
Glendale, California   1985

Contents

Illustrations

Preface

In baseball terms General Miles could best be equated with the "clean-up hitter," for it was he who always finished what most others had begun. That fact was as true for the 1876 Sioux Campaign as it was for the Nez Perce Campaign and later the Apache Campaign where Crook had failed so miserably. And in tribute to this remarkable—and often unsung—soldier-hero, this book is devoted. It came about in the following manner.

The United States Military Academy at West Point bought the original manuscript at auction some few years ago. It was originally from the Miles Reber estate, for it carried his book plate. The typescript of the manuscript was dated March 1929, and obviously was one created by some member of the family. Miles Reber was the son of Samuel Reber who, as Lieutenant Colonel of Volunteers, was the military secretary to General Miles. He married the General's only daughter, Cecelia, in 1901. It is upon this original manuscript that the present publication is based.

In 1980, I was visiting the library at West Point, when the archivist, Robert Schnare, placed into my hands the manuscript which addressed itself, in a chronological manner, to the military career of General Nelson A. Miles. Being attracted to our frontier military history in general, and to certain individuals in particular, I studied the manuscript for a while and saw in it the raw material for a book on the gentleman. After asking for and receiving a copy of it, I returned home and there it lay until by chance I uncovered it in a pile of "things to think about doing," when I was thinking about something to do next. Once more I studied what I had and this time I noticed the manuscript did not end with the man's career, but rather long before his retirement.

That meant a tedious research project in Washington, D.C., to bring it up to date in the same format as the original document. I showed the raw data to my friend Robert Utley, who shared my admiration for General Miles, and his comment was something like: "If you ever finish it and I like it, I'll make a written contribution to it." The end result speaks for itself.

At the moment, however, I was heavily committed for about ten books and I knew I could not get around to this one on Miles until much later, and knew also I needed to be in Washington, D.C., an expensive effort at best.

Quite luckily, I had at the same time been somewhat instrumental in a book then under contract with Brian Pohanka, a careful student, a thorough researcher and certainly an admirable scholar, traits I had long ago recognized. When I approached Brian on the possibility of a collaboration, he quickly agreed and then wound up doing all the work, and so by reflection, I shall share in all his kudos for the manner in which he completed the manuscript, the natural periods into which he separated the text, and the incisive and impressive bridges which he wrote connecting all the parts into a whole.

My only contribution will have been the two poems which had been inspired by General Miles, and this Preface. The poems were included only because I felt the poetic recognition of General Miles was important. Few officers have ever elicited a single rhyme, Custer being the lone exception. Poetically they are lacking in style and in art, but the admiration for the General in them is abundantly clear, and therefore I felt they should be recorded and preserved.

That's the story of how the book came to be, but the story of its publication by the Arthur H. Clark Co. is something else. It seems they had a choice at one time between this one and one which I had submitted about Wounded Knee. Very wisely they opted for this one, and for Brian and myself, thanks for the sagacity.

JOHN M. CARROLL
Bryan, Texas

A Khaki Kick

Back there in Washington, people may stare,
Easy-chair officers sputter and swear,
Bureaucrats legislate—what do we care?
Down in the ranks we don't follow the styles;
Here's health to the General, Nelson A. Miles!

I've been readin' in the papers and I'm feelin' pretty mad
At the shabby sort of treatment that a game old soldier's had.
And the soldier I'm referrin' to, who's so surprisin' game,
Is Miles, Lieutenant General—I guess you've heard the name?

Now, the pointers that a twelve-year duty sergeant hasn't got
On the secrets of the Service, are a quite extensive lot;
But he may make observations, while a-wearin' out his shoes,
Not just in strict accordance with the War Department's views.

I've seen some bits of service of a somewhat stirrin' brand
When the West was callin' lusty for the civilizin' hand,
And, myself, I've had some practice in that missionary work
With the men who did the business, from the buttes to Albuquerq'.

They've sent some stunnin' strategists, so history records,
To show the noble red man how the Nation loves its wards,
And some was politicians, and some was soft of heart,
And some was full of ginger, but couldn't make a start.

But the man who knew his business as the king-bird knows the hawk;
Who started with the rifle and finished with the talk;
Who wouldn't stop for bluffin' when he once got started right,
Was him I'm tellin' you about—you bet he came to fight!

I know he's no West Pointer—I've a notion, what is more,
That it isn't only Pointers who may know the game of war,
And if he's a little partial to the medals on his chest
He's got a darned good right to be; he earned 'em in the West.

For I've followed him in winter through those blamed Montana snows
When the hills was stiff as granite and the very air was froze,
And seen him ridin' out in front to lead the double-quick
When the lines went into action on the banks of Rosebud Creek.

I've lurched across the Painted Plains, my temples like to burst,
And seen men suckin' out their veins to quench their burnin' thirst,
With the sky a blazin' furnace and the earth a bakin' sea,
And he was there beside us—and was just as dry as we.

Oh, hang these army politics, when jealousy and spite
Can rob a veteran of his praise, his dearest, hard-earned right!
There's just one kind of officer enlisted men can like—
The kind who keeps his bearings when the shots begin to strike.

And that's the kind that Miles has been; he never ducked or flinched;
He was always in the mix-up when the lines of battle clinched;
He's whipped out Rebs and redskins and he's made some Dagos dance,
And he's good for lots more fightin' if he ever gets the chance.
And here's the moral to this talk—I'll ask no price, but thanks:
Miles may not have a stand-in, but he's solid with the ranks!

Back there in Washington, people may stare,
Easy-chair officers sputter and swear,
Bureaucrats legislate—what do we care?
Down in the ranks we don't follow the styles;
Here's a health to the General, Nelson A. Miles!

[From *Frontier Ballads* by Joseph Mills Hanson, 1910.]

Gen. Nelson A. Miles

The flag's today at half-mast
  For Gen. Nelson Miles,
A great old Indian fighter
  Whose name is in the files.

He served with Grant and Sherman,
  Hancock, McClellan, Meade;
He helped round up the rebels
  After slaves were freed.

When Sheridan took his great ride,
  And Sherman reached the sea,
Miles had charge of Davis
  And helped to capture Lee.

He later served with Custer,
  Merritt, Lorey, Crook;
In the wars with red men
  He scouted every nook.

Some famous chiefs he captured
  In the settling up the West;
Chief Joseph and his warriors
  Were routed from their nest.

Crazy Horse and Lame Deer,
  Broad Road and Elk Horn, too;
Also there was Sitting Bull,
  The leader of the Sioux.

Then he captured Geronimo
  When Indian fights were o'er
And rounded up the stragglers
  Who would continue war.

When Spain threw down her challenge,
  He answered America's call;
He gave the best he'd in him;
  For his land he gave his all.

He lived to see the World War;
  Greeted victory with his smiles.
Taps for a great American:
  Gen. Nelson Miles!

[From *Western Poems* by Col. Charles D. "Buckskin Bill" Randolph, 1925.]

Foreword

by Robert M. Utley

For a biographer, or for anyone attracted by character and achievement in history, Nelson A. Miles presents an immensely intriguing challenge. This is because he combines a record of indisputable achievement with a personality full of unappealing traits. Characters wedding achievement to personal appeal, or dubious attainment to unlikable personality, earn our acclaim or contempt, but in the end they are far less challenging and interesting. One must be especially fascinated, therefore, and torn between admiration and revulsion, when a significant historical figure mixes positive and negative in such proportion as did Nelson A. Miles.

Miles' record, set forth in this volume in his own words and those of others he assembled, is one of the most lustrous in the military history of his era. Civil War hero—Major General and Corps Commander by age 26—most consistently successful frontier commander and Indian fighter of all in the postwar years, head of the U.S. Army in the Spanish-American War, and finally Lieutenant General and the last General-In-Chief in the army's history, Miles was conspicuously successful most of the time and when not, at least prominent and influential. Even after his retirement he remained highly visible, and finally he outlived all Civil War generals save two. His death in 1925 was both dramatic and fitting. He took his grandchildren to the circus. The band played the national anthem. He stood erectly at attention, saluting. A heart attack struck him dead.

One cannot look very deeply into this outstanding record, however, without encountering a career badly disfigured by controversy and endless discord with associates. In Nelson A. Miles vanity and ambition powered a fierce competitiveness that drove him to revel tastelessly in his own genuine abilities and successes while minimizing or denying altogether those of others. "Brave Peacock," Theodore Roosevelt called him, not inaccurately. Pompous and dogmatic as well as ambitious and competitive, a shameless influence-peddler even in a time of widespread influence-peddling, he is a classic study in warped personality obscuring notable achievement.

It is therefore curious that Miles has escaped biographical treatment that thoughtfully probes the interplay of personality and achievement. He is a prime candidate for serious biography, especially since a considerable body of source material exists. Until such a work appears, however, we must be content with Miles' own memoirs (twice done, in fact), one well-written but uncritical biography, and, in this volume, Miles' compilation of his service record as filled out by Brian Pohanka. We are indebted to Pohanka, to John M. Carroll, and to the Arthur H. Clark Company for making available this further contribution to our knowledge of a complicated and fascinating man and his remarkable career.

Ten-year-old Nelson Miles
already projected self-confidence
tinged with arrogance.
Courtesy, Massachusetts Commandery,
Military Order of the Loyal Legion of
the United States. U.S. Army Military
History Institute.

The young lieutenant of the
22nd Mass. Miles at the outset
of his military career.
Courtesy Massachusetts Commandery,
as cited in above illustration.

I

A Career Begins

Nelson Appleton Miles was born August 8, 1839 in a small white frame farmhouse near the village of Westminster, Massachusetts, located seven miles from the larger manufacturing town of Fitchburg. His father, Daniel Miles, was a hard-working farmer who periodically engaged in the lumber business, with varying success; his mother, Mary Curtis Miles, was a stolid country woman, active in the local Baptist Church.

General Miles looked back on his rural childhood as an ideal preparation for the rigors of a military life. Held on his father's saddle as an infant, by age six he owned his own horse. Fond of the outdoors, when not busy with his farm chores, he delighted in swimming, hunting, ice-skating and sledding. Miles was never much of a scholar; one of his classmates at the local school recalled, "The study in which he seemed to take most delight was fighting."[1] In 1899 another boyhood acquaintance told how Miles had once defended a younger schoolmate from a crowd of bullies: "Aren't you ashamed of yourselves to tease a small boy, half your size, who is a total stranger here, and because his father is poor, cannot wear good clothes as the rest of you? All I have to say to you is, don't tease or touch him again during this term of school, for if you do, you touch me."[2] While this story may be apocryphal, it has the ring of truth in Miles' defensive pride of his own humble origins. This sensitivity about his middle class background, coupled with his lack of a college degree would in later years lead Miles to distrust politicians of the economic aristocracy and officers with a West Point education.

At age 16, having graduated from Professor John R. Galt's

---

[1] Boston *Sunday Post*, March 19, 1899, p. 17.
[2] Fitchburg *Sentinel*, March 24, 1899, p. 1.

Westminster Academy, Miles left his home town for Boston, where from 1855 to 1861 he was employed as a clerk in John Collomare's crockery store. Though most of his time was taken up in the mundane affairs of a small business, he managed to indulge his fondness for militaria as a member of the Salignac Drill Club, an informal corps of instruction run by an ex-Colonel of the French Army. In addition, he was not oblivious to the increasingly vehement political controversies that would bring the nation to a civil war. Having listened to the impassioned oratory of Charles Sumner and William Lloyd Garrison, Miles shared the anti-slavery sentiments prevalent in Boston.

There is every reason to believe that Nelson Miles welcomed the opportunities which war offered him. From the moment that he set about raising a company for the 22nd Massachusetts Regiment, to the surrender of Lee's army at Appomattox, he exulted in the knowledge that the profession of soldier was one at which he excelled. Indeed, Miles was one of several young men in their twenties—Wesley Merritt, George Armstrong Custer, Emory Upton, James Harrison Wilson, Ranald Slidell Mackenzie—who through dash, tenacity and personal bravery became invaluable to their superiors, Grant, Sherman and Sheridan.

Miles' career began with the bitter lesson of seeing his commission as captain revoked in order to place a political crony of the governor in that position. Through the course of the war, though his undenied merits on the battlefield won him his commission, he also began to display a trait that in later years would find him unabashedly lobbying for promotion using press, family connections and patronage to that end. Recovering from a severe wound received at Chancellorsville, Colonel Miles met with Senator Henry Wilson of Massachusetts, sponsor of the 22nd Massachusetts, and on August 12, 1863, pressured the Senator to obtain a Brigadier Generalcy for him:

> Can any officer bear better testimonials? There must be many vacancies, there are at least many *vacant places*. In this Army Corps there are but four General officers on duty. You kindly aided me once before to a *position* which was of much benefit to me, and has my record during the past two years repaid you? You can now assist

me to one higher grade of rank which will enable me to accomplish much more. And I promise the future shall equal the past.[3]

Ultimately the men who stood by young Miles and furthered his career were his superiors and comrades in the Army of the Potomac. In November of 1863, Brigadier General Francis Channing Barlow wrote Senator Wilson in another attempt to give the Colonel a star. In his enumeration of Miles' strengths, Barlow touched on many of those attributes that would characterize his later Indian campaigns:

> He is a man of untiring & sleepless energy who does not want to be told to do a thing, or when & how to do it, but who uses all the means in his power to attain success without waiting to be urged or quickened by anyone. If you send him with a body of troops to accomplish a certain purpose you know that he will do all that under the circumstances skill, determination & courage can do. To anyone who knows the habit of many military officers of fearing to take any responsibility & of sending at every step for orders & directions & of only doing just enough to escape censure or to obtain a reasonable degree of commendation, what I have said of Col. Miles will appear as high praise.
>
> He has also a remarkable talent for fighting battles. It is not only that he is very brave (for most officers are that) but he has that perfect coolness and self-possession in danger which is much more uncommon. The sound of cannon clears his head & strengthens his nerves.
>
> And his quickness of perception & skill in taking up positions & availing himself of advantages of ground & etc. in action I have not seen equalled. To all this he adds in an unusual degree the faculty of attracting men to him & arousing their pride & enthusiasm without relaxing discipline.
>
> In short I hardly know a military merit or quality (short of those higher powers of strategical combination whose presence he has yet had no opportunity to test or exhibit) which he does not possess...I think he is an unusual instance of military ability which ought to be brought out & encouraged.[4]

[3]Nelson A. Miles to Senator Henry Wilson, Aug. 12, 1863. Nelson A. Miles, CB File, M 1064, W 257-CB 1870, Roll 525, Nat. Arch.

[4]Letter of Francis Channing Barlow to Henry Wilson, Nov. 28, 1863. Miles/ Cameron Papers, Lby. of Cong.

Major General Winfield Scott Hancock, pre-eminent corps commander in the Army, echoed Barlow's assessment in his own comments to Miles:

> I have never met an officer in whose hands I would rather trust a Regiment, Brigade or Division in a campaign or on the field of battle than in yourself. I know of no commander from whom I would expect greater results in a campaign or battle, with either of those commands.
>
> For organizing, governing and commanding troops, I consider that you have high merit.
>
> You were always temperate, willing and anxious to perform difficult and dangerous service, and in the most trying times. I have never known you to be without resources, or to feel that hope was gone.
>
> My opinion of your faithful service is such that would I have a large command in the field, I would apply for you as one of my Lieutenants. And from none would I expect greater results.[5]

With recommendations such as these, Miles was assured a place in the post-war Regular Army; it would have been hard to ignore an ambitious 25-year-old Major General with such credentials.

---

[5]Letter of Winfield Scott Hancock to Nelson A. Miles, Dec. 15, 1866. Miles/Cameron Papers, Lby. of Cong.

A
Synopsis of Military Operations
and
Data of Rank and Command

with
Special Reference to the Military Record
of
Lieutenant General Nelson A. Miles, U.S. Army

from
the Commencement of the War of the Rebellion in
1861 to
the Concentration of Troops in the City of
Chicago in 1894, for the Purpose of Protecting
Life and Property and for the Maintenance
of Civil Law and Order.

(For a continuation of Military Operations
see Annual Reports of the Commanding
General of the Army from
1894 to 1903)*

---

*The Annual Reports of the Commanding General of the Army have been included in this work. Ed.

DATE OF RANK AND COMMAND, &c
NELSON APPLETON MILES

Captain Twenty-Second Mass. Inf., Sept. 9, 1861. (Honorably
mustered out, May 31, 1862.)
Lieut. Colonel Sixty-first New York Infantry, May 31, 1862.
Colonel Sixty-first New York Infantry, Sept. 30, 1862.
Brig. General Volunteers, May 12, 1864.
   Accepted, June 27, 1864.
Bvt. Major General Volunteers, August 25, 1864.
Major General Volunteers, October 21, 1865.
Colonel 40th U.S. Infantry, July 28, 1866.
Colonel 5th U.S. Infantry (transferred March 15, 1869, to date
July 28, 1866. Reorganization of Infantry.)
(In Command of the Military District of Fort Monroe, Va., from
May 21, 1865 to August 31, 1866.)
Brig. General by Brevet, March 2, 1867.
Major General by Brevet, March 2, 1867.

U.S.A.

Brigadier General—December 15, 1880.
Major General—April 5, 1890.
Lieutenant General—June 6, 1900.
   Sec. 2 of the Act of Congress approved June 6, 1900, making
appropriations for the support of the Military Academy for the
fiscal year ending June 30, 1901, and for other purposes provides:
"That the senior major general of the line commanding the
Army shall have the rank pay and allowances of a lieutenant-
general, and his personal staff shall have the rank pay and
allowances authorized for the staff of the lieutenant-general."
Per. G.O. 100. War Dept. A.G.O. Washington, Oct. 4, 1873.
   "Colonel Nelson A. Miles, appointed President of Board to
adopt plan for the building of a military prison: to frame
regulations for the government of the prisoners, &c. By the order
of the Sec. of War, E.D. Townsend, Adjutant General." Relieved by G.O. 108, Hd.Qrs. Army, A.G.O., Washington, Nov. 22,
1876.

Detailed on recruiting service per G.O. 43, June 27, 1878, as Superintendent. Relieved at his own request per G.O. 63, Aug. 27, 1878.

Appointed President of Equipment Board by S.O. 244, Nov. 11, 1878, and S.O. 266, Dec. 11, 1878. (See G.O. 76 of 1879, page 33.)

G.O. No. 37, Hdqrs. Army, A.G.O., Washington, April 20, 1881.

"11. Appointment—General Officers—Colonel Nelson A. Miles of the Fifth Infantry to be Brigadier General, Dec. 15, 1880, vice Ord. retired from active service. Commissions vacated by new appointment: by Brigadier General Nelson A. Miles—his commission of Colonel, Fifth Infantry, Dec. 18, 1880, the date of his acceptance."

IN COMMAND OF THE DEPARTMENT OF COLUMBIA

(Assumed command August 2, 1881—Relinquished command July 8, 1885.)

Per. G.O. No. 84, Hdqrs. of the Army, A.G.O., Washington, Dec. 18, 1880, "The President directs the following orders to be issued..." [Par. VI] "Brigadier General N.A. Miles is assigned to the command of the Department of the Columbia."

IN COMMAND OF THE DEPARTMENT OF THE MISSOURI

(Assumed command July 12, 1885. Relinquished command April 7, 1886.)

Per G.O. No. 75, Hdqrs. of the Army, A.G.O., Washington, July 10, 1885, "1. By direction of the President, Brigadier General Nelson A. Miles is relieved of the command of the Department of the Columbia and assigned to the command of the Department of the Missouri."

IN COMMAND OF THE DEPARTMENT OF ARIZONA

(Assumed command April 12, 1886. Relinquished command Nov. 23, 1888.)

Per G.O. No. 15, Hdqrs. of the Army, A.G.O., Washington, April 2, 1886. "By direction of the President the following changes of and assignment to command are ordered. . . Brigadier General Nelson A. Miles is relieved from the command of the Department of the Missouri and assigned to the command of the Department of Arizona. He will turn over the command of the Department of the Missouri to the senior officer on duty in that department."

In Command of the Division of the Pacific
and Department of California

(Assumed command Nov. 23, 1888. Relinquished command Sept.1, 1890.)

Per G.O. No. 97, Hdqrs. of the Army, A.G.O., Washington, Nov. 14, 1888. "By direction of the President the following changes of and assignment to command are ordered: Brigadier General Nelson A. Miles is relieved from the command of the Department of Arizona and assigned to the command of the Division of the Pacific and Department of California."

Per G.O. No. 46, Hdqrs. of the Army, A.G.O., Washington, April 22, 1890. "Appointments—General Officers. Brigadier General Nelson A. Miles to be Major General, April 5, 1890, vice Crook, deceased." (Vacated Commission as Brigadier General April 14, 1890.)

In Command of the Division of the Missouri

(Assumed command Sept. 15, 1890. Relinquished command July 10, 1891.)

Per G.O. No. 84, Hdqrs. of the Army, A.G.O., Washington, August 8, 1890. "By direction of the President the following changes of and assignments to command are ordered to take effect Sept. 1st next. . . 2d. Major General Nelson A. Miles is assigned to the command of the Division of the Missouri comprising the Departments of the Dakota and the Platte."

In Command of the Department of the Missouri

(Assumed command July 10, 1891. Relinquished command Nov. 14, 1894.)

Per G.O. No. 57, Hdqrs. of the Army, A.G.O., Washington, July 3, 1891. "The President directs that the military geographical divisions be discontinued and that the following assignments be made: ...Major General Nelson A. Miles assigned to the command of the Department of the Missouri, which will embrace the States of Michigan, Wisconsin, Indiana, Illinois, Missouri, Kansas and Arkansas, and Oklahoma and Indian Territories; headquarters at Chicago, Illinois."

IN COMMAND OF THE DEPARTMENT OF THE EAST

(Assumed command Nov. 20, 1894. Relinquished command Oct. 4, 1895.)

Per G.O. No. 60, Hdqrs. of the Army, A.G.O., Washington, Nov. 10, 1894. "By direction of the President the following changes of and assignments to command are ordered: ...Major General Nelson A. Miles is relieved from the command of the Department of the Missouri and assigned to the command of the Department of the East."

IN COMMAND OF THE ARMY OF THE UNITED STATES
AS MAJOR GENERAL

(Assumed command Oct. 5, 1895, to June 6, 1900.)

Per G.O. No. 53, War Department, Washington, Oct. 2, 1895. "By direction of the President, Major General Nelson A. Miles is assigned to the command of the Army of the United States."

IN COMMAND OF THE ARMY OF THE UNITED STATES
WITH THE RANK OF LIEUTENANT GENERAL FROM JUNE 6, 1900

COMMISSIONS CONFERRED FOR DISTINGUISHED SERVICES, BREVET RANK AND MEDAL OF HONOR

Brigadier General of Volunteers, May 12, 1864. "For distinguished services during the recent battles of the Old Wilderness and Spottsylvania Court House, Virginia."

Bvt. Brig. Gen., Mar. 2, 1867. "Gallant and meritorious services in the battle of Chancellorsville, Va."

Bvt. Maj. Genl., Mar. 2, 1867. "Gallant and meritorious services in the battle of Spottsylvania, Virginia."

Bvt. Gen. Vols., Aut. 25, 1864. "Highly meritorious and distinguished conduct throughout the Campaign, and particularly for gallantry and valuable services in the battle of Ream's Station, Virginia."

Medal of Honor. "For distinguished gallantry in the battle of Chancellorsville, Virginia, May 3d, 1863, while holding with his command a line of abatis and rifle pits against a strong force of the enemy until severely wounded; while Colonel 61st New York Volunteers, commanding the line of skirmishers in front of the 1st Division, 2nd Army Corps."

MILITARY RECORD OF NELSON APPLETON MILES

Born in Westminster, Massachusetts, August 8, 1839.

Enrolled as Capt. Co. "E" 22d Massachusetts Vols., Sept. 9, 1861.

Mustered in October 5, 1861 as: (Captain 22d Mass. Inf. to date Sept. 9, 1861.) (First Lieut. 22d Massachusetts Infantry.)[6]

Left Boston October 8th, 1861, and joined the Army of the Potomac at Washington, D.C. Regiment Brigaded in Porter's[7] Division, and encamped on Hall's Hill. Remained with regiment but a short time.

Detailed on staff of General Silas Casey[8] November 6, 1861, by order of General George B. McClellan.

Appointed Aide-de-Camp on the staff of Brigadier General O. O. Howard,[9] Commanding 1st Brigade, 1st Division, Second Army Corps, Army of the Potomac, to date from November 9th, 1861.

ENGAGED IN SCOUTING

February 4, 1862, under instructions from Division Head-quarters, made a scout with a detail composed of cavalry and infantry, 2 officers and 70 enlisted men, from Camp California on the Fairfax road 5 miles from Vienna, about 8 miles beyond Annandale on the Braddock road for the purpose of capturing a certain spy; captured two of the enemy's scouts, obtained important information and located the enemy's cavalry and picket line.

---

[6]Miles was commissioned and mustered in as Captain of Company E, 22nd Mass. (The Brewer Guard of Roxbury) on September 9, 1861. On the muster-in-roles, his age is given as 22, his residence Roxbury, and his occupation "salesman." His commission as Captain was cancelled by order of Governor Andrew on October 7, on which day Miles was commissioned 1st Lt. of Company E. By this act of political favoritism, William L. Coggswell became the new Captain.

[7]Thirty-nine year-old Brig. Gen. Fitz-John Porter, a graduate of United States Military Academy Class of 1845. A favorite of Army Commander George B. McClellan, his 1862 court-martial would be a cause celebre.

[8]Brig. Gen. Silas Casey, 54 (USMA 1826), perhaps best known as the author of *Infantry Tactics*, adopted by the Government in 1862. Gen. Casey asked for Miles, knowing that Gen. Howard wished to offer the Lieutenant a position on his staff.

[9]Thirty-one-year-old Col. Oliver Otis Howard (USMA 1854), 3rd Maine, had recently been appointed a Brig. General. Brave, pious and self-righteous, Howard could little foresee the checkered course of his career and the part that the impetuous Miles would play in it. Although their relationship would eventually become strained at best, at the start Howard took a brotherly interest in young Miles.

GENERAL CALDWELL AND STAFF, 1862
Soon after distinguishing himself at the Battle of Fair Oaks,
a bearded Lieutenant Miles stands at left as part of the staff of
Brigadier General John C. Caldwell (center) in June 1862.
Courtesy, Library of Congress.

Colonel Nelson A. Miles, 61st New
York. Miles was severely wounded
at Fredricksburg and Chancellors-
ville while in command of the 61st.
Carte-de-visite, circa 1863.
From the collection of the editor.

Brevet Major General
Nelson Miles, circa 1864
Courtesy, Henry Deeks

Miles received his Brevet
Major General rank
August 25, 1864
Courtesy, National Archives

In the Peninsular Campaign

As 1st Lieutenant 22d Mass. Infantry & Aide-de-Camp to Major General O.O. Howard. In siege of Yorktown April 5 to May 4, 1862, and Battle of Williamsburg May 5th.

Battle of Fair Oaks

In the Battle of Fair Oaks, or Seven Pines, June 1, 1862, and commanding the left wing of the 81st Pennsylvania Infantry, after Colonel Miller was killed. Miles was wounded in the foot,[10] and had his horse wounded. Referred to in General Howard's report at follows:

> I learned that Colonel Miller, 81st Pennsylvania Vols. was killed at the first fire of the enemy and that the right and left wings of that regiment had become separated and that one wing was without a field officer. I directed Lieutenant Miles, my Aide-de-Camp, to collect the companies of that wing and to make the best disposition of it he could. He continued with it during the day in the open field on the right of the railroad and checked the advance of the enemy in that direction... I am much indebted to the members of my staff for the assistance which they rendered me during the day. They were all brave in the face of the enemy, and each one of them cheerfully and faithfully performed his duties... Lieutenant Miles, Aide-de-Camp, as before remarked, commanded the left wing of the eighty-first Pennsylvania in a manner to my entire satisfaction and approval. He was wounded in the foot.

Referred to in Brigadier General Richardson's[11] report as follows: "During the whole of this severe and hotly contested battle I was ably assisted by all three of my Brigadiers with their staff, and among these staffs I would particularly mention as worthy of distinction... on the staff of General Howard... Lieutenant Miles (A.D.C.) wounded."

Acting Assistant Adjutant General on the staff of Brigadier General John C. Caldwell,[12] 1st Brigade, Richardson's Division 2nd Army Corps A. of P. June 5, 1862, to July 2, 1862.

---

[10]The wound was painful, but not serious—the bullet grazing his heel. At about the same time, Gen. Howard received the wound which would cost him his right arm.

[11]Forty-six-year-old Brig. Gen. Israel "Dick" Richardson (USMA 1841), soon to be promoted Major General.

[12]Caldwell, 28, was a Professor in Maine before the war. He would later command the famous 1st Division Second Corps, the "fightingest" division in the Army of the Potomac.

In the Seven Day's Battles

In the Seven Day's Battles: engaged at Peach Orchard or Allen's Farm and Battle of Savage Station June 29th, 1862; White Oak Swamp Bridge and Charles City Cross Roads; Glendale or Nelson's Farm June 30th, and Malvern Hill, July 1st. Specially mentioned by Brigadier General John C. Caldwell in his report as follows:

> Of Captain Miles I cannot speak in terms of sufficient praise. His activity was incessant. On Sunday he volunteered to cut a road through the woods from Allen's Farm to Savage Station, and collecting axmen from various regiments soon made a road practicable for Artillery, which was undoubtedly the means of saving three batteries. On Monday he most vigorously seconded my efforts, and on Tuesday although he was my only staff officer, I sent him to General Sumner[13] for re-enforcements which duty he performed in the most speedy and successful manner. Near the close of the engagement he conducted and placed a piece of artillery on the left, which by sending a shower of canister silenced a very effective musketry fire of the enemy. During the whole movement his services have been to me invaluable.

Colonel Barlow in his report remarks:

> If I may be permitted to speak of an officer not under my command, I desire to speak in terms of admiration of the good behavior of Captain N. A. Miles, Acting Assistant Adjutant General on the staff of General Caldwell. Captain Miles sought us out on Monday night, and in person brought us re-enforcements when under heavy fire. On Tuesday night he came repeatedly down into the field to look after our welfare and finally by much exertion succeeded in bringing down to our assistance a piece of artillery, which by a fire of grape succeeded in checking the fire of the enemy. I feel that both regiments under my command (81st Penn. & 61st N.Y.) are much indebted to Captain Miles.[14]

Referring to the battle of Charles City Cross Roads, Brigadier

---

[13] Maj. Gen. Edwin Vose Sumner, commanding the Second Corps. At age 64 he was the oldest active corps commander in the Civil War. He died March 21, 1863.

[14] Francis Channing Barlow, 26-year-old Colonel of the 61st N.Y. would become one of the great "boy generals" of the Civil War. A Harvard graduate and lawyer with no formal military training, he enlisted as a Private and by war's end held the rank of Major General. Barlow was a stern disciplinarian and cordially disliked by the enlisted men; however, his bravery and tactical skill in the field of battle were undisputed. So impressed was Barlow by Miles' conduct that he procured for the young staff officer the Lieutenant-Colonelcy of his

General Philip Kearny[15] states in his report of the battle which he remarks was "one of the most desperate of the war, the one the most fatal if lost;" "The 81st Penn. then nobly responded to my orders gallantly led by Lieut. Col. Connor and Captain Miles of General Caldwell's staff, dashed over the parapet, pursued, charged and with a few vigorous volleys finished the battle at 9:30 at night."

BATTLE OF ANTIETAM

In the Maryland Campaign as (Lieut. Col. 61st N.Y. Inf. 1st Brigade, 1st Div. 2d Army Corps, Army of the Potomac).

In the battle of Antietam September 17, 1862, commanding the Sixty-First and Sixty-Fourth New York Infantry regiments in the battle, after Colonel Barlow was wounded and especially mentioned in the official reports of the battle as follows: By Colonel Barlow:

> Lieut. Col. Nelson A. Miles, 61st New York Volunteers has been distinguished for his admirable conduct in many battles. The voice of every one who saw him in this action will commend better than I can his courage, his quickness, his skill in seeing favorable positions and the power of his determined spirit in leading on and inspiring the men.

Brigadier General John C. Caldwell, Commanding the Brigade says: "Of Lieut. Col. Miles it is perhaps sufficient praise to say that he added to the laurels he has acquired on every battlefield where he has been present. After the fall of Colonel Barlow he managed his two regiments in a masterly manner." Especially mentioned by Brigadier General Winfield Scott Hancock,[16]

---

own 61st N.Y., which position he assumed on July 10, 1862. From this time until his death in 1896, "Frank" Barlow was a close friend and ally, usually preaching moderation to his former protege. In 1887, when both men were middle-aged, Barlow would write: "Learn wisdom my boy, from your old father." [Francis C. Barlow to Brig. Gen. Nelson A. Miles, March 24, 1887. Miles/Cameron Papers, Library of Congress.]

[15] One-armed General Kearny commanded a division in the Third Corps.

[16] At McClellan's order, Hancock took the place of mortally wounded General Richardson in command of the 1st Division, Second Corps. Thirty-eight years old, the big-framed, six foot-two inch Hancock was known for his bravery, competence and battlefield presence. Assuming Command of the Second Corps in June 1863, he would play an instrumental part in the victory at Gettysburg, and thereafter be regarded as the finest corps commander in the Army of the Potomac. Always a supporter of Miles, it is interesting to speculate what course that officer's career would have taken had Hancock won the Presidential election of 1880, in which Hancock was narrowly defeated by James A. Garfield.

Commanding the Division among "those who by their position and the occasions presented had opportunities of acquiring the highest distinction and availed themselves thereof... Lieutenant Colonel N. A. Miles, 61st New York Vols. Commanding Sixty-First and Sixty-Fourth New York Volunteers after Colonel Barlow was wounded."[17]

BATTLE OF FREDERICKSBURG
December 11 to 15, 1862.

Colonel Commanding 61st and 64th New York Regiments 1st Brigade, 1st Division, 2nd Army Corps, Army of the Potomac. Brigadier General W.S. Hancock in his report says:

> Colonel Nelson A. Miles, severely wounded (in the throat)[18] Commanding the Sixty-First and Sixty-Fourth Regiments New York Volunteers consolidated, conducted himself in the most admirable and chivalrous manner. His battalion behaved with steadiness unsurpassed by any troops. The strength of his command was 27 Commissioned Officers and 408 enlisted men. Three officers were wounded and 105 enlisted men killed, wounded and missing.

Brigadier General Caldwell Commanding the Brigade in his report says: "Colonel Miles who has always signally distinguished

---

[17]The 61st N.Y. played an important role in this battle by charging and enfilading the Confederate line in "Bloody Lane." Barlow, struck in the groin by a shell fragment, would be out of action for several months, though he was comforted by promotion to Brigadier General. On the day after the battle of Antietam, Barlow wrote his mother, "Miles behaved splendidly and is unhurt." [Letter of Sept. 18, 1862, Francis C. Barlow Papers, Massachusetts Historical Society, Boston.] Miles' horse had been killed by a shell on Sept. 16.

[18]At the time he was wounded, Miles was about to lead a seemingly suicidal charge on the stone wall behind which the Confederate forces were sheltered. General Howard later recalled: "One of the most heroic acts I ever witnessed was at the battle of Fredericksburg, when Gen. [sic] Miles was shot in the chin and neck so badly that his comrades expected him to die at any time. Gen. [sic] Miles had some important word to convey to me, so holding together the lacerated pieces of flesh with his hands, he staggered to my headquarters, delivered his message and then fainted away. He was determined either to be killed or promoted." [Washington *Star*, May 16, 1925.]

On Dec. 16, 1862, Chaplain and acting Assistant Surgeon A.C. Vogelle described the wound as "a severe wound in the throat occasioned by a minie ball passing in at the front and coming out near the left ear."

Miles returned to duty in February 1863. Although for a time he covered it with a goatee, in later years Miles came to regard the prominent scar on his chin as a badge of honor.

himself on the battlefield displayed on this occasion the highest qualities of an officer's coolness, judgment and intrepidity." General John R. Brooke[19] 53rd Penn. in his report says:

> During the action the right was severaly assailed, and sending to the Colonel Commanding notice of the fact, I soon saw the gallant Colonel Miles of General Caldwell's brigade coming to my support. I directed him to place his regiment on the right of the road which he immediately did, but not a moment too soon as the enemy was evidently trying to turn our right.

In a letter to the Secretary of War, February 19, 1863, Major General Winfield S. Hancock says:

> It becomes my pleasant duty to bring to your favorable notice the name of Colonel Nelson A. Miles 61st New York Vols. Colonel Miles has an enviable reputation in this Army Corps. He has highly distinguished himself on many occasions. At the Battle of Fredericksburg he was severely wounded while gallantly leading the 64th New York Vols. and his own regiment into that severe action. I earnestly recommend him for the position of Brigadier General.

In a letter to the President of the United States June 22, 1879, recommending that Colonel & Brevet Major General N.A. Miles be promoted to Brigadier General U.S. Army, General Hancock says: "During the bloody assault on Marye's Heights, Battle of Fredericksburg December 13, 1862, he (Col. Miles) was conspicuous for brilliant conduct, in leading his command (the 61st and 64th New York Vols.) against the celebrated 'Stone Wall' which defended that position. He was severely wounded on that field."

IN THE CHANCELLORSVILLE CAMPAIGN

April 27th to May 3rd, 1863. (Col. Comdg. 61st N.Y. Inf.)

1st Brigade, 1st Division, 2d Army Corps, Army of the Potomac.

In the Battle of Chancellorsville May 1st, 2nd, & 3rd in command of the following troops: On the 2nd the 11th Mass., 2 companies 52d New York, 4 companies 2d Delaware, 6 companies 148th Penn., and 57th New York.

---

[19] Pennsylvanian John R. Brooke, 24, would not be promoted to Brigadier until May of 1864. he was one of several superb young volunteer officers in the Second Corps, and would later serve under Miles in the Regular Army.

May 3rd the 57th New York was relieved by the 66th New York and the companies of the 52d New York and 2nd Delaware by the 64th New York and a detachment of 250 men of the 154th Penn. General D.N. Couch,[20] Commanding the Corps in his report refers to operations of May 2nd as follows: "A strong picket on the road leading to Fredericksburg held its position under Colonel Miles, (Hancock's Division), after repeated assaults;" and in a subsequent report referring to the same operations: "Colonel Miles of the 61st New York with a strong body of skirmishers held some rifle pits in the forest to the front, and was attacked by the enemy but unsuccessfully."

General Hancock Commanding the Division in his report referring to operations on May 1st says: "The skirmishers on my right flank under command of Colonel Miles, 61st New York and Colonel Frank, 52d New York Vols. became engaged and lost some men;" and referring to operations on the 2nd says: "During the sharp contest of that day the enemy was never able to reach my principal line of battle, so stoutly and successfully did Colonel Miles contest the ground;" and referring to operations on the 3rd:

> I strengthened the advance position believing from the experience of the previous day and the well known ability and gallantry of Colonel Miles that it could be held. That line was frequently assaulted during the morning with great gallantry, the enemy marching their regiments up into the abatis... Colonel N.A. Miles 61st New York Vols. had great opportunity for distinction and availed himself thereof performing brilliant services.[21]

General Caldwell, 1st Brigade, in his report referring to the troops comprising the picket line in the operations of May 2d says:

With this force Colonel Miles skirmished all day long with the

[20] Forty-one-year-old Maj. Gen. Darius N. Couch (USMA 1846) commanded the Second Corps at Fredericksburg and Chancellorsville.

[21] So pleased was Hancock with Miles' handling of the skirmish line that after the repulse of one Confederate attack, he turned to his aide saying, "Captain Parker, ride down and tell Colonel Miles he is worth his weight in gold." General Couch was similarly impressed, commenting to his staff, "I tell you what it is, gentlemen, I shall not be surprised to find myself, some day, serving under that young man." [*History of the One Hundred and Fortieth Pennsylvania Volunteers* by Robert L. Stewart. 1912, p. 62.]

enemy and at 3 p.m. repulsed with signal loss a determined attack of the enemy made in two columns on each side of the road. I do not doubt that this repulse of the enemy, which kept them from our main lines, was due principally to the skill and gallantry of Colonel Miles, who, with a single line of skirmishers, deployed at three paces repelled a determined attack of the enemy made in column, a feat rarely paralleled... I greatly regret to report that Colonel Miles was severely, if not mortally wounded (in the abdomen)[22] on Sunday morning (May 3rd, 1863) while handling the picket line with masterly ability... I have had occasion to mention the distinguished conduct of Colonel Miles in every battle in which the brigade has been engaged. His merits as a military man seem to me of the very highest order. I know no term of praise too exaggerated to characterize his masterly ability. If ever a soldier earned promotion Colonel Miles has done so. If providence should spare his life, I earnestly recommend that he be promoted and entrusted with a command commensurate with his abilities.

---

[22]This was the third and most severe wound of Miles' military career. He later recalled the circumstances: "While riding down the line at Chancellorsville, one of the enemy's bullets struck, with great force, my metallic belt-plate. This caused a slight deviation as it entered the body. The result was an instant of deathly, sickening sensation; my sword dropped from my right hand; my scabbard and belt dropped to the left; I was completely paralyzed below the waist. My horse seemed to realize that had occurred; he stopped, turned, and walked slowly back, I holding onto the pommel of the saddle with my hands." ["My Forty Years of Fighting," *Cosmopolitan Magazine*, Vol. L, p. 412 (1912).]

Assistant Surgeon Calvin P.W. Fisher of the 148th Pa. was attending to a wounded private near the Chancellor House when he saw Col. Miles, supported in the saddle by a mounted comrade, encounter Gen. Hancock. As they met in the road, Miles said, "General Hancock, I am wounded," to which the General replied, "I am very sorry to hear it and hope it is not a serious wound." Hancock then ordered Dr. Fisher to accompany Miles to the Chancellor House. Fisher recalled, "When I reached the house, I had the Colonel laid on a table and proceeded to dress his wound. He had been shot by a large musket ball which entered near the center of the abdomen between one and two inches below the naval. I thought, of course, the wound would prove mortal. I dressed it as well as I could, not venturing to remove the ball." [p. 184, *The Story of Our Regiment* (148th Pa.), J.W. Muffley, Editor. Des Moines, Iowa, 1904.]

So severe was Miles' wound that the regimental returns of May 13 listed him as "mortally wounded." Escorted home to Massachusetts by his brother Daniel, it was two weeks before the Colonel's paralysis abated and the bullet could be safely removed on May 23. Dr. Alfred Hitchcock of Fitchburg, Mass., described the track of the bullet as "entering obliquely near the umbilicous and fracturing the margin of the pelvis." [Nelson A. Miles, ACP File, National Archives, Washington, D.C.]

Miles would be away from his regiment for three months and would ever after regret his absence from the decisive Battle of Gettysburg.

Lieutenant Colonel Broady,[23] 61st New York in his report says: "We all, officers and men, feel the loss and deplore sadly the fate of our beloved and highly esteemed Colonel N.A. Miles, who was severely wounded on the morning of the third (May) but our hopes and prayers are, that he soon may be restored to us again and to usefulness in the service of his country."

In a letter to the President of the United States June 22, 1879, recommending General Miles' promotion to Brigadier General U.S. Army, General Hancock says: "He was highly distinguished at Chancellorsville where he commanded an advanced portion of my line, and held it against great odds until he received a wound which well nigh cost him his life."

Received Brevet of Brigadier General, March 2, 1867, for gallant and meritorious services in the battle of Chancellorsville, Virginia (May 3, 1863) and Medal of Honor,

> For distinguished gallantry in the Battle of Chancellorsville, Va., March 3rd, 1863, while holding with his command a line of abatis and rifle pits against a strong force of the enemy until severely wounded; while Colonel 61st New York Volunteers, commanding the line of skirmishers in front of the 1st division 2d Army Corps.

IN THE GETTYSBURG CAMPAIGN[24]
June 11 to July 5, 1863.

July 6, 1863. Assigned as Acting Brigadier General in command of troops rendezvoused at Huntington, Penn., by S.O. No. 21 of 1863, Headquarters Department of the Susquehanna.

Major General D.N. Couch, Commanding Department of the Susquehanna in his report says: "Colonels Beaver and Miles, both of the 2nd Army Corps, dangerously wounded at Chancellorsville, commanded Camps Curtin and Huntington, Penn."

Colonel Miles' Command at Huntington was: 29th Penn.

---

[23]Thirty-year-old Knut Oskar Broady was a native of Sweden and a veteran of that country's navy. Emigrating to the United States in 1855, he became an assistant Professor of Theology at Madison (now Colgate) University, Hamilton, N.Y. In 1861 he led a company of college students to war with the 61st N.Y. Broady ably seconded Miles in many bloody engagements.

[24]On May 26, 1863, General Barlow wrote Miles urging him to accept command of a brigade in Barlow's First Division, Eleventh Corps. It was fortunate for Miles that he turned down his friend's offer since the Division was routed and nearly destroyed at the battle of Gettysburg, where Barlow himself was terribly wounded.

Militia—5 companies, Penna. Militia—unattached companies, 46th Penn. Militia, Penn. Cavalry Co.

Major General D.N. Couch in a communication dated Headquarters Department of the Susquehanna July 23, 1863 says:

> Colonel Nelson A. Miles, 61st New York Vols. has been on duty in this Department since the invasion of Penn. by the rebel army. Colonel Miles' services have been of great value to the service and he did his duty as he ever did whether in the camp or in battle, in the best manner. I have recommended Colonel Miles for the position of Brigadier General and know none in our army worthier of the appointment.

In S.O. 39 of July 20, 1863, Couch "tenders his thanks to Colonel Miles for the valuable services rendered by him in the emergency through which we have just passed" (Gettysburg Campaign).

By S.O. 39 Headquarters Department of the Susquehanna July 20, 1863, Colonel Miles was relieved from command of the forces at Huntington, Penn., and directed to turn over the command to the senior officer present, and proceed to Washington and report to the Adjutant General of the Army.

NOTE: In the organization of the Army of the Potomac, Major General George G. Meade Commanding, July 31, 1863, Colonel Miles is shown to have resumed command of his brigade thus:

First Brigade
First Division, Second Army Corps, Army of the Potomac
Colonel Nelson A. Miles
61st New York—Lieut. Col. K. Oscar Broady.
81st Penn.—Colonel H. Boyd McKeen.
148th Penn.—Colonel James A Beaver.
Bristow (Virginia) Campaign, October 1863.
Colonel Commanding 1st Brigade, 1st Division, 2d Army Corps.
(61st New York, 81st Penn. 140 Penn. Infantry regiments.)
ARMY OF THE POTOMAC
In the Bristow (Virginia) Campaign October 9 to 22, 1863.
Major General G.K. Warren,[25] Commanding the Corps in his

[25]Thirty-three-year-old Gouverneur Kemble Warren (USMA 1850) commanded the Second Corps from August 1863 to March 1864, during Hancock's recuperation from a severe wound received at Gettysburg. Thereafter he led the Fifth Corps until his removal from command at Five Forks in April, 1865.

report says: "General Caldwell in covering the crossing of Cedar Run at Auburn, and in guarding the rear thence to Bristow performed a duty always difficult from its uncertain requirements, with perfect success and he was ably sustained by his Colonels. Both he, Colonel Brooke, and Colonel Miles are worthy of promotion." Brigadier General Caldwell in his report says: "Colonel Miles, though not engaged in an infantry fight, handled his brigade with skill in the support of batteries. This officer has been repeatedly recommended for promotion and I most earnestly renew the recommendation."

MINE RUN VIRGINIA CAMPAIGN
November 26 to December 2, 1863.

Colonel Commanding 1st Brigade, 1st Division, 2d Army Corps, Army of the Potomac.

In the Mine Run (Va.) Campaign, Nov. 26, marched in the advance from Mountain Run; crossed Rapidan at Germania Ford, Nov. 27, developed the enemy's line near Robertson's Tavern, but not engaged. Enemy fell back at night. Advanced to Mine Run, found enemy strongly entrenched. Brigade in line all day Nov. 28th. On 29th marched to New Hope Church made dispositions for attack; advanced 3 miles without support; halted one hour for reinforcements. Advance so rapid and unexpected the enemy was surprised and dislodged, broke and fled in confusion. Nov. 30 moved to Orange Plank Road; Dec. 1, marched to camp at Mountain Run, crossing Rapidan at Culpeper Mine Ford.

Major General G.K. Warren Commanding the Corps in his report says:

> We pushed on, and at the head of Mine Run, having driven the enemy three miles we found him in trenches. Colonel Miles' Brigade especially acquitted itself in this movement, and at this time Colonel Miles' Brigade held the extreme left, and from the railroad around the right of the enemy. He was, however, nearly two miles distant from the main force.

CAMPAIGN FROM THE RAPIDAN TO THE JAMES RIVER
(WILDERNESS CAMPAIGN)
May 4 to June 12, 1864.

Brigadier General Nelson A. Miles, Commanding First Brigade, 1st Division, 2nd Army Corps, Army of the Potomac consisting of:

> 26th Michigan—Major Lemuel Saviers.
> 61st New York—Lieut. Col. K. Oscar Broady.
> 81st Penn.—Colonel H. Boyd McKeen.
> 140th Penn.—Colonel John Fraser.
> 183rd Penn.—Colonel George P. McLean.
> May 29th, 1864.

2nd New York Artillery-Colonel Whistler assigned to brigade.

June 1st, 1864, reinforced by 5th New Hampshire Volunteers.

Synopsis of Operations.

May 3—Broke camp at Stevensburg.

May 4—Crossed the Rapidan at Ely's Ford and marched to Chancellorsville.

May 5—Marched through the Wilderness to Orange C.H. where engaged.

May 6—Moved to extreme left and fortified.

May 7—Part of 27th Michigan deployed as skirmishers, charged the enemy driving him from position on Brock road capturing prisoners.

May 8—Marched to Todd's Tavern, engaged at Corbin's Bridge on Catharpin Road.

May 9—Crossed the Po River.

May 10—Engaged the enemy in battle at the Po River.

May 11—Reconnoitering across the Po River and in the vicinity of Todd's Tavern driving the enemy's skirmishers.

May 12—Fought battle of Spottsylvania, C.H. carrying the enemy's works with the bayonet, capturing colors, guns and prisoners. During the day, enemy made repeated attempts to retake position but were repulsed with heavy loss.

May 13—Volunteers from regiments of the brigade captured between the lines (under fire) 2 guns with caissons and limbers.

May 15—In reserve in rear of Ninth Corps.

May 17—Returned to former position in line.

May 18—Moved to extreme left of line and engaged the enemy and encamped in reserve.

May 20—Marched through Milford, crossed the Mattapony River and went into position at 4 p.m. of the 21st. Remained until—

May 23—and marched south to North Anna River. Lay under arms on North Bank till 24th.

May 24—Crossed at Jericho Bridge where the enemy was in force, part of brigade deployed as skirmishers and advanced driving the enemy to his works: relieved by Ninth Corps and withdrew to position of railroad near river.

May 26—Recrossed North Anna and bivouacked till morning of 27th.

May 27—Marched for Pamunkey crossing near Hanovertown.

May 28—Went into position and built breastworks. At dark marched to Haws Shop withdrew and returned to former position.

May 29—Marched via Richmond Road encountered and drove enemy's pickets across Totopotomy Creek.

May 30—Part of brigade advanced to a crest overlooking enemy's position and threw up breastworks, when the entire brigade advanced continuing the line to the left.

June 1—Skirmish line advanced part of the enemy's line taken and prisoners captured.

June 2—Marched from Totopotomy Creek to Cold Harbor.

June 3—Engaged in Battle of Cold Harbor charged and carried the enemy's works by assault capturing prisoners and driving the enemy, but unable to hold position on account of fire on both flanks, but gained advance position which was fortified and held till June 12 when withdrew and marched southward.

General Meade in his report referring to operations on May 8th says: "Miles' Brigade repulsing and driving a brigade of the enemy who attacked him at Corbin's Bridge."

Major General Hancock in his report referring to operations of May 4th to 7th says: "Colonel (now Brigadier General) N.A. Miles, Commanding First Brigade of Barlow's Division, checked several attempts of the enemy to advance on my left. In these encounters General Miles displayed his usual skill and courage;" and referring to operations of May 8th about 11 a.m.,

Colonel (now brevet Major General) Miles, made a reconnoissance on the Catharpin road towards Corbin's Bridge with his own brigade of Infantry, one brigade of Gregg's Cavalry and one battery. This force proceeded to within one-half mile of Corbin's

Bridge where the enemy opened upon it with artillery from high ground on the south side of the Po opposite the bridge. General Miles formed his infantry in line of battle along a wooded crest facing the river, his artillery replying to the enemy's fire. He held this position until ordered to return to Todd's Tavern later in the day... At 5:30 p.m. when General Miles was returning from his reconnoissance towards Corbin's Bridge he was attacked by Mahone's Brigade of Hill's Corps which was then marching to Spotsylvania Court House. As soon as the firing commenced on Miles' front, I directed General Barlow to send a brigade to his support. The remaining troops were held in readiness to march in the same direction if required. About this time I was informed that the enemy's infantry was also advancing on the Brock Road to attack my right. I therefore directed that General Miles should retire slowly towards my main line of battle at Todd's Tavern. This movement was executed with great skill and success by that officer who while accomplishing it repelled two spirited attacks of the enemy inflicting severe loss upon him. After the second repulse of the enemy, I withdrew Miles' command inside the intrenchments at Todd's Tavern.

In closing his report General Hancock remarks: "Colonel (now brevet Major General) Miles' 61st New York performed marked and distinguished services, especially at the Catharpin Road on the 8th, at the battle of the Po on the 10th and at Spottsylvania on the 12th and 18th of May."

Major General George G. Meade, Commanding Army of the Potomac in a letter to General Grant May 16, 1864, requests that "Colonels Brooke, Miles and Hayes[26] be appointed Brigadier Generals in the volunteer service for distinguished gallantry on several occasions in the face of the enemy" and says:

Independent of the conspicuous bravery they have exhibited on the field of battle, the above named officers are in all other respects well qualified for the positions for which they are recommended. Colonels Brooke and Miles have for a long time commanded brigades with marked ability and have repeatedly been recommended for promotion.

Brigadier General Francis C. Barlow, in a letter to General Hancock May 13, 1864, recommending promotions to Brigadier

---

[26]Twenty-six-year-old Col. Joseph Hayes, 18th Mass., had been wounded at the Battle of the Wilderness.

Generals of Volunteers and referring to the battle of Spottsylvania
Court House says:

> The distinguished services which both these officers (Colonel
> Brooke and Colonel Miles) have repeatedly rendered and the
> previous strong recommendations for their promotions which
> they have received, are well known to the War Department. I
> consider that the part which this division took in the assault of
> yesterday, the importance of the success of which cannot be too
> strongly stated, entitles it to receive some signal reward in the way
> of promotions, and the two officers above named are unquestion-
> ably those upon whom the honors should fall, because, in addition
> to the services rendered by them yesterday, they have very strong
> previous claims. The brigades commanded by these two officers
> constituted the first line of columns and Colonels Brooke and
> Miles charged with their men and by their gallantry, skill and
> confidence powerfully contributed to the success of the assault and
> the battle.[27]

General Hancock forwarded May 14th the foregoing recommendation approved, saying: "These are highly distinguished
officers and with Colonel Carroll[28] are those officers whom I
would recommend for promotion. These officers have been often
distinguished, and have been recommended for promotion for
services by every commander under whom they have served."

Received the Commission of Brigadier General of Volunteers
to date May 12, 1864, "For specific distinguished services... For
distinguished services during the recent battles of the Old
Wilderness and Spottsylvania Court House, Virginia," and the
brevet of Major General, March 2, 1867, "for gallant and
meritorious services in the Battle of Spottsylvania, Virginia."

IN THE RICHMOND CAMPAIGN
June 13 to July 31, 1864.
(Including Petersburg Mine operations)
Brigadier General Nelson A. Miles, Commanding First Bri-

---

[27] Barlow refers here to Hancock's brilliant May 12 assault on the "Muleshoe Salient" at
Spottsylvania, which netted some three thousand Confederate prisoners, thirty flags and
twenty cannon.

[28] Thirty-one-year-old Col. Samuel Sprigg Carroll (USMA 1856), commanding 3rd Brigade,
2nd Division, Second Corps. Carroll was wounded at the Wilderness and again at
Spottsylvania.

gade, 1st Division, 2d Army Corps, Army of the Potomac,
Consisting of:

28th Mass.—Capt. James Fleming.

26th Michigan —Captain Asa G. Dailey.

5th New Hampshire—Major James E. Larkin.

2d New York Hy. Arty.—Major George Hogg.

61st New York—Col. K. Oscar Broady.

81st Penn.—Lt. Col. William Wilson.

183rd Penn.—Lt. Col. James C. Lynch.

140th Penn.—William A.F. Stockton, Captain.

Synopsis of Brigade Operations

June 13—Crossed Chickahominy 9 a.m. at Long Bridge, marched towards Charles City; arrived on banks of James River at Swynyards' Landing at 4 p.m. and encamped.

June 14—Remained in camp until 11:45 p.m.; moved to the landing.

June 15-At 2:30 a.m. we embarked; crossed the James and landed at Wind-Mill Point. At 6 a.m. marched about one mile from landing and bivouacked in an open field all forenoon. At 1:20 we moved, and arrived within three miles of Petersburg at 11:30 p.m.

June 16—At 3 a.m. moved to within sight of Petersburg, and from thence to the left about two miles. At 5:30 a.m. formed the second line for a charge on the enemy's works.

June 17—At 4 a.m. charged the enemy's works in conjunction with Burnside.

June 18—At 6 a.m. moved forward and occupied the enemy's works, the enemy having fallen back during the night. At 12:00 m. we marched to near the railroad, in rear of Petersburg, and took up a position on a crest commanding the railroad.

June 20—At 10 p.m. we were relieved by a portion of Burnside's troops and moved about one mile to the rear.

June 21—At 6 a.m. we moved to the left; marched until 2 p.m. and arrived near the Weldon Railroad.

June 22—At 4 p.m. resisted a determined assault of A.P. Hill's Corps on our breastworks and captured 40 prisoners.

June 23—Moved to the left in front and relieved a Brigade of the Sixth Corps.

June 24—At 6:30 p.m. marched back to our old position behind the breastworks and remained in the second line the rest of the month.

July 10—At 1 a.m. we moved from our position about two miles to our left and relieved the Sixth Corps picket, and remained on picket until 2 p.m. the 12th.

July 12—At 5 p.m. we moved out on the Jerusalem Plank Road, and at 11 p.m. we were ordered back to our old position at Williams House.

July 13—At 5:30 a.m. we marched to the right and arrived opposite Petersburg at 10:30 a.m.

July 14—The whole Brigade worked on the trenches.

July 20 to 25—Work on the trenches.

July 26—At 5 p.m. we moved towards the Appomattox. At 11:30 p.m. we crossed.

July 27—At 1 a.m. crossed the James, marched a short distance and bivouacked in an open field. At 6 a.m. we threw out skirmishers. At 7 a.m. charged the enemy and captured four 20 pounder Parrott guns and about 20 prisoners. At 11 a.m. we advanced our skirmish line about one mile through the woods.

July 28—At 6 p.m. we went back about one mile to the edge in the open field where we charged the battery on the twenty-seventh.

July 29—At 8:30 p.m. we moved back across the James and Appomattox, arriving opposite Petersburg at 5 a.m. of the thirtieth.

July 30—Remained all day in supporting distance of the Ninth Corps. About 6 p.m. we moved back in the same camp which we occupied before the march across the James.

Major General Hancock Commanding 2d Army Corps in his report of operations June 13 to July 26 says:

The conspicuous valor and good conduct of the officers and men under my command during the marches, battles, and siege operations embraced in this epoch of the campaign, gave me complete satisfaction and merit the highest commendation... The following General Officers Commanding Brigades and Divisions, are entitled to my thanks for their distinguished and valuable services: Brigadier General (now Brevet Major General) Miles commanding First Brigade, First Division.

And in his report July 26 to 29 says:

Meanwhile the skirmish line of Miles' brigade of Barlow's Division (composed of the One-Hundred and Eighty-third Pennsylvania, Twenty-eighth Massachusetts, and Twenty-sixth Michigan Volunteers) under command of Colonel J.C. Lynch One-Hundred and Eighty-third Pennsylvania Volunteers, engaged the enemy farther to the left, driving him into the rifle-pits along the New Market and Malvern Hill Road, and by a well executed movement captured four 20 pounder Parrott guns, with their caissons, and drove the enemy from their works... In my own command special mention is made by subordinate commanders, referring to the Twenty-eighth Massachusetts, Twenty-sixth Michigan, and One-Hundred and Eighty-third Pennsylvania Volunteers, under command of Colonel Lynch, of the One-Hundred and Eighty-third Pennsylvania Volunteers. The last named regiments captured the enemy's battery of four 20 pounder Parrotts as heretofore mentioned.

This capture is also referred to in General Orders No. 25, Headquarters 2nd Army Corps, July 31, 1864, as follows: "The Major General Commanding desires to express to the troops his gratification with their conduct during the late movement across the James River." The following organizations seem to merit particular mention:

The Fifth New Hampshire, Twenty-eighth Massachusetts, One-Hundred and Eighty-third Pennsylvania and Twenty-sixth Michigan Volunteers, under command of Colonel Lynch, One-Hundred and Eighty-third Pennsylvania Volunteers all from General Miles' Brigade constituting part of the skirmish line of General Barlow's Division, for their gallantry in the capture of the enemy's battery on the morning of the 27th (June 1864).

General Miles was detailed by Special Orders No. 258 War Department, Adjutant General's Office, Washington, D.C., August 3, 1864, a member of the Court of Inquiry on the Mine

Explosion on the 30th of July 1864,[29] which first met August 6, 1864, and was in session till Sept. 9, 1864. For proceedings see Vol. xl Part 1, pages 42 to 163. Official Records War of the Rebellion.

NOTE: General Barlow in his report of the foregoing operations says: "No operations of importance were executed by the Division on the 29th (July 1864)... On the evening of that day I left the front upon leave of absence;"[30] consequently by virtue of seniority, General Miles was in command of the First Division July 29th and Major W.G. Mitchell (Senior Aide-de-Camp to General Hancock) in a memorandum referring to the position of the troops of the Corps says: "First Division, General Miles in command from "Gate Posts" on New Market Road (Malvern Hill), connecting with Gibbon's[31] left, to edge of wood near the potteries, holding the rifle pits." General Miles also sent and received dispatches as commander of First Division on July 29th, 1864.

IN THE RICHMOND CAMPAIGN (VA.)
Aug. 1 to Dec. 31, 1864.

Brigadier General Nelson A. Miles commanding First Division, Second Army Corps, Army of the Potomac. (From return of July 31, 1864.)

FIRST BRIGADE

Colonel James C. Lynch
28th Mass.—Capt. James Fleming.
26th Mich.—Capt. Asa G. Dailey.
5th New Hampshire—Major J.E. Larkin.
61st New York—Major George W. Scott.
81st Penn.—Capt. Lawrence Mercer.
140th Penn.—Capt. William A.F. Stockton.
183rd Penn.—Major George T. Egbert.
2nd N.Y. Heavy Arty.—Major Willaim A. McKay.

---

[29] This was the famous battle of the Crater, a Union fiasco start to finish.
[30] Barlow's young wife Arabella, a nurse, died of typhoid on July 28.
[31] Maj. Gen. John Gibbon (USMA 1847), 37, Commander of the Second Division, Second Corps. His later career included major roles in the Indian Wars' Little Big Horn and Nez Perce campaigns.

CONSOLIDATED BRIGADE
Colonel Levin Crandell
7th N.Y. 4 Cos.—Capt. J. Schen.
39th N.Y.—Capt. David A. Allen.
52d New York—Capt. Henry P. Ritzius.
57th New York—Capt. Geo. W. Jones.
88th N.Y. (4 Cos.)—Capt. John Smith.
63rd N.Y. (6 Cos.)—Capt. M.H. Kermeally.
69th N.Y. (6 Cos.)—Lieut. James T. Smith.
111th New York—Capt. Lewis W. Husk.
125th New York—Capt. Nelson Penfield.
126th New York—Lieut. Henry M. Lee.

FOURTH BRIGADE
Lieut. Colonel K. Oscar Broady
64th New York—Capt. W. Glenny.
66th New York—Lieut. Nathaniel P. Lane.
53rd Penn.—Capt. Philip H. Schreyer.
116 Penn.—Capt. Garret Nowlan.
145th Penn.—Capt. James H. Hamlin.
148th Penn.—Capt. James F. Weaver.
7th New York Heavy Arty.—Maj. Edward A.
Springstead.

1st. Operations Aug. 12 to 20. Movement to Deep Bottom and return to camp near Deserted House.

2nd. Operations Aug. 22 to 26. Destroying Weldon Railroad and Battle of Ream's Station.

3rd. Operations Oct. 27 to 30. Demonstrations on work opposite Fort Morton and enemy's picket line opposite Fort Sedgwick.

4th. Operations Dec. 9 & 10. Including Reconnaissance to Hatcher's Run with engagement at Hatcher's Run Dec. 9 obtained important information and withdrew under orders Dec. 10, 1864.

Itinerary of the First Division

Aug. 12—Struck camp and marched to City Point, embarked and sailed up the James River to Deep Bottom.

Aug. 14—Landed at Deep Bottom and pushed out to the New Market Road skirmishing all day. At night took up position opposite enemy's works and intrenched.

Aug. 16—First Brigade made reconnoissance to White Tavern, on the New Market Road.

Aug. 20—Recrossed James and Appomattox Rivers, returning to position in front of Petersburg.

Aug. 21—Marched to Gurley's House.

Aug. 22—Marched to the Weldon Railroad and commenced its destruction.

Aug. 23—Destroyed Railroad to Ream's Station.

Aug. 25—Fought the enemy at Ream's Station (Battle of Ream's Station) and marched to William's House.

Aug. 27—Took position in reserve near Avery's House in front of Petersburg. Reinforcements Fourth New York Heavy Artillery 57 officers and 1,557 enlisted men; one company 7th New York Vols. Three Commissioned officers and 91 enlisted men. Reductions: Captain James M. Favill, 57 New York Vols. Company "F"—Aug. 11 and Capt. Jones 57th New York Vols. Company "I" Aug. 13.

Sept. 5—Division moved from Camp at Deserted House to Jerusalem plank road where it built a line of works.

Sept. 9—Moved into camp near the Jones House.

Sept 24—Moved into line of works from the Appomattox to Fort Meikel headquarters at the Friend's House.

Oct. 1—Division occupied line in front of Petersburg from Fort Spring Hill to Fort Meikel; headquarters at Friends' House.

Oct. 5—Were relieved by Second Division from Fort Meikel to Fort Morton, inclusive.

Oct. 25—Relieved by Second and Third Divisions, taking up the line as far to the left as battery No. 24; moved headquarters to Avery's house; occupied this line on October 31st.

Nov. 4—Moved into position to support line of works. Remained until Nov. 30, when the Division moved to line of works on left of Fifth Corps.

Dec. 9—Broke camp at daylight and marched on the Vaughan Road towards Hatcher's Run, encountered the enemy's pickets, which were driven across the Run; forced a crossing and advanced to Armstrong's Mill; remained until 1 p.m. of the tenth when the Division returned to present camp. No other movements.

General Meade Commanding Army of the Potomac, in his report of operations August 22 to 26 says:

On the 22d of August, Hancock having moved up to the vicinity of the Weldon Railroad, Miles' Division Second Corps, and Gregg's Division of cavalry were sent to Ream's Station with instructions to destroy the road. On the 23rd General Hancock, with Gibbon's Division, was sent to reenforce Miles. The work of destruction was continued on the 24th; but on the 25th, the enemy appearing, Hancock concentrated his force at Ream's Station, where late in the afternoon, he was heavily attacked by a superior force of cavalry and infantry and pressed with so much vigor that a part of his line was boken and five pieces of artillery fell into the hands of the enemy.[32] Upon learning the condition of affairs, Wilcox's division, Ninth Corps, was sent to support Hancock but did not reach the ground till the action was over. At night Hancock withdrew, the enemy leaving the ground at the same time. This terminated the efforts of the enemy to dislodge us from the Weldon Railroad. A line was at once formed connecting the Jerusalem plank road with our new position and the necessary defensive works laid out and constructed.

Battle of Ream's Station

Major General Hancock, Commanding Second Army Corps, in his report of operations Aug. 12 to 20 says:

On the eighteenth General Barlow was compelled by sickness to give up the command of his division to General Miles. This day passed with skirmishing and reconnoitering the enemy's position until 5:30 p.m. when the enemy came out of their works above Fussell's Mill and attacked General Birney. The fight lasted about thirty minutes, when the enemy were repulsed with considerable loss. General Miles with the First and Fourth brigades of his command, took part in the affair, attacking the enemy on his left flank.

Referring to operations on Aug. 25th (Battle of Ream's Station) General Hancock says: "At 12 o'clock the enemy drove in the pickets of the First Division on the Dinwiddie Road and at about 2 p.m. made a spirited advance against Miles' front, but

---

[32]This disaster was due in large measure to the influx of draftees and "bounty men" into what had previously been reliable regiments.

were speedily repulsed. A second and more vigorous attack followed at a short interval and was likewise repulsed, some of the enemy falling within a few yards of the breastworks." Referring to the reverse in General Gibbon's Division during the battle, General Hancock says:

> Affairs at this juncture were in a critical condition and but for the bravery and obstinacy of a part of the First Division and the fine conduct of their commander (General Miles) would have ended still more disastrously. General Miles succeeded in rallying a small force of the Sixty-first New York Volunteers and forming a line at right angles with the breastworks swept off the enemy, recapturing McKnight's guns and retook a considerable portion of his line.

And referring to the attack on Gregg's Cavalry after General Gibbon's division had fallen back, General Hancock says:

> Woerner's battery, First New Jersey Artillery, rendered efficient service during and after this attack. With the aid of this battery and the troops under General Miles the road running to the Plank Road was held until dark, the enemy being checked in every attempt to advance beyond that part of the line they had captured...
> At this time General Miles and General Gregg offered to retake their breastworks entire, but General Gibbon stated that his Division could not retake any of his line.

In his report of operations—25 to 28 October General Hancock says:

> For the operations of General Miles respectfully refer to his report, as he was not under my immediate command. It will be seen that he was not idle, though holding a line several miles in length with but a little over 6,000 men. On the night of the 27th (Oct.) he carried one of the enemy's forts near the crater with a storming party of the One Hundred and Forty-eighth Pennsylvania Volunteers, led by Captain Brown of that regiment and Lieut. Price of the 116th Pennsylvania. . . Lieutenant Price was unfortunately killed. This party held the work for a short time capturing several prisoners including two field officers, but were finally forced to retire as General Miles had not the troops at his disposal to pursue his advantage. On the same night he captured a part of the enemy's picket line on the Jerusalem Plank Road, holding it for two or three hours and retiring at leisure.

These operations are also referred to in General Orders No. 40, Headquarters 2nd Army Corps, Nov. 4, 1864, as follows: "The troops under General Miles forming a part of the force holding the intrenchments at Petersburg are also entitled to great commendation for their services while detached."

Major General George G. Meade Commanding Army of the Potomac in forwarding a list of officers recommended for promotion in that Army—2d Army Corps, Major General Hancock Commanding recommended: "To be Major General by Brevet... 2. Brigadier General Nelson A. Miles 'For highly meritorious and distinguished conduct throughout the campaign and particularly for gallantry and valuable services at the battle of August 25th, 1864, at Ream's Station, Va. To date from August 25th, 1864.'"

Brigadier General Nelson A. Miles received the brevet of Major General of Volunteers for highly meritorious and distinguished conduct throughout the campaign and particularly for gallantry and valuable services in the Battle of Ream's Station, Virginia, to date from August 25, 1864, (the date of the battle).

IN THE RICHMOND CAMPAIGN

Operations Feb. 5, 6 & 7, and Mar. 25, 1865

In front of Petersburg

Brevet Major General Nelson A. Miles, Commanding

1st Division (From return of Dec. 31, 1864)

Second Army Corps, Army of the Potomac,

consisting of 1st Brigade

Brevet Brigadier General Geo. N. Macy

26th Michigan—Major Nathan Church.

5th New Hampshire—Lieut. Col. Welcome A. Crafts.

61st New York—Col. George W. Scott.

81st Pennsylvania—Lieut. Col. William Wilson.

140th Penn.—Capt. William A.F. Stockton.

183rd Penn.—Col. George T. Egbert.

2nd New York Heavy Arty.—Lieut. Col. George Hogg.

SECOND BRIGADE

Colonel Robert Nugent

28th Massachusetts (5 cos.)—Lt. Col. John Conner.

63rd New York (6 Cos.)—Lieut. Col. John H. Gleason.
69th New York—Major Richard Moroney.
88th New York (5 Cos.)—Lieut. Col. Dennis F. Burke.
7th New York Heavy Arty.—Major Samuel L. Anable.

THIRD BRIGADE
Col. Clinton D. MacDougall
7th New York—Col. George W. von Schack.
39th New York (7 Cos.)—Capt. David A. Allen.
52d New York (7 Cos.)—Lt. Col. Henry M. Karples.
111th New York—Lieut. Col. Lewis W. Husk.
125th New York—Lieut. Col. Joseph Hyde.
126th New York (5 Cos.)—Capt. John B. Geddis.

FOURTH BRIGADE
Lieutenant Col. William Glenny
64th New York (6 Cos.)—Capt. Victor D. Renwick.
66th New York—Capt. Nathaniel P. Lane.
53rd Penn.—Lieut. Col. George C. Anderson.
116th Penn.—Capt. David W. Megraw.
148th Penn.—Capt. James F. Weaver.
145th Penn.—Capt. Peter W. Free.
4th New York Heavy Arty.—Major Frank Williams.

Synopsis of Operations, First Division

Feb. 5—The Fourth Brigade of the Division was ordered to Hatcher's Run and formed in line on the right of the Third Division.

Feb. 9—It returned not having been engaged. On the same day the Division moved to the left, its right resting at Fort Gregg, its left at the chimneys of the Westmoreland House, and threw up a line of works.

March 25—The Division remained in camp in the breastworks near Squirrel Level Road, until the morning of this date when attacking parties were sent out from the First and Fourth Brigades to occupy the enemy's picket line. This was done and the movement was followed by the advance of the entire command to the new position gained. During the afternoon three determined attacks were made by the enemy, with the view of dislodging us, all of which were repulsed. A strong picket line was left upon the ground occupied when the Division returned to its former camp behind the entrenchments.

General Meade in his report of operations of March 25 says:

> Major General Humphreys,[33] Commanding Second Corps likewise advanced his skirmishers, well supported by the First and Third Divisions and carried the enemy's entrenched skirmish line taking over 200 prisoners; subsequently the enemy was reenforced and made several vigorous and determined attacks all of which were repulsed. Humphreys capturing in the last affairs 2 battle flags and over 400 prisoners. The fighting on this part of the line continued till near 8 o'clock.

And in General Orders No. 13, Headquarters Army of the Potomac, March 26, 1865, General Meade says:

> The Major General Commanding announces to the Army the success of the operations of yesterday... The enemy being driven from the front of the Ninth Corps (Fort Stedman and Batteries 9, 10, and 11, which the enemy had captured), the offensive was assumed by the Sixth and Second Corps; the enemy by night was driven from his entrenched picket line and all his efforts to recover the same, which were particularly determined and persistent on the Second Corps front, were resisted and repulsed with heavy losses, leaving with the Sixth Corps over 400 prisoners and with the Second Corps 2 battle flags and over 300 prisoners... Of the Second Corps, Major General Humphreys mentions Miles and Motts divisions, etc.

Memorandum relating to General Miles in Command of the Second Army Corps.

On the morning of February 15, 1865, Major General A.A. Humphreys, then in command of the Second Army Corps, Army of the Potomac, started on leave of absence, and Brevet Major General Nelson A. Miles assumed command of the Corps on that same morning by virtue of seniority. By direction of the

---

[33] Fifty-four-year-old Major General Andrew A. Humphreys (USMA 1831) assumed command of the Second Corps in November of 1864 when Hancock's Gettysburg wound reopened. Humphreys ably led the Corps till the end of the War.

Commanding General, Army of the Potomac, Brevet Major
General G. Mott[34] assumed command of the Corps on the
evening of the same day under the presumption that the Senate
had confirmed his (General Mott's) nomination as Brevet Major
General to date from August 1, 1864, but this was found to be an
error from the fact that such nomination was confirmed to date
from September 9, 1864, whereas, the nomination of General
Miles as Brevet Major General was confirmed to date from
August 25, 1864, (the date of the Battle of Ream's Station). On
February 17, 1865, General Mott was informed that as his
confirmation as Brevet Major General from September 9, 1864,
instead of August 1, 1864, fixed his rank as such junior to that of
Brevet Major General Miles, and was directed by the Commanding General, Army of the Potomac, to turn over the
command of the Second Corps to that officer and resume the
command of his division, whereupon Brevet Major General
Miles resumed command of the Second Army Corps February
17, 1865, (in accordance with the following order) remaining in
command to February 25, when General Humphreys resumed
command of the Corps.

> Headquarters Army of the Potomac,
> February 17, 1865.

Brevet Major General N.A. Miles,
  Commanding First Division, Second Corps.
General: The Commanding General directs me to enclose a copy
of a despatch just received from the War Department, and to say
that as it thus appears that your rank as Brevet Major General is
senior to that of Brevet Major General Mott you will relieve that
officer in Command of the Second Corps.

> Yours respectfully,
> George D. Ruggles,
> Assistant Adjutant General.

In the Appomattox Campaign
March 29 to April 9, 1865
Brevet Major General Nelson A. Miles, Commanding First

[34] Brig. Gen. Gershom Mott, a forty-one-year-old New Jerseyan, commanded the Third
Division of the Second Corps. This squabbling over rank was typical of Mott's rather
uneven career.

Division, Second Army Corps, Army of the Potomac, composed of:

FIRST BRIGADE
Colonel George W. Scott
26th Michigan—Capt. Lucius H. Ives.
5th N.H. (battalion)—Lt. Col. Welcome A. Crafts.
2d New York Heavy Arty.—Maj. Oscar F. Hulser.
61st New York—Maj. George W. Schaffer.
81st Penn.—Lieut. Col. William Wilson.
140th Penn.—Capt. William A.F. Stockton.

SECOND BRIGADE
Colonel Robert Nugent
28th Mass. (5 Cos.)—Capt. Patrick H. Bird.
63rd New York (6 Cos.)—Capt. William H. Terwilliger.
69th New York—Lieut. Col. James J. Smith.
88th New York (5 Cos.)—Lieut. Col. Dennis F. Burke.
4th New York Heavy Arty.—Maj. Seward F. Gould.

THIRD BRIGADE
Bvt. Brig. Genl. Henry J. Madill*
7th New York—Bvt. Brig. Genl. Clinton D. MacDougall.
—Lieut. Col. Anthony Pokorny.
39th New York—Col. Augustus Funk.†
—Maj. James Mc. E. Hyde.
52nd New York—Lieut. Col. Henry M. Karples.
—Maj. Henry P. Ritzius.
—Lieut. Col. Henry M. Karples.‡
111th New York—Bvt. Brig. Gen. Clinton D. MacDougall
—Lieut. Col. Lewis W. Husk.
125th New York—Lieut. Col. Joseph Hyde.
126th New York (battalion)—Capt. John B. Geddis.*
—Capt. I. Hart Wilder.

FOURTH BRIGADE
Bvt. Brig. Genl. John Ramsey
64th New York (battalion)—Lieut. Col. William Glenny.
66th New York—Capt. Nathaniel P. Lane.
53rd Penn.—Col. William M. Mintzer.
116th Penn.—Maj. David W. Megraw.†
—Capt. John R. Weltner.

145th Penn.—Capt. James H. Hamlin.
148th Penn.—Capt. Alfred A. Rhinehartt.†
        —Capt. John F. Sutton.
183rd Penn.—Col. George T. Egbert.
*Wounded Apr. 2; †Wounded Mar. 31; ‡Temporarily disabled April 2.

Synopsis of Operations

March 29—The Division marched by the left flank across
  Hatcher's Run, and formed line on the left of the Third
  Division. Advanced in line to Dabney's Mill Road next day,
  with the left resting at the Boydton Plank Road.

March 31—Moved to the left relieving the Fifth Corps from the
  position held by them at 12:30 p.m. the Division advanced to
  the relief of the Fifth Corps, then engaged with the enemy.
  The Third and Fourth Brigades striking the rebels in flank
  and driving them to their works, capturing large numbers of
  prisoners and a flag. Obtained possession of the White Oak
  Road. Subsequently moved to the right intrenched the line and
  bivouacked.

April 1—At 3:30 a.m. moved back to position on Boydton Road
  occupied the previous day by the Third and Fourth Brigades, the
  left extending towards Gravelly Run Bridge and remained
  until about 5:30 p.m. when advanced again and occupied
  White Oak Road. Remained till 11 p.m. frequent demonstrations being made upon the enemy's line. At 11 p.m. marched
  (movement to reinforce Sheridan) via White Oak Road, to the
  vicinity of Five Forks, and reported for duty to Major General
  Sheridan; bivouacked.

Five Forks

April 2—Moved at 7:30 a.m. upon White Oak Road to the point
  held the previous night at 9 a.m.; the enemy abandoned his
  works which were immediately occupied by this division. The
  pursuit of the enemy was at once commenced and he was
  closely followed to a point near Sutherland's Station where he
  was found in position behind breastworks with artillery after
  two attacks were repulsed—the enemy being able to concentrate his force opposite any threatened point, but at 2:45 p.m.
  the position was carried by a flank movement, a large number

of prisoners captured and the remainder of the enemy put to flight. The Division capturing 600 prisoners, one battle flag and two pieces of artillery. As General Sheridan's directions were to drive the enemy towards Petersburg, advanced in that direction by river and South Side roads about two miles when met by Second Division moving on latter road in opposite direction. Returned to vicinity of Sutherland's Station. Division disposed so as to hold the railroad and bivouacked for the night.

April 3—Marched from Sutherland's Station on the river and Namozine Roads to near Winticomack Creek and bivouacked.

April 4—Marched on Namozine Road to Deep Creek, and bivouacked at 7 p.m. During the march of this day the Third Brigade was ordered back to assist in bringing up the trains, roads being in very bad condition.

April 5—Resumed the march at 1 a.m. crossing Deep Creek at 6 a.m. and arrived at Jetersville about 3 p.m. Took up position west of the railroad and on the left of the corps facing northward, and bivouacked.

April 6—Marched northward toward Amelia Court House at 5:30 a.m. The pursuit of the enemy continued all day, the troops moving in line of battle, over all kinds of ground, skirmishers almost constantly engaged with the rear guard of the enemy. At one position taken up they were successfully charged by the 26th Michigan and 140th Penn. Vols., who captured 100 prisoners. On arriving in the vicinity of Sailors Creek[35] about sunset the enemy was found strongly posted on a commanding ridge, covering the crossing of the creek, evidently determined to make a fight to gain time to cross his train. The First Brigade advanced splendidly, charged with a cheer and drove the enemy in perfect confusion into and across the creek, capturing two guns, four colors, his entire train of about 250 wagons and ambulances, etc., together with mules, horses and all appurtenances, and a large number of prisoners. The Third Brigade followed closely on the right of the First, crossed the stream, and possessed themselves of the crest. The First Brigade then crossed and went into position on the other

---

[35]The correct spelling is "Sayler's."

side also the Fourth and Second Brigades were moved down to the bank of the creek without crossing. At 8 p.m. the command bivouacked. The captures by the Division of this day were 5 flags, 3 guns, the enemy's train and several hundred prisoners.[36]

April 7—At 6 a.m. marched from Sailor's Creek to Appomattox River at High Bridge, 2nd Division skirmishers had crossed the river, but were being driven rapidly back when a strong line of skirmishers of the First Division was deployed, and with the use of artillery the enemy was driven and the two divisions crossed the river and marched to a point near intersection of the Farmville Plank and Old Stage roads where the enemy was found in position behind breastworks with artillery; after an unsuccessful flank movement the enemy advanced over their works in pursuit of the attacking party, but were quickly driven back. A picket line was established in connection with the Second Division and the command bivouacked.

April 8—Marched at 6 a.m. through the enemy's works (he having abandoned them during the night to a point near Holliday Creek on the Stage Road halting at 4 p.m. At 9 p.m. moved forward again about five miles and bivouacked. The negotiations of this day, by flag of truce, looking to the surrender of the rebel army, were carried on through the skirmish line of this Division.

April 9—At 6 a.m. marched as on the previous day preceded by a skirmish line. After advancing about six miles a flag of truce from the enemy was observed. At 2 p.m. the order had been given to advance, when the Division was directed to halt until further orders. Soon afterward the surrender of the rebel army was announced.

SUTHERLAND'S STATION, APRIL 2

Lieutenant General Grant in a dispatch to Colonel Bowers[37] April 2nd says: "I have just heard from General Miles. He attacked

---

[36]The wagon train was carrying a sizeable portion of the Confederate treasury, and Miles watched with amusement as his soldiers gambled with the worthless currency. There was also a prize of another kind: "A litter of bright-eyed rollicking puppies was rescued from one of the wagons before the torch was applied, and fell to the lot of the Major-General commanding the Division, who frequently enjoyed their antics in front of his tent in the days of relaxation which followed the surrender of Lee's Army." [Stewart, *History of the 140th Pa.*, pp. 263-64.]

[37]Col. Theodore Bowers, Assistant Adjutant General on Gen. Grant's staff.

what was left of Heth's and Wilcox's divisions at Sutherland's
Station and routed them, capturing about 1,000 prisoners...
General Miles also captured two field pieces in this attack," and in
a dispatch to General Meade April 2nd, General Grant says:
"Miles has made a big thing of it and deserves the highest praise for
the pertinacity with which he stuck to the enemy until he wrung
from him victory." General Grant in his report referring to these
operations, says:

> The enemy south of Hatcher's Run retreated westward to
> Sutherland's Station where they were overtaken by Miles' Divi-
> sion. A severe engagement ensued and lasted until both his right
> and left flanks were threatened by the approach of General
> Sheridan, who was moving from Ford's Station towards Peters-
> burg, and a division sent by General Meade from the front of
> Petersburg when he broke in the utmost confusion, leaving in our
> hands his guns and many prisoners.

Major General Meade in his report, referring to the operations
on March 31st says:

> On the 31st about 10 a.m. Ayres,[38] under General Warren's orders
> advanced to dislodge the enemy in position on the White Oak
> Road; Ayres' attack was unsuccessful and was followed by such a
> vigorous attack of the enemy that Ayres was compelled to fall back
> upon Crawford,[39] who in turn was so strongly pressed by the
> enemy as to force both divisions back in considerable disorder to
> the position occupied by Griffin,[40] when the pursuit of the enemy
> ceased. Immediately on ascertaining the condition of affairs Major
> General Humphreys was ordered to move to Warren's support,
> and that officer sent Miles' division to attack in flank the force
> operating against Warren... This movement was handsomely
> executed by Miles, who, attacking the enemy vigorously, drove
> him back to his former position on the White Oak Road,
> capturing several colors and many prisoners.

And referring to the operations at Sutherland's Station April
2nd, General Meade reports:

[38]Thirty-nine-year-old Brig. Gen. Romeyn B. Ayres (USMA 1847) commanded the 2nd
Division, Fifth Corps.
[39]Thirty-five-year-old Brig. Gen. Samuel W. Crawford of Pennsylvania commanded the
3rd Division, Fifth Corps.
[40]Brig. Gen. Charles "Black Jack" Griffin, 39, (USMA 1847), commanded the 1st Division,
Fifth Corps. The next day, at the battle of Five Forks, Sheridan relieved Warren and
placed Griffin in command of the Fifth Corps.

Early in the morning Miles reporting his return to his position on the White Oak Road, was ordered to advance on the Claiborne Road simultaneously with Mott and Hays. Miles perceiving the enemy were moving to his right, pursued and overtook him at Sutherland's Station, where a sharp engagement took place, Miles handling his single division with great skill and gallantry, capturing several guns and many prisoners. On receiving intelligence of Miles being engaged, Hays was sent to his support, but did not reach the field till the action was over.

In concluding his report of the operations General Meade again calls attention to the operations of the First Division, thus:

> To the brilliant attack of Miles' Division, Second Corps at Sutherland's Station [and] To the energetic pursuit and attack of the enemy by the Second Corps on the 6th instant, terminating in the battle of Sailor's Creek, and to the prompt pursuit the next day, with Barlow's and Miles' attacks—as all evincing the fact that this army, officers and men, all nobly did their duty and deserve the thanks of their country. Nothing could exceed the cheerfulness with which all submitted to fatigue and privations to secure the coveted prize—the capture of the army of Northern Virginia.

General Sheridan in his report referring to operations of April 2 says:

> At daylight on the morning of April 2nd General Miles' Division of the Second Army Corps reported to me coming over from the Boydton Plank Road. I ordered it to move up the White Oak Road towards Petersburg and attack the enemy at the intersection of that road with the Claiborne road where he was in position in heavy force, and I followed General Miles immediately with two divisions of the Fifth Corps. Miles forced the enemy from this position and pursued with great zeal, pushing him across Hatcher's Run and following him up on the road to Sutherland's Depot. On the north side of the run I overtook Miles who was anxious to attack, and had a very fine and spirited division. I gave him permission, but about this time General Humphreys came up and receiving notice from General Meade that General Humphreys would take command of Miles' Division, I relinquished it at once, and facing the Fifth Corps by the rear (I afterwards regretted giving up this division as I believe the enemy could at that time have been crushed at Sutherland's Depot) I returned to Five Forks and marched out the Ford Road to Hatcher's Run.

General Sheridan in his Personal Memoirs, vol. 2, page 172 says:

The night of the 1st of April, General Humphrey's Corps—the Second—had extended its left toward the White Oak Road, and early next morning, under instructions from General Grant, Miles' Division of that corps reported to me, and supporting him with Ayres' and Crawford's Divisions of the Fifth Corps, I then directed him to advance toward Petersburg and attack the enemy's works at the intersection of the Claiborne and White Oak roads.

Such of the enemy as were still in the works Miles easily forced across Hatcher's Run, in the direction of Sutherland's Depot, but the Confederates promptly took up a position north of the little stream, and Miles being anxious to attack, I gave him leave, but just at this time General Humphreys came up with a request to me from General Meade to return Miles. On this request I relinquished command of the Division, when, supported by the Fifth Corps it could have broken in the enemy's right at a vital point; and I have always since regretted that I did so, for the message Humphreys conveyed was without authority from General Grant, by whom Miles had been sent to me, but thinking good feeling a desideratum just then, and wishing to avoid wrangles, I faced the Fifth Corps about and marched it down to Five Forks, and out the Ford Road to the crossing of Hatcher's Run. After we had gone, General Grant, intending this quarter of the field to be under my control, ordered Humphreys with his other two divisions to move to the right, in toward Petersburg. This left Miles entirely unsupported, and his gallant attack made soon after was unsuccessful at first, but about 3 o'clock in the afternoon he carried the point which covered the retreat from Petersburg to Richmond.

General Sheridan in a letter to General Miles dated Aug. 2, 1866, referring to the foregoing operations says: "Your ability and courage while under my command, and the spirit and discipline of your division, satisfied me that the very high compliments which had been coupled with your name were well earned and deserved."

Major General Humphreys in his report of April 21 referring to operations of March 31 says:

Being informed by a staff officer from Major General Warren that they (Ayres' and Crawford's Divisions) were being pressed back and needed support, I ordered General Miles to throw forward two of his brigades and attack the enemy and subsequently to follow it up with his whole division, at the same time extending Mott's left to maintain the connection and give support. This order was complied with in the promptest and most spirited manner. The brigades of General Madill[41] and General Ramsey[42] supported by that of Colonel Nugent[43] advanced rapidly to the attack, struck the enemy in flank and drove him back into his intrenchments, with severe loss of killed and wounded and one flag and many prisoners and occupied the White Oak Road.

And referring to General Miles' operations of April 2nd at Sutherland's Station General Humphreys says:

Taking the 2nd Division, I moved rapidly as possible by the Cox Road towards Sutherland's Station, expecting if the enemy was still in front of Miles to take them in flank. Upon nearing the Station however, I found that General Miles had, at about 3 o'clock, made a third and successful assault, striking the enemy's left flank and driving him out of his breastworks, taking one flag, two guns and 600 prisoners. Brevet Brigadier General Madill and Brevet Brigadier General MacDougall,[44] commanding Third and First Brigades, were among the wounded, the former severely. Captain Clark's Battery, B, First New Jersey, rendered great asistance in the assault by keeping up a vigorous and well directed fire upon the enemy.

Referring to the operations of April 6th including the Battle of Sailor's Creek, General Humphreys says: "The whole result of the day's work to the corps was 13 flags, 4 guns, about 1700 prisoners and over 300 wagons, including ambulances with their contents;" and in closing his report the General says: "I beg leave to ask the attention of the commanding general to the services of Brevet Major General Miles, whose division had the good fortune to be most frequently and heavily engaged with the enemy... For the prompt and intelligent manner in which all orders were carried out, my thanks are due to Brevet Major General Miles [and others]," and in a circular to the officers and soldiers of the Second Army Corps by Major General Humphreys he says:

[41]Col. (Brevet Brig. Gen.) Henry John Madill of Pennsylvania.
[42]Col. (Brevet Brig. Gen.) John Ramsey of New Jersey.
[43]Col. (Brevet Brig. Gen.) Robert Nugent of New York.
[44]Col. Clinton D. MacDougall of New York.

I congratulate you on the glorious success that has attended the operations just closed.

While awaiting the expressions of approbation from the country, from the Commander of the Armies and of the Army of the Potomac, for the manner in which you have performed your part in the general plan, I cannot refrain from expressions of admiration at the noble spirit that has animated you throughout, at the brilliant exhibition of those soldierly qualities for which the Second Corps has been conspicuous. The rapid manner in which you pressed the pursuit, from the moment the enemy was discovered in retreat, driving him before you by constant combat, over an unknown country, through dense undergrowth and swamps, from positions which his advanced troops had intrenched, has, I believe, been unexampled.

Being in direct pursuit the opportunities for large captures were not yours; but despite the disadvantages you labored under, the results to the Corps have been the capture of 35 guns, 15 flags, and 5,000 prisoners, and the capture or destruction of 400 wagons, with their contents, besides tents, baggage, and other material, with which the road was strewn for miles... In addition you have contributed eminently to the general success, and to captures made by other corps, by hemming in the enemy and preventing his escape, and have done your full share in the grand closing scene.

In the operations before Petersburg your success was brilliant, General Miles, with the First Division was ordered to advance and attack the enemy. Flushed with success over two divisions of another Corps, which they were pressing back; this was done in the promptest and most spirited manner. The enemy was driven back rapidly into his intrenchments, with severe loss in killed, wounded and prisoners. . .

During the night of the 1st instant, General Miles' [First] Division had been detached under orders of Major General Sheridan, and in the pursuit of the following day attacked the enemy, intrenched in a strong position which was finally carried in the handsomest manner, with the capture of two guns, one flag and 600 prisoners...

In this brief glance of what you have done I cannot attempt to award to each the full merit due, but must content myself with thanking the division commanders—Major General Miles [and others].

MILES AT THE WAR'S END
This photo was taken shortly before his assignment to Fort
Monroe as guardian of the ex-Confederate President. He wears
the badge of mourning for the assasinated Abraham Lincoln.
Courtesy, Library of Congress.

II

Reconstruction

As Commander of the Military District of Fort Monroe, Virginia, Miles' principal duty was to serve as jailor to ex-Confederate President Jefferson Davis, confined to a casemate within the fort. As such, the young general soon found himself the target of hard-hitting attacks in the public press. In examining the official records of Miles' tenure at Fort Monroe, it becomes clear that though he may have been over-zealous in obeying the orders of his superiors—Secretary of War Stanton, Assistant Secretary Dana and Major General Halleck—he was not guilty of intentional cruelty to his prisoner.

On May 22, 1865, Miles was "authorized and directed" to manacle Davis, "whenever he may think it advisable."[45] The next day, leg irons were forcibly placed on the struggling and near-hysterical prisoner, ostensibly to prevent his escape while the doors to his cell were changed. These remained until May 28, when Secretary of War Stanton ordered them removed.

By July, Davis was allowed to receive books and carefully scrutinized letters, and permitted a daily walk, on which Miles accompanied him. The general was made responsible for daily reports on the ex-President's health, to counter growing charges of mistreatment.

Although Davis regarded Miles as a "miserable ass,"[46] the general did, in September, move his ailing prisoner to former officers' quarters in Carroll Hall. This was no easy transfer to accomplish given the vindictive and confused administration in Washington.

Following the arrival of Mrs. Varina Davis at Fort Monroe in

[45] *Official Records of the War of the Rebellion*, Series II, Vol. VIII, p. 565.
[46] *Ibid.*, p. 841.

May 1866, popular condemnation of Miles reached such fever-pitch that he requested reporters be allowed inside the post to assess Davis' condition. This was refused, despite Miles' assertion that "the gross misrepresentations made by the press impinges severely upon my honor and humanity."[47]

On August 24, 1866, having learned of his imminent muster-out, Miles addressed the Secretary of War in a final attempt to clear his name:

> HEADQUARTERS, MILITARY DISTRICT OF
> FORT MONROE, VA.
> August 24, 1866.
>
> Hon. E.M. STANTON, Secretary of War:
>
> SIR: I have received the order of the President mustering me out of service September 1. As I have received no other appointment I fear that the President is dissatisfied with my course here, or perhaps credits some of the base slanders and foulest accusations which the disloyal press have heaped upon me. I am ready to vindicate my course to all honorable men, and here state that as far as the confinement of Jefferson Davis is concerned he has received impartial treatment—better than any other Government would have given him, and as much leniency as the dignity of the Government would justify.
>
> As I have been here fifteen months since his first imprisonment I would have preferred to remain one month longer until he was removed from this place, at which time I intended to tender my resignation. I would now ask this slight consideration in justice to my own reputation, which has cost many sacrifices and is as highly prized as life. If I am to receive another appointment in the reorganization of the Army of course I cheerfully abide any orders; if not, I would most respectfully request to remain until October 5 and then be allowed to resign. I regret being obliged to trouble you with so small a matter, but it is very important to me and one which I feel very sensitive about. You have been more than a friend to me, and I hope some day to be able to serve you in return for your many kindnesses to me.
>
> I have the honor to remain, with the highest respect, your obedient servant,
>
> NELSON A. MILES,
> Major-General, U.S. Volunteers[48]

---

[47] *Ibid.*, p. 914.   [48] *Ibid.*, p. 954.

Unsuccessful in this request, Miles ever after regarded the sixteen months at Fort Monroe as one of the low points of his career, glossing over the period in his voluminous writings. If nothing else, he had learned to appreciate the power and fickle nature of the American press.

Miles counted himself lucky to have obtained the Colonelcy of the 40th U.S. Infantry, though given the glowing list of testimonials from his superiors in the late war the position was virtually his for the taking. He assumed the command of the 40th, a Black regiment, in October 1866, and his commission was predated to July 28. From March of the following year until March 1869, the young colonel witnessed first hand the implementation of Reconstruction in the state of North Carolina. Much of his service was under the direction of his Civil War comrade General Oliver Otis Howard, who administered the Freedman's Bureau with moral sincerity and unfortunate naiveté. Political opportunism and corruption was rife within the Bureau; Congressional investigations further damaged Howard's already checkered career. Through it all Miles seems to have performed his duties capably, his sympathies firmly on the side of the Republican architects of Reconstruction.

In the summer of 1867 Miles met Mary Hoyt Sherman at the Washington home of her uncle, influential Senator John Sherman. Mary's father was Judge Charles Sherman of Cleveland, Ohio; another uncle, the redoubtable Lieutenant General William Tecumseh Sherman, soon to be General-in-Chief of the Army. By autumn, he was ready to propose to Mary Sherman, and they were married at Cleveland's Trinity Church on June 30, 1868. Through his wife Miles obtained the ear, if not always the support, of two powerful men; later, his sister-in-law Elizabeth Sherman would marry Senator Don Cameron of Pennsylvania, providing another friend in Washington. Much has been made of this liaison as a marriage of convenience of Miles' part; be that as it may, it is quite certain that genuine love, not political opportunism, was at the heart of the matter.

On March 15, 1869, Miles was posted to the newly reconstituted 5th U.S. Infantry, headquartered at Fort Hays, Kansas. He was extremely fortunate in his assignment to what became the finest Indian-fighting regiment on foot in the Army; soldiers of the Fifth winning more Medals of Honor than any other "walk-a-heaps" on the frontier. From the time of his arrival at Fort Hays in April, Miles fell in love with the straightforward military life on the plains. He soon formed a close friendship with Lt. Col. George A. Custer, whose 7th Cavalry was stationed at the post. Custer; when Mrs. Miles died in 1904, Libbie Custer wrote him a hunting, while their wives too became fast friends. In later years Miles would always champion the memory of the controversial Custer; when Mrs. Miles died in 1904, Libbie custer wrote him a touching letter of condolence.

When the 5th Infantry was assigned to Fort Leavenworth, the Miles' settled in one of the large well-landscaped homes on that sprawling post. There in the autumn of 1869, their first child, Cecelia was born. Though he had little to complain about, Colonel Miles was not content with an endless round of drill, paperwork and courtmartial duties. He envied the success of officers such as Col. Ranald Mackenzie of the 4th Cavalry, and Lieutenant Colonel George Crook of the 23rd Infantry, soon to be promoted Brigadier General; Miles itched to try his hand at Indian warfare but it was some time before he got his chance.

MILITARY DISTRICT OF FORT MONROE

Special Orders No. 243.   Headquarters of the Army, A.G.O.
                                 Washington, May 19, 1865.
...7. Brevet Major General N.A. Miles, U.S. Volunteers is hereby relieved from duty in the Army of the Potomac, and will immediately proceed to Fort Monroe, and from there report by telegraph to, and await orders from Major General H.W. Halleck,[49] Commanding Military Division of the James. He has permission to take with him the following named officers serving on his staff while commanding First Division, Second Army Corps; Major N. Church, twenty-sixth Michigan Volunteers; Captain J.D. Black, one hundred and forty-fifth Pennsylvania Volunteers.

By command of Lieutenant General Grant:

                                        E.D. Townsend,
                                        Assistant Adjutant General.

---

[49] Maj. Gen. Henry Wager "Old Brains" Halleck (USMA 1839). He had been commander in Chief of the Army from 1862-64.

See Rebellion Records—Series I Vol. XLVI part 3—pages 1191 & 1192.

> Headquarters Military Division of the James,
> Fort Monroe, Va., May 21, 1865.

Special Orders No. 2.

I. Brevet Major General Miles is hereby appointed to the command of the Military District of Fort Monroe with his headquarters in the fort. Major General E.O.C. Ord[50] will fix the limits of the district inland.

II. Colonel Pritchard[51] and his command will be subject to the orders of General Miles for prison guards, and will be quartered in the fort.

> By order of Major General H.W. Halleck:

> > D.C. Wagner,
> > Assistant Adjutant General.

NOTE: For correspondence while in command and in reference to Jefferson Davis, a prisoner, see vol. VIII series II, Prisoners of War, etc.

See Rebellion Records—Series I Vol. XLVI part 3, page 1192.

> Headquarters Department of Virginia,
> Army of the James, Richmond, Va., May 21, '65

Special Orders No.

1. By direction of the Major General Commanding Military Division of the James, Brevet Major General Miles is assigned to the command of the Military District of Fort Monroe, with his headquarters in the fort.

2. General Miles' district will include the Peninsula west as far as Henrico, and Hanover counties, exclusive; also Mathews, Gloucester, Accomack and Northampton counties. In all that relates to the command of troops or military affairs the commanding officers of the sub-districts of the Eastern Shore and Peninsula will report to General Miles. In all that relates to the Department of Negro Affairs they will report to these headquarters direct, as will Brevet Major General Miles.

> By command of Major General E.O.C. Ord:

> > Ed. W. Smith,
> > Assistant Adjutant General.

---

[50] Maj. Gen. Edward Otho Cresap Ord (USMA 1839).
[51] Lt. Col. Benjamin D. Pritchard, 4th Michigan Cavalry.

G.O. 130, War Dept., A.G.O., Washington, July 28, 1865.

The following General Officers assigned as indicated below will report in accordance with the instructions herein given...

VIII. To report for duty to Major General A.H. Terry,[52] Commanding Department of Virginia.

Brigadier and Brevet Major General N.A. Miles.

By command of Lieutenant General Grant.

> War Department Adjutant General's Office,
> Washington, August 29, 1866.

Special Orders No. 431.

. . .5. Major General N.A. Miles U.S. Volunteers is relieved from duty at Fort Monroe, Va., and will report in person to the Adjutant General. He will bring with him the confidential records pertaining to his late command and deliver them to the Adjutant General...

By order of the Secretary of War:

> E.D. Townsend,
> Assistant Adjutant General.

RECONSTRUCTION

Major General Edward R.S. Canby,[53] Commanding Second Military District embracing the States of North Carolina and South Carolina in his official report for 1867 says: "In March 1867 the 40th United States Infantry, Brevet Major General Nelson A. Miles Colonel Commanding, arrived in the Department and was assigned to duty."

In December 1867 the stations of the 40th Infantry in North Carolina and South Carolina according to G.O. 145, Second Military District December 6th, were as follows:

Post of Goldsboro N.C.—Headquarters and Companies A, C, E, G, H and K 40th Infantry; Colonel and Brevet Major General N.A. Miles Commanding and the Major of the 40th Infantry.

The Command to embrace the counties of Halifax, Northampton, Nash, Wilson, Wayne, Samson, Duplin, Lenoir, Onslow, Jones, Carteret, Craven, Pitt, Beauford, Hyde, Martin, Bertie,

---

[52] Maj. Gen. Alfred Howe Terry, a lawyer from Connecticut, won promotion in the Regular Army and the thanks of Congress for his successful campaign against Fort Fisher on the coast of North Carolina. Although at this period he was one of Miles' friends, relations between them would deteriorate in the coming decade.

[53] Maj. Gen. Edward R.S. Canby (USMA 1839). He would meet his death at the hands of Modoc Indians in the Lava Beds of California on April 11, 1873.

Hertford, Washington, Tyrrell, Chowan, Perquimans, Gates, Pasquotank, Camden, Currituck, Greene and Edgecombe.

Fort Macon, N.C., Companies "B" and "I" 40th Infantry, Captain and Brevet Lt. Col. Charles B. Gaskill,[54] 40th Infantry commanding.

Post of Charleston, S.C. Companies "D" and "F" 40th Infy.

Assistant Commissioner Bureau Refugees Freedmen and Abandoned Lands

April 6, 1867. Brevet Major General Nelson A. Miles was appointed Assistant Commissioner Bureau Refugees Freedmen and Abandoned lands for the State of North Carolina, and Major General O.O. Howard Commissioner, in his report for 1867, says:

> General Miles has actively cooperated with the various agencies established for the benefit of freed people, correctly appreciating the interests of all classes. He has to a considerable extent succeeded in relieving the Colored people of unjust exactions and in restoring public confidence throughout the State.

In his annual report for 1868 General Howard says:

> Brevet Major General Miles has continued to discharge the duties of Assistant Commissioner for the State of North Carolina.
>
> Orders from headquarters second military district having constituted commanders of posts, sub. assistant Commissioners of the Bureau for their respective commanders, General Miles directed the following arrangements of bureau sub-districts, to take effect March 1, 1868. The State is divided into sub-districts of Goldsboro, Raleigh, Wilmington, and Morganton each of which is again subdivided into sections—comprising on an average three counties each under the charge of an officer or agent.
>
> The Assistant Commissioner (General Miles) bears emphatic testimony to the exemplary conduct of the freed people through the entire canvass which resulted in the adoption of the new State Constitution and the election of State and local officers.

Memorandum
Concerning Indian Affairs in the Department of the Missouri from 1869 to 1873 Inclusive

[54] Lt. Col. Charles B. Gaskill of New York had risen from Private to Colonel during the Civil War, much of his service being with U.S. Colored Troops.

1869

Major General Schofield[55] Commanding Department of the Missouri in his annual report for 1869 says:

> During the summer large portions of the Fifth United States Infantry have been distributed in small guards at short intervals along the Kansas Pacific Railroad and detachments of the Third and Fifth at the stage stations between Forts Wallace and Lyon. They will soon be concentrated at their proper stations for winter quarters and their better instruction and discipline.

The distribution of the Fifth Infantry during the year was as follows:

Fifth Infantry, Brevet Major General Miles Commanding, headquarters and two companies at Fort Harker, two companies at Fort Hays; three companies at Fort Wallace; one company at Fort Lyon; one company at Fort Reynolds; one company and recruits at Leavenworth Depot.

1870

General Pope[56] Commanding Department of the Missouri in his annual report for 1870 says:

> Speaking generally there has been little trouble with the Indians in this Department during the season. The result is mainly due to the fact that these Indians have been fed and furnished with nearly everything they ask for, and by these means much temptation to depredate removed.
>
> In May a raid was made by Indians on the working parties of the Kansas Pacific Railroad beyond Kit Carson and 10 or 12 persons killed and several head of stock (mainly mules) driven off. The railroad was then being guarded and completed between Kit Carson and Denver, and a large force of laborers distributed with as much heedlessness of danger as if employed in the streets of St. Louis. They were without arms and observed not the least precaution. Every man killed was without arms of any kind...
>
> As soon as news of the raid reached me by telegraph, I directed

[55] Maj. Gen. John McAllister Schofield (USMA 1853), Secretary of War from 1868-69 and General in chief of the Army (1888-95).

[56] Brig. Gen. John Pope (USMA 1842). As Maj. Gen. of Volunteers he commanded the Army of Virginia in the disastrous Second Battle of Bull Run, the stigma of which he would carry to his grave, despite a creditable administration of his Western department.

Colonel C.R. Woods,[57] Fifth Infantry, Commanding Fort Wallace to take charge of the region of country along the railroad from Wallace to Denver and to transfer his headquarters to some convenient point between these places. I gave him general command for this service of the troops at Wallace, Lyon and Reynolds, and re-enforced him with two cavalry troops from Hays and one Infantry Company from Larned. Colonel Woods promptly distributed his infantry force along the line of the roads and sent out four troops of cavalry under Major Reno,[58] Seventh Cavalry, in pursuit of the raiding party. The Indians, however, had too much the start and escaped across the Platte. Another attack was attempted soon after near River Bend, but the troops were at their stations, and easily repulsed it. Since that time there have been no further troubles from Indians in that region.

The Fifth Infantry was distributed at Forts Harker, Hays, and Wallace along the line of the Kansas Pacific Railroad, also a company each at Forts Lyon and Reynolds, during the year, employed in protecting settlers and railroads, furnishing escorts for authorized exploring expeditions, and in the protection of Indian Agents on Reservations, and ready at all times to take the field as necessity required.

1871

Brigadier General John Pope, Commanding the Department of the Missouri in his annual report for 1871 says:

I am happy to be able to say that with the exception of some few robberies of stock, etc., by Reservation Indians in the Western part of New Mexico, and the killing of four or five men by Apaches in the Southwestern corner of New Mexico on the line of Arizona and near Fort Stanton, there has not been a depredation or murder committed by Indians in this Department for the past twelve months.

Fifth Infantry Stations in 1871 were headquarters and 3 Cos. at Fort Leavenworth, Kan., 1 Co. Fort Harker, 2 at Fort Hays, 3

[57] Lt. Col. Charles R. Woods (USMA 1852) a Brigadier General and Brevet Major General in the Civil War. He became Colonel of the 2nd Infantry February 18, 1874.
[58] Maj. Marcus A. Reno (USMA 1857) a Brevet Brigadier General in the Civil War, he would become notorious in the Regular Army for his part in the Battle of Little Big Horn in 1876.

companies Fort Wallace, 1 company Fort Reynolds, and during the year these troops were employed in duties similar to those performed in 1870.

1872

Brigadier General John Pope, Commanding Department of the Missouri in his annual report for 1872 says: "The report is necessarily and I trust, satisfactorily brief as I have no Indian hostilities, depredations or disturbances of any moment to recount, and nothing except the relation of a very quiet and peaceful administration of my office."

The Fifth Infantry was stationed as follows, Aug. 31, 1872: Headquarters, Non-commissioned Staff and Battallion, Fort Leavenworth, Kansas; Cos. A, G, H, I, K, Fort Leavenworth, Kansas; Co. B, Fort Scott; Co. C, Fort Dodge; Cos. D & F, Fort Larned; Co. E, Fort Hays.

During the year these troops were employed in duties similar to those performed in 1870.

1873

Brigadier General John Pope, Commanding Department of the Missouri referred to operations in his annual report for 1873 as follows: "I am glad to say that, with very trifling exceptions I have no difficulties nor troubles with Indians anywhere in the Department to report."

The Fifth Infantry was stationed as follows: Aug. 31, 1873: Headquarters, Non-Commissioned Staff and Band, Fort Leavenworth, Kansas; Cos. A, G, H, I, K, Fort Leavenworth, Kansas; Co. B, Fort Gibson, I.T.; Cos. C, E, & F., Fort Larned; Co. D, Fort Dodge, Kansas.

During the year these troops were employed in duties similar to those performed in 1870.

MILES IN 1874
Although Miles variously dated this portrait, made by E. Decker
of Cleveland, as 1874 and 1876, the earlier date is probably correct.
Courtesy, Custer Battlefield National Monument.

III

The Red River War

The Red River War of 1874-75 gave Colonel Miles his first experience in conducting a protracted Indian war campaign. His command was one element of a five pronged offensive intended to force rampaging Kiowa, Commanche and Cheyenne tribesmen back to their established reservations. With four companies of his 5th Infantry and eight companies of the 6th Cavalry, Miles pushed southward into the Texas Panhandle from Fort Dodge, Kansas. The other columns were led by Maj. William R. Price, 8th Cavalry, advancing east from New Mexico; Lt. Col. John W. Davidson, 10th Cavalry, and Lt. Col. George P. Buell, 11th Infantry, moving west from Indian Territory (now Oklahoma); and famed Indian-fighter Col. Ranald S. Mackenzie, 4th Cavalry, heading north from Fort Concho, Texas.

Miles' was a long and frustrating campaign waged against an elusive foe under the worst possible physical conditions. On the barren Staked Plains' savage heat, in which some thirst-crazed soldiers drank their own blood, alternated with torrential downpours. Later came the frozen misery of a winter war. After initial success against the Cheyennes at Red River on August 30, a critical shortage of supplies forced Miles to halt on the Washita River until more could be brought south from Camp Supply. During its return the supply train was attacked and besieged from September 9 to 12; and September 12 also saw the famous "Buffalo Wallow" fight between six of Miles' couriers and over 100 warriors. The Colonel's fears that Mackenzie would win whatever glory the campaign had to offer were partially realized in that officer's September 28 victory at Palo Duro Canyon.

By November, having without orders assumed control of Major Price's four companies of cavalry, Miles was able to mount renewed efforts. These included Lt. Frank D. Baldwin's November 8 capture of a Cheyenne village on McClellan Creek, in which two white hostages, Adelaide and Julia German (or, as often spelled, Germaine) were rescued. Despite frigid temperatures, the indefatigable Miles continued to press operations through January of 1875, and with Mackenzie deserves much credit for the successful conclusion of the campaign.

The Red River War showed Miles to be an energetic perfectionist willing to lead his command to the limits of human endurance. As he wrote his wife, "I find I have to be Captain and Sergeant and Wagon Master and a little of everything."[59] He had no patience or respect for "incompetent and inefficient officers who have no interest in their duties,"[60] nor did he hold high regard for his superior, Brig. Gen. John Pope, who commanded the Department of the Missouri from distant Fort Leavenworth. The dearth of supplies led Miles to a vehement denunciation of 59-year-old Colonel Stewart Van Vliet, Pope's Chief Quatermaster, of whom he wrote, "This command has been actually starved to death by his bad management."[61] He forthrightly and outspokenly expressed the opinion that he, Miles, ought to have been given control of all five columns—exhibiting a tendency to question the wisdom of his superiors which would become an increasingly abrasive character trait that only battlefield success would offset.

Indian Operations 1874-75

August 22, 1874—A column consisting of eight troops of the Sixth Cavalry and four companies Fifth Infantry, with a section of artillery,[62] commanded by Colonel N.A. Miles,

[59] Letter to Mrs. Miles, Camp South of the Washita, Texas, Aug. 25, 1874.
[60] Letter to Mrs. Miles, Red River, Sept. 6, 1874.
[61] Letter to Mrs. Miles, Washita, Dec. 2, 1874.
[62] Miles' force was composed of Companies A, D, F, G, H, I, L and M of the 6th Cavalry, inter battalion commanders Maj. James Biddle and Maj. Charles E. Compton; Companies C, D, E, and I, 5th Infantry, under Capt. Henry B. Bristol; one ten-pounder Parrott Gun and two Gatling Guns, commanded by 2nd Lt. James W. Pope, 5th Inf.; and a force of Civilian and Indian scouts, under the direction of 1st Lt. Frank D. Baldwin, 5th Inf.

Fifth Infantry, was also advanced against the Indians from Camp Supply Indian Territory via the Antelope Hills. Another column consisting of three troops of the Eighth Cavalry and a couple of mountain howitzers under Major W.R. Price,[63] Eighth Cavalry, from Forts Bascom and Union New Mexico moved down the main Canadian to join Colonel Miles at or near the Antelope Hills.

August 30—The column of Colonel Miles encountered the Indians near the headwaters of the Washita[64] and kept up a running fight for several days, the Indians steadily falling back until they reached the hills, about eight miles from Salt Fork of Red River, where they made a stand, but were promptly attacked, routed, and pursued in a Southwesterly direction, across the main Red River and out into the Staked Plains with a loss of 3 killed besides animals and camp equipage captured. The troops had one soldier and one civilian wounded.

Sept. 9—Indians attacked Colonel Miles' supply train, escorted by about 60 men, Commanded by Captain Lyman,[65] Fifth Infantry, on the Washita River, Texas, keeping it corraled for several days until relief arrived from Camp Supply Indian Territory; one enlisted man was killed, one soldier, a wagon master, and Lieutenant G. Lewis Fifth Infantry were wounded.[66]

Sept 11 and 12—Near the Washita River a detachment of two scouts and four soldiers from Colonel Miles' command, in endeavoring to communicate with that of Major Price, was attacked by Indians and four of the six wounded, one of the

[63] Maj. William R. Price, 8th Cav., brevetted Brigadier General for his service with the 3rd Pa. Cavalry during the Civil War. Miles would repeatedly find fault with him during the Red River War.

[64] At the start of the attack Capt. Adna R. Chaffee, 6th Cav., shouted the famous command, "Forward! If any man is killed I will make him a corporal!" Lieutenant Baldwin's 20 Delaware Scouts, led by Falling Leaf, were conspicuous for their bravery in this affair.

[65] Capt. Wyllys Lyman, 5th Inf., commanding a mixed force of men from his own regiment and the 6th Cav., escorting 36 wagons. Scout William F. Schmalsle rode for help, and on September 14 a relief force arrived from Camp Supply. Lyman was brevetted Lt. Col. for gallantry in this engagement.

[66] 1st Lt. Granville Lewis, 5th Inf., was shot through the left knee. He was later brevetted Captain for gallantry in this fight.

wounded dying in a hole in which the party desperately
defended themselves for two days until relieved by troops in
that vicinity.[67]

November 8—near McClellan Creek, Texas, Lieut. F.D. Baldwin, Fifth Infantry, with a detachment consisting of Troop
"D" 6th Cavalry, and Company "D" Fifth Infantry attacked a
large camp of Indians, routing them with a loss of much of
their property.[68] Two little white girls, Adelaide and Julia
Germaine aged five and seven years were rescued from these
Indians. The children stated that two older sisters were still
held captive by the Indians. The story of their woe and
suffering in captivity was pitiable in the extreme, not even their
tender years sparing them from the most dreadful treatment.
Their father, mother, brother, and one sister were all murdered
at the time the four sisters were captured. At the close of the
campaign the other two sisters were rescued from the Indians,
and all four provided a comfortable home with the Army at
Fort Leavenworth, Kansas. General Miles became their
guardian and Congress authorized the stoppage of an amount

[67]This was the famous "Buffalo Wallow" fight. The couriers were, from the 6th Cavalry:
Sgt. Z.T. Woodall, Co. I; Pvt. Peter Rath, Co. A; Pvt. John Harrington; Co. H and Pvt.
George W. Smith, Co. M. The two scouts were Amos Chapman and William Dixon. All
were wounded or otherwise injured, Smith mortally so. Of them Miles wrote:

   The simple recital of their deeds and the mention of the odds against which they
   fought; how the wounded defended the dying, and the dying aided the wounded by
   exposure to fresh wounds after the power of action was gone; these alone present a
   scene of cool courage, heroism and self-sacrifice which duty, as well as inclination,
   prompts us to recognize, but which we cannot fitly honor. (Miles, *Personal
   Recollections*, p. 174.)

The men received the Medal of Honor.

[68]1st Lt. Frank D. Baldwin, 5th Inf., led Companies D, 6th U.S. Cav., and D, 5th Inf. in
this attack on Chief Graybeard's Cheyennes. He was brevetted Captain and awarded his
second Medal of Honor for his gallantry in this battle; his first Medal had been awarded for
Civil War service at the Battle of Peachtree Creek, Georgia, when he was Captain in the
19th Michigan.

   A loyal and capable subordinate, Baldwin also became one of Miles' closest friends, in
part, perhaps, because he posed no threat to the Colonel's far-reaching ambition. In his
memoirs Miles praised Baldwin: "His qualities were of the highest and noblest character.
He was one of those men who did not come in with a plausible excuse for failure. He
always accomplished good results." (Miles, *Personal recollections*, p. 230.)

   Miles wrote to his wife of Baldwin: "He is a very safe and gallant officer and I have great
confidence in him. He is one of those officers that I am willing to trust a long way out of my
sight." (Letter to Mrs. Miles, Cantonment on the Yellowstone, Jan. 21, 1877.)

for the support of the children from the annuities of their captors, the Southern Cheyennes.[69]

Major General John Pope, Commanding Department of the Missouri in his annual report for 1875, referring to the foregoing operations says:

> At the date of my last annual report the expedition against the hostile Indians in the Indian Territory and Texas under Command of Colonel N.A. Miles, Fifth United States Infantry, had just fairly entered upon active operations. On the 30th of August 1874, after a rapid pursuit for seven successive days of a body of the Cheyenne Indians, among whom were a number of Indians belonging to the Kiowas and Comanches, Colonel Miles overtook the combined force on the banks of Red River, and after a spirited conflict the Indians were routed and driven from the field, leaving their lodges and much of their property in the hands of the troops. Everything was destroyed, and the pursuit of the scattered bands was continued for 30 miles farther on to the Staked Plains. Being so far from his supplies, and those he was able to carry being nearly exhausted, Colonel Miles retraced his steps, to meet the trains which were on the way to overtake him.

1875

The Military operations against the bands in the Indian Territory, described during the last half of the year 1874, were continued during the winter of that year and well into the Spring of 1875. The force brought from New Mexico, under Major Price, Eighth Cavalry, was consolidated with that under Colonel Miles, and the whole expedition from the Department of the Missouri fell under the immediate command of the latter during the rest of the field operations. It consisted of eight troops of the Sixth Cavalry under Majors Compton and Biddle, four troops of the Eighth Cavalry under Major Price, and four companies of the Fifth Infantry. From July 21, 1874, to February 12, 1875, the whole of this force was actively and incessantly employed in

[69]The westward-bound family of John German was attacked on Sept. 11 by Medicine Water's Cheyennes. Of the seven children, Katherine, 17, Sophia, 13, Julia, 7, and Adelaide, 5, were taken hostage. In the following weeks all were brutalized and the elder two were repeatedly raped by their captors. Medicine Water traded the younger girls to Gray Beard shortly before the fight on November 8. On March 6, 1875, Katherine and Sophia were surrendered to Lt. Col. Thomas H. Neill, 6th Cav., at Cheyenne Agency.

scouting the entire section infested by the Indian Territory Bands, keeping the Indians so constantly on the move that they were unable to lay in any stock of provision. This active work was continued by the troops upon the exposed and barren plains of that region during the whole of a winter of unprecedented severity, and as the season advanced the difficulty of supplying the necessary forage and subsistence increased so that no little hardship and privation resulted, but the troops bore everything with fortitude and courage and without complaint. By extra-ordinary efforts enough supplies reached the troops to keep them in the field until their work was done, and at length early in March 1875, the Southern Cheyennes, completely broken down, gave up the contest and under their principal Chief, Stone Calf, the whole body of that tribe, with trifling exception, surrendered themselves as prisoners of war, restoring at the same time the two elder Germaine girls who had been captives among them for nearly eight months. In surrendering, the Indians gave up their horses, which were sold, and with the proceeds were purchased herds of young cattle for the pastoral education of the Indians. Although the conditions of surrender required the Indians to deliver up their arms, only some guns and a large quantity of bows and arrows were turned in, the greater part of their more valuable fire arms being hidden away where no search by the troops would be likely to find them.

INDIAN OPERATIONS 1874-1875

General Sheridan in his annual report for 1874, referring to the operations of the troops under command of Colonel N.A. Miles, Fifth Infantry says:

> On the 21st of July authority was received from the Department of the Interior, through the Secretary of War, to invade, if necessary, the special Indian Reservations set aside for these Indians (Cheyenne, Kiowas, and Commanches) within the limits of Indian Territory, or, in other words to punish them wherever they may be found. General Pope was then authorized to push his troops into the field and carry out this condition to the best of his ability.
>
> The result has been the organization of a column under Colonel Nelson A. Miles, Fifth Infantry, which advanced against the

Indians from Camp Supply Indian Territory, via: Antelope Hills, and another column under Major W.R. Price, Eighth Cavalry who moved down the Canadian River from Forts Bascom and Union to join Colonel Miles, at or near the Antelope Hills.

Colonel Miles encountered the Indians near the headwaters of the Washita River and kept up a running fight for several days, the Indians steadily falling back until they reached the hills, eight miles from Salt Fork of Red River when they made a bold stand, but were promptly attacked and routed, and pursued in a Southwesterly direction across Main Red River, and out on to the Staked Plains, losing heavily in men, animals and baggage. Owing to a want of supplies, Colonel Miles was at length forced to abandon the pursuit and return to a point near Antelope Hills where supplies had been sent him. This train of supplies which met him at the point indicated, had been attacked by a large force of Indians, principally Kiowas from the Wichita Agency, while moving on the Washita River above that place, but had been most gallantly and successfully defended by Captain Lyman and Lieutenant Lewis with a small train guard of about 60 men, Lieutenant Lewis receiving a severe wound in the action.

Colonel Miles has by this time in all probability resumed the pursuit of the hostile tribes, and in conjunction with the column of Colonel Mackenzie who is moving up from Texas towards the headwaters of Red River, almost to the very spot where Colonel Miles has driven the Indians, and Lieutenant Colonel Davidson, who has been moving with his command since the 10th of September up the Washita River together with Lieutenant Colonel Buell, who is moving from Fort Sill up the main Red River, we may well anticipate lively times for these unruly Indians.

All of these columns were pushed out much sooner than was desirable, especially that of Colonel Miles and Major Price, but I deemed it necessary that we should take the field at once to prevent hostile Indians from forcing out those of their tribes who had made up their minds to remain at peace, and, also, to prevent the accumulation of Winter supplies from the buffalo herd. As these hostile Indians have their families and stock with them and as Colonel Miles has given them but little time to hunt for the last six or eight weeks, and as all of our columns are now in the field, we may hope for good results soon. Still the country is large, and it may take us until mid-winter to accomplish the object in view namely, the definite settlement of Indian troubles in the Southwest forever.

In concluding his report General Sheridan says:

It will thus be seen that the operations of Colonel Miles, Lieutenant Colonel Davidson, Lieutenant Colonel Buell, and Major Price, (who came down the Canadian from Fort Bascom) will result in forcing the hostiles to the vicinity of Colonel Mackenzie. All these arrangements have worked admirably so far, and it is hoped that the very best results which could be expected will be accomplished, and that we may settle the Indian question forever so far as the Kiowas, Comanches and Cheyennes in the Southwest are concerned.

General Sheridan in his annual report for 1875, describing operations in the Department of the Missouri and mainly referring to the operations of the troops under General Miles' Command says:

In the Department of the Missouri the Campaign against the Cheyennes, Kiowas and Comanches was finished early in the Spring, and the ringleaders and worst criminals separated from the tribes and sent to Fort Marion, Florida. This campaign was not only very comprehensive, but was the most successful of any Indian Campaign in this country since its settlement by the whites; and much credit is due to the officers and men engaged in it.

IV

Avenging Custer

At Cimarron, New Mexico, in late November 1875, a party of Muache Utes and Jicarilla Apaches expressed dissatisfaction with the poor rations and shabby conditions of reservation life by shooting up their agency and fleeing for the mountains. On December 1 General Pope ordered Miles to proceed from Fort Leavenworth to Cimarron, assume control of the troops at that point plus two 5th Cavalry companies at Trinidad and force the recalcitrant Indians to return to their reservation. Arriving in Cimarron on November 6, Miles soon found that the Indians' grievances were well-founded in fact; "As near as I can ascertain the whole trouble arises from whisky, bad rations and a want of proper discretion in their management."[70] Within twenty-five days he negotiated a peaceful return to the agency, leaving New Mexico with the confirmed opinion that corrupt inefficiency of the Indian Bureau lay at the heart of the matter. As time went on he would become convinced that the Army, not the political bureaucracy, should govern the reservations.

The next seven months passed uneventfully for Miles and his family at Fort Leavenworth, as thousands of Sioux and Cheyennes left their reservations to follow the militant mystic Sitting Bull. The Colonel was peeved not to have a place in the Army's grand campaign of 1876 in which his rival, Brig. Gen. George Crook seemed destined to play a major role. However, on July 5, 1876, the terrible news of Custer's disaster at Little Big Horn reached Leavenworth, followed shortly thereafter by orders of six companies of the 5th Infantry to join the forces led by General Alfred H. Terry and Col. John Gibbon in the field. If army commander Sherman thought his ambitious relation would be content to

[70] Letter, Miles to Mrs. Miles.

remain at his station while Lt. Col. Joseph Whistler led the 5th Infantry to war as originally planned, he was sadly mistaken. Within days Miles had badgered his way to field command and was steaming up the Missouri with his foot soldiers.

On July 23 the steamer arrived at Fort Lincoln, Dakota Territory, home station for the doomed 7th Cavalry. Miles gave what comfort he could to Mrs. Custer, and wrote his wife Mary, "You can have no idea of the gloom that overhangs that post with twenty-seven widows. I never saw anything like it."[71] It was a sobering prelude to the difficult work ahead.

From Fort Buford at the mouth of the Yellowstone, Miles proceeded up that river, sticking to a regimen of thrice-daily drills and officers' instruction. Upon debarking August 2 at the Terry/Gibbon camp at the mouth of Rosebud Creek, eager and confident, Miles was in for a rude surprise. "I never saw a command so completely stampeded as this, either in the volunteer or regular service, and I believe entirely without reason."[72] As usual, he did not cast blame on the enlisted men, but on their officers, "both high and low."[73] In his view Terry was a beaten man, Gibbon slow and plodding, Crook vacillating and unreliable. "This campaign thus far would not have been creditable to a militia organization."[74] Frustrated that his superiors seemed unwilling to press the offensive against the victorious Sioux and Cheyennes, Miles concluded, "The more I see of movements here the more admiration I have for Custer, and I am satisfied his like will not be found very soon again."[75]

On August 8 Terry's army, 1,700 strong, began slowly marching up the Rosebud, rendezvousing with Crook's column two days later. It was obvious to anyone with an understanding of Indian warfare that such a ponderous force could never bring their elusive foe to bay; subsequently Crook struck off to the Southwest for the Black Hills, while the Terry/Gibbon command ultimately disbanded at Glendive on the Yellowstone River. Miles with his entire regiment, and six companies of the 22nd

---

[71] Letter, Miles to Mrs. Miles, Fort Lincoln, July 23, 1876.

[72] Letter, Miles to Mrs. Miles, Camp opposite Rosebud, Montana, Aug. 4, 1876.

[73] *Ibid.*

[74] *Ibid.*

[75] Letter, Miles to Mrs. Miles, Camp at Mouth of Rosebud, Aug. 7, 1876.

Infantry under Lt. Col. Elwell S. Otis, was ordered to patrol the Yellowstone between the Tongue and Powder Rivers. It was hoped that by stationing troops at all possible crossing points, and patrolling the 210 mile stretch by steamer, that any significant Indian movement north would be detected and stopped. In addition Miles received orders from Sherman to construct and supply a winter cantonment at the junction of the Tongue and Yellowstone.

Despite these plans few officers held hopes for a successful conclusion of the 1876 campaign, least of all Miles. On August 20 he wrote Mary from the mouth of Powder River,

> Terry means well enough, and is decidedly the best man but he has had little experience and is too much under the influence of those slow inefficient men like Gibbon to reap good results. This business to be successful should be conducted on sound military principles first, and then with great energy and persistency.[76]

As Terry and Gibbon abandoned the campaign, Crook pressed his famous "Starvation March." Save for a minor victory against American Horse's Miniconjous at Slim Buttes on September 9, this effort failed to defeat or coerce Sitting Bull's followers to return to their reservations.

In the course of supplying the Tongue River Cantonment, the trains escorted by Otis' 22nd Infantry were threatened, prompting Miles to sally forth with his "walk-a-heaps." Moving down the Yellowstone, on October 20 he came face to face with the redoubtable Sitting Bull before his camp at Cedar Creek. After two inconclusive negotiations, Miles attacked the Indian village. A two-day running battle cost the hostiles much of their winter food stock, and led to the surrender of a number of Sans Arcs and Miniconjous. Encouraged by this success against the most formidable of opponents, Miles wrote his wife, "It was a good thing for the Regiment as it was all engaged, every company, and the fact of whipping and routing Sitting Bull's body of Sioux has inspired them with great confidence and spirit."[77]

Following the return march to Tongue River Cantonment,

---

[76]Letter, Miles to Mrs. Miles, Mouth of Powder River, M.T. Aug. 20, 1876.
[77]Letter, Miles to Mrs. Miles, Near the Camp Fire on the Yellowstone 20 miles above Glendive, Oct. 25, 1876.

Miles determined not to pass the winter in camp but to continue his offensive operations. As supplies were stockpiled the troops were outfitted with fur caps, gloves, leggings and buffalo coats, while their Colonel persistently lobbied for Sibley tents, cannon and cavalry reinforcements. Presenting these demands to his uncle-in-law General Sherman, Miles wrote,

> If you expect me to be successful see that I am supported or give me command of this whole region and I will soon end this Sioux war. And I would be very glad to govern them afterwards for the more I see of them the more respect I have for them and believe their affairs can be governed to their entire satisfaction as well as for the interests of the govt.[78]

Through November and December the Fifth Infantry battalions under Miles and his capable subordinates Captains Frank Baldwin and Simon Snyder braved blizzards and sub-zero temperatures seeking hostile villages between the Yellowstone and Missouri. On December 23 the ever-reliable Baldwin attacked and destroyed a village of 122 lodges on Redwood Creek.

Envious of Col. Mackenzie's November 25 victory over Dull Knife's Cheyennes on Powder River, Miles launched another campaign at the end of December. At Wolf Mountain on January 8, 1877, he confronted Crazy Horse's Oglalas with five companies of the Fifth Infantry, two of the 22nd and two cannon ingeniously disguised as wagons. Indecisive though it was, the tactical success boosted morale; "I never saw troops behave better or fight with more coolness or pluck."[79]

The glow of victory began to wear off after Miles returned to Tongue River. From his superiors, he received no troops, few supplies and little encouragement. In letters to Mrs. Miles he heaped scorn and derision on General Terry, who was sitting out the winter at Department of Dakota Headquarters in St. Paul. Sherman was bombarded with complaints and demands from the ambitious Colonel. In a letter of January 20, after charging Terry and his quartermasters with "criminal neglect of duty" and "a determination that I shall not accomplish anything," Miles continued in an unbelievably presumptuous vein,

[78] Letter, Miles to General Sherman, Opposite Fort Peck, Montana, Nov. 18, 1876. William T. Sherman Papers, Lby. of Cong.
[79] Letter, Miles to Mrs. Miles, Cantonment on the Yellowstone, Montana, Jan. 19, 1877.

Now if I have not earned a command I never will, and if I have not given proof of my ability to bring my command into a successful encounter with Indians every time I never will, besides I now have a better knowledge of this country than any other white man and unless you can give me a command and it should be no less than a department, you can order my Regt. out of this country as soon as you like for I have campaigned long enough for the benefit of thieves and contractors. If you will give me this command & *one half the troops now in it, I will end this Sioux war once & forever in four months.*[80]

Though he did not get the department and promotion he craved, Miles' success where so many others had failed was not unappreciated by Sherman and Sheridan. He received additional troops, including cavalry, and was allowed greater leeway in the breadth and scope of his operations. In the months that followed, military victories coupled with successful peace negotiations conducted by Crazy Horse's uncle, Spotted Tail, fragmented the coalition of tribes forged by Sitting Bull. That defiant chief fled to Canada with his Hunkpapas, while Crazy Horse with over 2,000 tribesmen surrendered at Red Cloud Agency on May 6, 1877.

There remained at large some 60 lodges under the Miniconjou Lame Deer, who had refused to surrender with Crazy Horse. On May 1, 1877, Miles started after him with two companies of the 5th Infantry, four of the 22nd, a four company squadron from the 2nd Cavalry, and a force of loyal Cheyennes and Miniconjous. At dawn on May 7 Miles launched his cavalry on Lame Deer's village. For a few minutes it seemed the chief would surrender; he approached Miles accompanied by the warrior Iron Star, laying his rifle on the ground. As the Colonel bent down from his saddle to shake hands, a nervous white scout in his escort pointed his weapon at the Indians, who, fearing treachery, promptly seized their guns and opened fire. Lame Deer's shot missed Miles by inches, killing a trooper behind him. The subsequent exchange of fire left fourteen Sioux dead, including both Lame Deer and Iron Star. The village was burned and much of the pony herd killed; the remaining animals were used to convert four companies of Miles' regiment to mounted infantry. For a loss of four dead

---

[80] Letter, Miles to General Sherman, Cantonment on the Yellowstone, Jan. 20, 1877. William T. Sherman Papers, Lby. of Cong.

and seven wounded, Miles crushed this last immediate hostile threat, less than a year after Little Big Horn. By summer's end there remained only the elusive Sitting Bull ensconced in Canadian territory.

In June, having been separated from his family for almost a year, Miles welcomed his wife, daughter Cecelia and sister-in-law Elizabeth Sherman Cameron to Tongue River Cantonment. Proud of his success in avenging Custer, he little suspected that within three months he would be called upon to deal with another military crisis.

INDIAN OPERATIONS 1876-77

After the Custer Massacre in June 1876 on the Little Big Horn, the bands which had broken off from the main body of hostiles, and young warriors, from the agencies, continued their old well known methods of warfare, stealing horses on the frontier and killing small parties of citizens, while the constant communications of the hostiles with Indians at the agencies, made it evident that supplies of food and ammunition were still being drawn from those places.

To prevent this it had been deemed necessary that the military should control the agencies, and on May 29 the Interior Department had been requested to cooperate with the military so as to enable the latter to carry out the policy of arresting, disarming, and dismounting such of the hostiles as made their appearance at these agencies.

At last on July 22, Congress having passed a bill authorizing the construction of the two posts in the Yellowstone country recommended long before this war began, preparations were made to begin them at once and all the material was prepared as rapidly as possible but the season had now become so far advanced that it was found impracticable to get the supplies up the Yellowstone River, on account of low water, so the building of the posts had to be deferred until the following Spring. However, a temporary cantonment was ordered to be immediately constructed at the mouth of Tongue River, the place selected for one of the permanent posts (Fort Keogh) and a strong garrison, under the command of Colonel Miles, Fifth Infantry, was detailed to occupy it.

October 10, Captain C.W. Miner,[81] Twenty-second Infantry, with companies H, G and K, 22nd Infantry, and Company C, 17th Infantry, escorting a train of ninety-four wagons, started from the camp at mouth of Glendive Creek, Montana, for the cantonment at mouth of Tongue River. The train was attacked in its camp that night by Indians estimated at from four to six hundred, several of the animals wounded and forty-seven mules stampeded and captured. In this crippled condition the train attempted to reach Clear Creek, eight miles further on, being constantly harrassed by the hostiles in large force, but finding it impossible to continue returned to Glendive Creek for reinforcements.

The teamsters having become too demoralized to proceed, forty-one of them were discharged and soldiers were detailed to drive. The escort, now consisting of five companies of infantry, numbering eleven officers and one hundred and eighty-five men, under command of Lieutenant Colonel E.S. Otis,[82] Twenty-Second Infantry, again attempted to carry these much needed supplies to the garrison at Tongue River.

October 15 on Spring Creek the Indians increased to an estimated strength of from seven to eight hundred warriors, again attacked the train, which, however, formed in compact lines, pressed on, the infantry escort charging the Indians repeatedly and driving them back while the wagons slowly advanced. Three or four scouts from Colonel Miles' Command were met here, having been attacked by Indians and one of their party killed. The train proceeded, with the escort skirmishing, until Clear Creek was reached, the point from which Captain Miner had previously been obliged to return. Here the Indians made the most determined attack, firing the prairie. The wagons proceeded, being obliged to advance through the flames compactly arranged

[81]Capt. Charles W. Miner of Ohio; he was brevetted Major for gallantry in the affair on Spring Creek.
[82]Lt. Col. Elwell S. Otis of New York had been brevetted Brigadier General for his Civil War service. Although Miles sometimes thought him lacking in talents, Otis' career was a noteworthy one; he would later serve as Major General of Volunteers in the Philippine Islands campaign.

in four lines, with the entire escort being engaged in alternately charging the Indians, driving them back and then regaining the moving teams; three or four of the escort were wounded and a considerable number of Indian saddles emptied. On October 16th, while advancing, an Indian runner approached and left upon a hill the following communication:

Yellowstone

I want to know what you are doing traveling on this road. You scare all the buffalos away. I want to hunt in this place. I want you to turn back from here. If you don't I will fight you again. I want you to leave what you have got here and turn back from here.

I am your friend,
Sitting Bull

(P.S.) I mean all the rations you have got and some powder. Wish you would write as soon as you can.

Colonel Otis sent out a scout named Jackson,[83] with a reply to Sitting Bull's note stating that he intended to take the train through to Tongue River, and would be pleased to accommodate the Indians with a fight at any time. The train proceeded, the Indians surrounding it, and keeping up firing at long range. After proceeding a short distance, two Indians appeared with a flag of truce and communication was again opened with the hostiles, who stated they were hungry, tired of war and wanted to make peace. Sitting Bull wanted to meet Colonel Otis outside of the lines of the escort, which invitation however Colonel Otis declined, though professing a willingness to meet Sitting Bull inside the lines of the troops. This the wary savage was afraid to do, but sent three Chiefs to represent him. Colonel Otis made them a present of one hundred and fifty pounds of hard bread and two sides of bacon, said that he had no authority to treat with them, but that the Indians could go to Tongue River and there make known their wishes regarding surrender. The train moved on and the Indians fell to its rear, finally disappearing altogether.

On the night of the 18th of October, Colonel Otis met Colonel Miles with his entire regiment, who, alarmed for the safety of the train, had advanced to meet it. Colonel Otis succeeded in reaching Tongue River, delivered his supplies, and returned safely with his wagons to Glendive on October 26th.

---

[83] Scout Bob Jackson.

Shortly after meeting Colonel Otis and learning from him the immediate situation, Colonel Miles, with the entire Fifth Infantry started after Sitting Bull, overtaking him near Cedar Creek, Montana, north of the Yellowstone, Colonel Miles met Sitting Bull between the lines of the troops and of the Indians, the latter having sent a flag of truce to Miles, desiring to communicate.

Sitting Bull simply desired to hunt buffalo and trade for ammunition; he would agree that the Indians should not fire on the soldiers if unmolested; in short he wanted simply "an old fashioned peace" for the winter. He was informed of the terms of the government, told how he could have peace and that he must bring his tribe near the camp of the troops. The interview closed unsatisfactorily, and Colonel Miles' column, numbering three hundred and ninety-eight rifles, moved and encamped on Cedar Creek, so as to intercept more easily the movement of the Indians, which was northward, Sitting Bull being told to come again next day.[84]

While the command was moving north between the Indian camp and the Big Dry River, the Indians again appeared and desired to talk. Another council followed between the lines, October 21, Sitting Bull and a number of principal men being present. Sitting Bull wanted peace if he could have it upon his own terms. He was told the conditions of the government, which were that he should either camp his people at some point on the Yellowstone River, near to the troops, or go into some Agency and place his people under subjection to the government. He said he could come in to trade for ammunition, but wanted no rations or annuities, and desired to live free as an Indian. He gave no assurance of good faith, and, as the Council broke up, he was told that a non-acceptance of the terms of the government would be considered an act of hostility. The Indians took positions instantly for a fight, and an engagement followed (October 21, 1876) the Indians being driven from every part of the field, through their camp ground, down Bad Route Creek, and pursued forty-two miles to the south side of the Yellowstone. In

[84] Miles suspected that Sitting Bull might attempt to assassinate him during one of their meetings, as General Canby had been in the Lava Beds. Given his own predeliction for taking hostages, it would be safe to assume that had Miles been given the chance he would have held the Sioux Chief by force of arms.

their retreat they abandoned tons of dried meat, quantities of lodge poles, camp equipage, ponies, and broken down cavalry horses. Five dead warriors were left on the field, besides those they were seen to carry away. Their force was estimated at upwards of one thousand warriors.

On October 27th over four hundred lodges of Indians, numbering about two thousand men, women, and children, surrendered to Colonel Miles; five chiefs giving themselves up as hostages for the delivery of men, women, children, ponies, arms and ammunition at the agencies;[85] Sitting Bull himself escaped northward with his own small band, and was joined later by "Gall"[86] and other chiefs with their followers. Having returned to Tongue River Cantonment General Miles organized a force numbering four hundred and thirty-four rifles and moved north in pursuit of Sitting Bull, but the trail was obliterated by the snow in the vicinity of Big Dry River. A band of one hundred and nineteen lodges under "Iron Dog" crossed the Missouri in advance of the command and dissolved itself in the Yanktonnais camp, Sitting Bull continuing to hover about the neighborhood of the Missouri River and its branches for sometime afterwards.

The operations of Colonel Miles against Sitting Bull and his confederates were continued. On December 7th, First Lieutenant F.D. Baldwin, with companies G, H and I Fifth Infantry, numbering one hundred officers and men, overtook Sitting Bull's camp of one hundred and ninety lodges, followed and drove it south of the Missouri, near the mouth of Bark Creek. The Indians resisted Baldwin's crossing of the river for a short time and then retreated into the Bad Lands. On December 18th this same force under Lieutenant Baldwin, surprised Sitting Bull's band of one hundred and twenty-two lodges near the head of the Redwater, a southern affluent of the Missouri, capturing the entire camp and its contents, together with about sixty horses, ponies and mules. The Indians escaped with little besides what they had upon their persons and scattered southward across the Yellowstone.

---

[85] Many of these Indians subsequently left the agencies a second time, if they ever in fact arrived. The holding of hostages did not always guarantee decisive results.

[86] Gall was perhaps the most redoubtable chief after Sitting Bull and Crazy Horse. He had played a crucial role in destroying Custer's battalion at the Little Big Horn.

1876

General Sherman in his report for 1876 referring to the foregoing operations says:

Colonel Miles had nearly completed his cantonment at the mouth of Tongue River and Lieutenant Colonel Otis of the 22nd Infantry was at Glendive Creek, a post intermediate between Tongue River and Fort Buford, when a train carrying stores for Tongue River, escorted by two companies of the Sixth Infantry, was, on the 10th of October attacked by hostile Indians, estimated as high as 500 warriors, who captured sixty mules from the train. The train returned to Glendive, but was reinforced and conducted by Lieutenant Colonel Otis in person, and performed its journey in safety. As soon as the intelligence of this reached Colonel Miles, he started with his regiment, the Fifth Infantry, taking a course northeast, to intercept the Indians on their way towards Fort Peck, and struck their trail and camp on the 21st of October, when the Indians appeared in large force on the surrounding hills but presented a flag of truce and asked a conference. Colonel Miles met Sitting Bull in person, with some of his leading men, who wanted an "old fashioned peace" with privileges of trade, especially in ammunition. Colonel Miles explained that he could only accept surrender on terms of absolute submission to the will of the general government. They separated that evening with an understanding to meet the next day. The next morning Colonel Miles moved his command north so as to intercept retreat in that direction, and while he was in motion the Indians again appeared and desired further "talk." A council was again held with Sitting Bull, Pretty Bear, Bull Eagle, John, Standing Bear, Gall, White Bull and others, who all professed a wish for peace, but such a peace as Colonel Miles could not concede; and as they gave him no assurance of good faith, the council ended and an engagement immediately followed. The Indians were driven from their camp and ground down Bad Route Creek and across the Yellowstone a distance of 42 miles; the Indians abandoned "tons of dried meat, lodge poles, camp equipage, ponies &c." The troops on foot followed rapidly, not stopping to count the dead or gather the plunder and the consequence was that on the 27th of October five principal Chiefs surrendered themselves to Colonel Miles on the Yellowstone, opposite the mouth of Cabin Creek as hostages for the surrender of their whole people represented as between 400 and 500 lodges, equal to about 2,000 souls. The hostages were sent

under escort to his Commanding General, Terry, at St. Paul, and
the Indians were allowed five days in their camp to gather food,
and thirty days to reach the Cheyenne agency, near Fort Sully, on
the Missouri River, where they are to surrender their arms and
ponies to the Commanding Officer, and remain either as prisoners
of war, or subject to treatment such as is universally accorded to
Indians living at peace with the United States. Had Colonel Miles
taken these to his camp at Tongue River, they would have
required strong guards, and would have eaten up the provisions
collected for his own men during the severe winter now at hand,
and he could not afford to escort them to the Cheyenne Agency
three hundred miles away without neglecting his paramount
duties in that quarter; he was therefore fully justified in taking
hostages for their good faith, and I doubt not early in December
these Indians will reach their proper Agency, and receive the usual
treatment.[87]

Meantime, Colonel Hazen,[88] 6th Infantry, commanding at
Fort Buford, has started up the Missouri River for Fort Peck with
4 companies of his regiment, 6th Infantry, to head off Sitting Bull,
who is reported by the surrendered Chiefs, to have slipped out,
with thirty lodges of his special followers, during the retreat down
Bad Route Creek, and to have resumed his course for Fort Peck or
the British possessions. Colonel Miles reports his purpose to
replenish his supplies, to turn north and follow this last desperate
band to the death. The winter is close at hand and there is great
danger from the weather in that high latitude, but a reasonable
certainty of finding some food at Fort Peck, and abundance at Fort
Buford, or his own cantonment on the Yellowstone, he will be sure
to catch up at one or the other, and, I trust, enroute, will make an
end of Sitting Bull.

Lieutenant General Sheridan, in his annual report for 1876,
referring to operations says:

> While this was going on, the hostiles attacked the trains
> carrying supplies to the Tongue River cantonment, and Colonel
> Nelson A. Miles, 5th Infantry, marched out his command, and
> after an engagement on the 21st of October and a successful
> pursuit, over 400 lodges of the Missouri River Indians surrendered
> to him, giving hostages for the delivery of men, women, children,
> ponies, arms and ammunition of the Cheyenne River Agency on

---

[87] As noted above, not all of these Indians actually arrived at the agencies.
[88] Col. William B. Hazen (USMA 1855) had been Major General of Volunteers in the Civil
War, one of Sherman's most valued subordinates.

the 2nd of December; Sitting Bull with his band of about 30 lodges escaping to the north, and, no doubt, to the British possessions... The surrender of the Indians from the Missouri River Agencies to Colonel Miles on the 27th of October, numbering in men, women and children at least 2,000 and the escape of Sitting Bull and his small band to the north, leaves now out and hostile, only the Northern Cheyennes and the band of Crazy Horse and his allies on the Red Cloud Agency.

Brigadier General Alfred H. Terry, commanding Department of the Dakota referring to the foregoing operations says:

Colonel Miles, having received information that Sitting Bull was about to cross the Yellowstone and go to the Dry Fork of the Missouri for the purpose of hunting buffalo moved from Tongue River with the 5th Infantry with the design of intercepting or following him. When on Custer's Creek he received news of the attack on Captain Miners' train and of Colonel Otis' engagement. Moving in a northeasterly direction from Custer's Creek he was approaching the Sioux camp when a flag of truce appeared and was received. Two conferences between Colonel Miles and Sitting Bull followed. The Indians were informed of the terms upon which alone they could surrender. These terms were not accepted, and an engagement of which the result was the complete discomfiture of the Indians, nearly all of whom were driven across the Yellowstone, abandoning in their flight tons of dried meat, lodgepoles, travois, camp equipage, ponies, and broken down cavalry horses. Sitting Bull with about thirty lodges escaped to the northward. Colonel Miles estimates the number of Indians engaged at 1,000. On the 27th of October, 4 principal chiefs and one head warrior of the hostile bands surrendered themselves to Colonel Miles and agreed to conduct their bands to Cheyenne Agency and there to remain at peace subject to the orders of the government. It was understood also that they would on arrival give up their arms and horses. Five days were allowed the Indians to obtain meat and thirty days to make the journey to the agency. Chiefs and head warriors above mentioned who represent the Minneconjou and Sans-Arc tribes placed themselves in the hands of the military authorities as hostages for the faithful fulfillment of this agreement and have been sent to Cheyenne under guard.

1877

The large cantonment at the mouth of the Tongue River

having been established from this point as a base, the pursuit of
the remnants of the Sioux and Northern Cheyennes with Sitting
Bull and Crazy Horse was energetically pressed by the troops
under Colonel Miles. The low state of the water in the river now
gave the troops on the Yellowstone a threefold task of great difficulty to shelter themselves by building huts, to bring up their
supplies by tedious hauling from the head of navigation, and to
prosecute simultaneously, in the midst of winter, vigorous field
operations against the hostiles.

On the 29th of December Colonel Miles with companies A, C,
D, E and K, Fifth Infantry, and companies E and F Twenty-
Second Infantry, numbering four hundred and thirty-six officers
and men, with two pieces of artillery, moved out against the Sioux
and Cheyennes under Crazy Horse, whose camp had been
reported south of the Yellowstone in the valley of Tongue River.
As the column moved up the Tongue River the Indians abandoned their winter camps consisting of about six hundred lodges
and the column had two sharp skirmishes on the 1st and 3rd of
January driving the Indians up the valley of Tongue River until
the night of the 7th when the advance captured a young warrior
and seven Cheyenne women and children, who proved to be
relatives of one of the head men of the tribe. A determined
attempt was made by the Indians to rescue the prisoners, and
preparations were made for the severe fight to be expected the
next day. On the morning of January 8th about six hundred
warriors appeared in front of the troops and an engagement
followed, lasting about five hours. The fight took place in a cañon,
the Indians occupying a spur of the Wolf Mountain Range, from
which they were driven by repeated charges. The ground was
covered with ice and snow to a depth of from one to three feet, and
the latter portion of the engagement was fought in a blinding
snow storm, the troops stumbling and falling, in scaling the ice
and snow covered cliffs from which the Indians were driven, with
serious loss in killed and wounded, through the Wolf Mountains
and in the direction of the Big Horn Range. The troops lost three
men killed and eight wounded. The column then returned to the
cantonment at the mouth of Tongue River.

The prisoners which Colonel Miles' command captured from
Crazy Horse's village on the night of January 7th proved a

THE QUINTESSENTIAL MILES
Nokh-ko-Ist-sa (Bear Coat) as he
appeared in the winter
campaign of 1876-77
Courtesy of Brian C. Pohanka

MILES AND STAFF IN THE FIELD, JANUARY 1877
Photographed at the Tongue River Cantonment, from left to right are:
"Yellowstone" Kelly (in background, mounted), 2nd Lt. Oscar F. Long,
Surgeon Henry Remson, 2nd Lt. James W. Pope, Col. Miles, 1st Lt. Frank D.
Baldwin, 2nd Lt. Charles E. Hargous, 2nd Lt. Hobart K. Bailey.
Courtesy, National Archives.

valuable acquisition in communicating with the hostiles and in arranging negotiations for their surrender. On February 1st Colonel Miles sent out a scout,[89] with two of the captives, offering terms on which a surrender would be accepted, informing the hostiles that a noncompliance would result in a movement of the troops against them. Following up the trail from the scene of the engagement of January 8th, near the Wolf Mountains, the Indians were found camped on a tributary of the Little Big Horn. The mission was successfully executed and on February 19th the scout returned with nineteen Indians, mainly Chiefs and leading warriors, who desired to learn the exact conditions upon which they could surrender. The terms were repeated, viz: unconditional surrender and compliance with such orders as might be received from higher authority. The delegation returned to their village, the camps moved to near the forks of Powder River for a general council, and a large delegation of leading Chiefs came in, March 18th, to learn whether further concessions could be obtained from Colonel Miles. They were informed that there would be no change in previous conditions and that it would be equally satisfactory if the Indians surrendered at the more southern agencies, but that they must do one thing or the other, or troops would be immediately sent out after them. Crazy Horse's uncle named "Little Hawk," with others, then guaranteed to either bring the Indian camp to the cantonment at Tongue River, or to take it to the lower agencies, leaving in Colonel Miles' hands as a pledge of good faith nine hostages, prominent men and head warriors of both tribes. Three hundred Indians, led by "Two Moons,"[90] "Hump"[91] and other Chiefs, surrendered to Colonel Miles on April 22nd. The largest part of the bands numbering more than two thousand, led by Crazy Horse, Little Hawk and others moved southward and surrendered at the Red Cloud and Spotted Tail Agencies in May.

Crazy Horse and his people were placed on the reservation near Camp Robinson, where, for a time, they appeared quiet and peaceable, but in a few months the restraints of this new position

[89] The half-breed interpreter John Brughier, who with Luther S. "Yellowstone" Kelly was one of Miles' effective cadre of scouts.

[90] Two Moon had been one of the Cheyenne chiefs at Little Big Horn.

[91] Hump would become a scout for the Military, and was badly wounded at the Bear Paw battle with Joseph's Nez Perces in September.

became so irksome to Crazy Horse, that he began to concoct schemes again involving his people in war. It was determined, therefore, to arrest and confine him. Whilst on his way to the guard-house he broke from those around him and attempted to escape by hewing his way with a knife, through the circle of sentinels and by-standers. In the melee he was fatally wounded and died on the night of Sept. 7.

In the meantime Sitting Bull's camp had gathered near the Yellowstone, and when Crazy Horse and his confederates decided to place themselves under subjection to the Government, Sitting Bull's band, in order to avoid surrendering and to escape further pursuit, retreated beyond the northern boundary and took refuge on Canadian soil, the party being in a very destitute condition, almost out of ammunition and having lost nearly everything excepting their guns and horses.

From those who had surrendered Colonel Miles learned that a band of renegades, chiefly Minniconjous under "Lame Deer" had determined not to yield, had broken off from those who surrendered at Tongue River, and had moved westward. This was about April 22nd, and as soon as the necessary forage could be obtained on May 1st Colonel Miles with a force consisting of troops F, G, H and L Second Cavalry, companies E and H Fifth Infantry, and E, F, G and H Twenty-Second Infantry started up Tongue River. At a point sixty-three miles from its mouth, they cut loose from the wagons, struck across to and moved up the Rosebud, and after a very hard march, with scarcely a halt during two nights and one day, the command surprised Lame Deer's band on May 7th near the mouth of Muddy Creek, an affluent of the Rosebud. The village was charged in fine style and the Indian herd of animals cut off and secured. The Indians were called on to surrender; Lame Deer and Iron Star his head warrior, appeared desirous of doing so, but after shaking hands with some of the officers, the Indians either meditating treachery or fearing it, again began firing. This ended peace making and the fight was resumed, the hostiles being driven, in a running fight, eight miles across the broken country, to the Rosebud. Fourteen Indians were killed including Lame Deer and Iron Star, four hundred and fifty horses, mules and ponies, and the entire Indian camp outfit were captured including fifty-one lodges well stored with supplies. Lieutenant Alfred M. Fuller,[92] 2nd Cavalry was slightly wounded; four enlisted men were killed and six were wounded. The Indians who escaped subsequently moved eastward to the Little Missouri and the command returned to the cantonment, where four companies, B, F, G, and I Fifth Infantry, were mounted with the Indian ponies and continued to serve as cavalry until after the Nez Perce campaign in the following Autumn.

During the remainder of May and the early part of June the force under Colonel Miles, commanding the district of the Yellowstone, was increased by eleven troops of the Seventh Cavalry, four companies of the First Infantry, and two of the Eleventh Infantry. A portion of these were sent to assist in the construction of the new post on the Big Horn (now Fort Custer) and field operations were continued by several separate columns from Colonel Miles' force.

[92]2nd Lt. Alfred M. Fuller (USMA 1876) was brevetted Captain for gallantry in this affair.

V

The Nez Perce Campaign

No event in the history of the Indian Wars remains as poignant and dramatic as the Nez Perce Campaign of 1877. The hopeless 1700 mile odyssey of 800 men, women and children through some of the most formidable terrain in North America; the hard-driven, futile pursuit by one-armed General Howard's exhausted soldiers; the nobility and skill of chiefs Joseph, White Bird, Ollokot, Toohoolhoolzote and Looking Glass, and the fundamental justness of their stand in the face of settlers' encroachment on their homeland, all epitomize the fundamental tragedy of the Indian Wars.

The refusal of the so-called "Nontreaty" Nez Perces to move from their Wallowa Valley homeland of Oregon to the Lapwai Reservation in Idaho had been confronted with military pressure brought to bear by Brig. Gen. Oliver O. Howard, Miles' old commander of Civil War days, now in charge of the Department of Columbia. Grudging acceptance of their fate gave way to violence when three young Nez Perces murdered several of the settlers who represented the source of their unhappiness. Then began the three-month fighting exodus aimed at attaining a safe haven with Sitting Bull's Sioux in Canada. On June 17 the Nez Perce displayed their military prowess by routing two companies of the 2nd Cavalry at White Bird Canyon; following other victories, they fought Howard's pursuing command to a standstill at the Battle of the Clearwater on July 11-12. Stung by press criticism and reprimanded by Sherman, the zealous General passed on into Terry's Department of Dakota. On August 9, Colonel John Gibbon's detachment of the 7th Infantry drawn from his District of Montana was nearly annihilated after striking the Nez Perce camp on the Big Hole River.

By August 22, as the Indians entered Yellowstone Park safely in the lead of their pursuers, it became necessary to alert Colonel Miles in his District of the Yellowstone to prepare to enter the campaign. Preoccupied as both Terry and Miles were with the ever-present threat of Sitting Bull just over the Canadian border, all either could do was detach Colonel Samuel D. Sturgis with six companies of his 7th Cavalry to catch the Nez Perce as they emerged from Yellowstone Park and crossed the Absaroka Range. The uninspired Sturgis, intimidated by the loss of half of his regiment and his only son the year before, was highly critical of the lack of cooperation from the Territory of Montana. He wrote to Miles on August 21,

> If the good people of Montana, with Howard's large force close on the heels of Joseph, allow him to escape I do not think they deserve much sympathy. . . Knowing that my force is so far up the Yellowstone, they may think it strange that I do not *go on* (or rather "come on") but it would be an absolute waste of force, whether they can appreciate it or not.[93]

Unfortunately for the lethargic colonel, he was called upon to play a part in the campaign. On August 31, the Nez Perces adroitly outmaneuvered Sturgis and passed through Clarks Fork Canyon, continuing up that river to the Yellowstone. On September 13, spurred on by Howard's arrival, Sturgis again engaged the Indians, and was checked, with slight loss at Canyon Creek. On September 12 Howard had written Miles, "Earnestly request you to make every effort in your power to prevent the escape of this hostile band, and at least hold them in check till I can overtake them."[94] Now, in the face of Sturgis' apparent failure and the exhausted condition of his men and horses, the General dispatched an even more urgent message to Miles. He would ease his pursuit to grant the Nez Perces a false sense of security, while Miles attempted to head off their northward flight at the Missouri River. Several days later, after learning that Miles was in the field, Howard wrote his former protegé: "My command gets tired but I myself am in sound strength—all will go right now that your loyal head is awake. God bless you & yours."[95]

[93] Sturgis to Miles, Aug. 21, 1877. Miles/Cameron Papers, Lby. of Cong.
[94] Howard to Miles, *Report of the Secretary of War, 1876-77*, p. 623.
[95] Howard to Miles, Sept. 20, 1877. Miles/Cameron Papers, Lby. of Cong.

Anxious for word of events, Miles personally met the courier from Howard outside Tongue River Cantonment on the evening of September 17. By next morning he had a command of 350 men across the Yellowstone and on the move. There were two cavalry battalions, Companies F and H of the 2nd Cavalry and A, D and K of the 7th; Companies B, F, G and I of the Fifth Infantry mounted on their captured Indian ponies; Company K of the 5th, dismounted, escorting the pack and wagon trains, which included a 12-pound Napoleon gun; with the advance went a breach-loading Hotchkiss gun manned by a detachment of 5th Infantrymen. In addition Miles could call upon a force of white scouts and loyal Sioux and Cheyennes.

Miles pushed his men hard, covering 52 miles on September 21, and 38 the next day. On September 23, fortune twice smiled on the indefatigable Colonel. The steamer *Fontenelle* was encountered on the Missouri, and used to ferry the 2nd Cavalry battalion across the river to scout possible Nez Perce crossings, and ultimately to escort General Terry's Peace Commission to Sitting Bull. Miles intended the bulk of his command to patrol the Missouri above the mouth of the Musselshell; but as the steamer chugged away, three civilians arrived by boat with news that the Nez Perce had already crossed the river at Cow Island, some 60 miles to the west. As Miles later admitted, "This was one of the occasions in military affairs when, acting upon the best information obtainable, you suddenly find yourself greatly embarrassed by new information that is directly contradictory."[96] The Hotchkiss gun was hastily unlimbered and fired, causing the steamer to reverse its course—whereupon the entire column was carried to the northern bank of the Missouri, and pressed on after the elusive foe.

The battle of the Bear Paw, or Snake Creek, on Sunday, September 30, 1877, was one of the hardest fought of the Indian Wars. When Miles' soldiers thundered down on the Nez Perce camp, only 40 miles from potential refuge in Canada, he little anticipated the hot reception he received. Superior marksmanship caused 30% casualties in the initial engagement; the five day siege that followed was perhaps the tensest period of Miles' military career. At one point he fully intended to hold Joseph hostage

---

[96] Miles, *Personal Recollections*, p. 265.

when the chief came out under a white flag to negotiate a truce. Unfortunately for Miles' scheme, Lieutenant Jerome of the 2nd Cavalry blundered into the Indian camp, necessitating an exchange. Though the Indians' pony herd had been driven off in the opening moments of the fight, there was the ever-present threat of intervention by Sitting Bull's warriors, who received word from those Nez Perces who managed to escape the trap. On October 4, Howard arrived on the scene with a small escort, graciously permitting Miles to continue in command, and it was "Bearcoat" who accepted Joseph's eloquent surrender the following day.

In many ways Miles' success in cutting off the flight of the Nez Perces and thereby salvaging a campaign that had been a series of blunders on the part of the Army, was the highlight of his Western career. Unfortunately, true to character, he set about trumpeting his victory as a vehicle to promotion, thereby slighting the unfortunate Howard, and causing a round of backbiting and recriminations that soon involved most of the Department and District commanders on the Northern Plains. More commendable was his sincere effort to see justice done a chief and a tribe he considered the worthiest of opponents. Since Joseph had surrendered under Miles' promise that the Nez Perces would be returned to their far-off homeland, he watched with anger and chagrin as they were shipped first to Bismarck, then to Leavenworth and Indian Territory. Two years later he would write to his superiors: "From all I can learn, the Nez Perces' trouble was caused by the rascality of their Agent, and the encroachment of the whites, and have regarded their treatment as unusually severe."[97] He championed their cause as he would that of no other Indian tribe, and ultimately managed to arrange the return of the surviving Nez Perces to the Department of Columbia, then under his command. Unfortunately most of these proud people, Joseph included, would never see their beloved Wallowa Valley again. Like so many Indian lands, it fell irrevocable prey to the expanding white America.

[97] Mark H. Brown, *The Flight of the Nez Perce*, New York, 1971, p. 429.

INDIAN OPERATIONS
1877

Pursuit—Engagement with, and surrender of Nez Perces

On the night of September 17th Colonel Miles received the communication informing him of the movements of the Nez Perces; he at once started from Tongue River September 18th, and marched rapidly in a northwest direction to intercept the enemy. His force consisted of troops F, G & H 2nd Cavalry, A, D, and K 7th Cavalry, and companies B, F, G, I and K Fifth Infantry (mounted) two pieces of light artillery, and a detachment of white and Indian scouts; he decided to push for the gap between the northern end of the Little Rocky and the Bear Paw Mountains. On September 23rd the Nez Perces crossed the Missouri at Cow Island, destroying the public and private stores there. A detachment of twelve men under Sergeant Molchert, 7th Infantry was stationed at that point in a slight intrenchment, they were repeatedly charged by the Nez Perces, who were however as often repulsed by the little garrison consisting of but four citizens and Sergeant Molchert's detachment. Two of the citizens were wounded.

On September 25th Colonel Miles received, through the citizens who had escaped from Cow Island, information that the Indians had crossed the Missouri so he began very rapid forced marches, which brought his command to the Bear Paw range on September 29th. On September 30th, at seven o'clock in the morning, after a march of two hundred and sixty-seven miles, Colonel Miles' command was upon the trail of the Nez Perces and their village was reported only a few miles away. It was located within the curve of a crescent-shaped cut bank in the vicinity of Snake Creek and this with the valley rendered it impossible for his scouts to determine the full size and strength of the camp. The whole column, however, advanced at a rapid gait, the leading battalion of the Second Cavalry[98] being sent out to make a slight detour, attack in rear, and cut off and secure the herd. This was done in gallant style, the battalion in a running

[98]Commanded by Capt. George L. Tyler, ably seconded by 2nd Lt. Edward J. McClernand.

fight capturing upwards of eight hundred ponies; the battalions of
the Seventh Cavalry and the Fifth Infantry charged mounted,
directly upon the village.

The attack was met by a desperate resistance and every advance
was stubbornly contested by the Indians, but with a courageous
persistence, fighting dismounted, the troops secured command of
the whole Indian position excepting the beds of the ravines in
which some of the warriors were posted. A charge was made on
foot by a part of the Fifth Infantry[99] down a slope and along the
open valley of the creek into the village but the fire of the Indians
soon disabled thirty-five per cent of the detachment which made
this assualt, and attempts to capture the village by such means had
to be abandoned. (The engagement is known as Snake or Eagle
Creek near Bear Paw Mountain, Montana.)

In the first charge by the troops and during the hot fighting
which followed Captain O. Hale,[100] 7th Cavalry, Lieutenant
J.W. Biddle,[101] 7th Cavalry, and twenty-two enlisted men were
killed; Captains Miles Moylan [sic][102] and Edward S. Godfrey,[103]
7th Cavalry, First Lieutenant George W. Baird[104] and Henry
Romeyn[105] Fifth Infantry and thirty-eight enlisted men were
wounded.

The Indian herd having been captured, the eventual escape of
the village became almost impossible. The casualties to the troops
had amounted to twenty per cent of the force engaged, there were

---

[99]Commanded by 1st Lt. Mason Carter, who received the Medal of Honor.

[100]Capt. Owen Hale commanded the battalion of the 7th Cavalry in this affair. He was shot
through the neck and killed while on his line of battle overlooking the Nez Perce
positions.

[101]Youthful 2nd Lt. Jonathan W. Biddle of Hale's Company K, 7th Cavalry. From a
prominent Pennsylvania family, he was fatally struck by several bullets in this, his first
battle.

[102]Capt. Myles Moylan was struck in the thigh as he rode up to Hale's beleagured Troop
K. He was awarded the Medal of Honor.

[103]Capt. Edward S. Godfrey (USMA 1867), famous for his writings on the Little Big Horn,
was shot through the side and nearly killed; he was awarded the Medal of Honor.

[104]1st Lt. George W. Baird was Regimental Adjutant of the 5th Infantry; he was shot
through the arms and ear while carrying an order from Miles. Awarded the Medal of
Honor.

[105]1st Lt. Henry Romeyn, an outspoken but meritorious officer, was seriously wounded by
a shot through the lungs while signalling a charge. He was awarded the Medal of Honor
and in later years wrote many articles on his experiences.

many wounded to care for, and there were neither tents nor fuel, a cold wind and snow storm prevailing on the night of Sept. 30th, so Colonel Miles determined to simply hold his advantage for a time, notifying General Howard and Colonel Sturgis of the situation; Colonel Sturgis received General Miles' dispatch on the evening of October 2nd, and at once started his troops for the battle field.

On the morning of October 1st, however, communication was opened between Colonel Miles' troops and the Indians, and Chief Joseph with several of his warriors, appeared under a flag of truce. They expressed a willingness to surrender and brought up a part of their arms (eleven rifles and carbines) but being suspicious, the Nez Perces remaining in camp hesitated to come forward and lay down their arms. While Chief Joseph remained in Colonel Miles' camp, Lieutenant Lovell H. Jerome,[106] Second Cavalry was sent to ascertain what was going on in the village. He went into the Indian camp and was detained there by the Nez Perces unharmed until Joseph returned on the afternoon of October 2nd. General Howard with a small escort arrived upon scene on the evening of October 4th, in time to be present at the full surrender of the Indians.

During the fight with Colonel Miles' command seventeen Indians were killed and forty wounded. The surrender included eighty-seven warriors, one hundred and eighty-four squaws and one hundred and forty-seven children. The prisoners were first sent to Fort A. Lincoln, thence to Fort Leavenworth, Kansas, and were finally located in the Indian Territory.

In the annual report for the year 1877, Colonel Miles commanding the District of the Yellowstone, the following summary of the operations of his troops against Indians in that district for the years 1876, and 1877, appears. Aggregate distance marched, over four thousand miles; besides the large amount of property captured and destroyed, sixteen hundred horses, ponies and mules were taken from the hostiles; each principal engagement was followed by important surrenders of bands and upwards of

[106] 2nd Lt. Lovell H. Jerome (USMA 1870) upset Miles' plans to hold Joseph as hostage pending an unconditional surrender, when he wandered into the Indian camp after being dispatched on a reconnaisance. Jerome was an unstable officer with a penchant for the bottle.

seven thousand Indians were either killed, captured, forced to
surrender or driven out of the country.

General Sherman in his annual report for 1877 says:

> In referring to the Nez Perces war I will again refer to the troops
> under General Sheridan's command, for although that war
> originated in the Department of Columbia, the retreat of the Nez
> Perces brought into the theater of operations of General Sheridan's
> troops, who in fact made the capture. . . The Nez Perces then
> passed north across the Muscleshell [sic] through Judith Basin (a
> region once densely filled with buffalo and large game) to the
> Missouri River at Cow Island. This is a steamboat landing, one
> hundred and twenty-five miles below Fort Benton, used for some
> weeks after the boats stop running to Benton. Near this place First
> Lieutenant Edward Maguire,[107] United States Engineers, with a
> small guard of the 7th Cavalry, was engaged in removing
> obstructions in the river. With these the Indians lightly skir-
> mished; burning some stores on the landing; forded the river, and
> September 23rd, pushed on north toward Milk River, and the
> British boundary, evidently aiming to reach the same harbor of
> refuge which had been gained by Sitting Bull last winter. But on
> the 17th of September Colonel Miles, Commanding District of the
> Yellowstone, received at his post at the mouth of Tongue River the
> two dispatches of General Howard and Colonel Sturgis (herewith
> marked etc.) He instantly organized the available force of his
> garrison and on the morning of the 18th was across the Yellow-
> stone and off in the direction of the mouth of Muscleshell, aiming
> to head off and capture the Nez Perces. His command reached the
> Muscleshell where he crossed the Missouri River on the 27th.
> Here he learned that the Nez Perces had crossed at Cow Island on
> the 23rd. He accordingly moved with extreme rapidity northwest,
> passed the Little Rockies and Bear Paw mountains on the 29th
> struck the trail, and on the morning of September 30th found the
> camp on Eagle Creek, near the head of Snake River which is a
> tributary of Milk River. The result was complete viz. the capture
> of Joseph and the surviving remnant of his brave but dangerous
> body of Indians. The Indians in this fight lost in killed six of their
> leading chiefs,[108] and twenty-five warriors with forty-six wounded.

---

[107]1st Lt. Edward Maguire (USMA 1867) famous for his map of the Little Big Horn
battlefield.

Colonel Miles reports his own loss at two officers and twenty men killed; four officers and forty-one men wounded.

General Howard with a small escort arrived on the field a short time before the surrender, but did not exercise any command. Of course Colonel Miles and his officers and men are entitled to all honor and praise for their prompt, skillful and successful work; while the others, by their long toilsome pursuit are entitled to corresponding credit because they made success possible.

General Sheridan in his report for 1877, refers to the capture of the Nez Perces as follows:

Meanwhile General Howard had sent word to Colonel Miles Fifth Infantry, at Tongue River, of the flight of the Indians and Colonel Miles with characteristic and highly commendable energy moved across the country with such troops as he had at hand, and, turning north across the Missouri River at or near the mouth of the Muscleshell, and on the 30th, overtook the Nez Perces near the mouth of Eagle Creek, and after a severe engagement in which 2 gallant officers and 21 men were killed and 4 officers and 38 men wounded, succeeded in capturing this band of hostiles, numbering in all men women and children between four hundred and five hundred.

[108]The dead Nez Perces included Toolhoolhoolzote, Ollokot, Pile of Clouds, Hahtalekin, and Lean Elk.

VI

Indian Campaigns in Montana

The year 1878 began with Miles once again pestering General Sherman for promotion and increased command responsibilities, this time with a view of striking against Sitting Bull's force in Canada. Pleading his case, Miles wrote, "In every military sense I cannot see why I am denied a similar command to that given to Harney, Sumner, Auger, Davis, Crook and many others." He launched into yet another diatribe against Department Commander Terry, whose Peace Commission to Sitting Bull had failed, and who had recently irked Miles by refusing to place Fort Buford under his jurisdiction:

> . . .the way he has organized this District *I could not order an inspection—drill—or target practice—by the very troops that I am expected to take out and risk my life with.* . . . He has been in charge of this Dept. a good part of the time for eleven years during which time there has been a chronic state of war and during the last fifteen months I have cleared this country twice of hostile Indians, yet I would as soon be called a slave-hunter as an "Indian fighter" simply—if the authorities consider me good only for that kind of work.[109]

By this point Sherman had had enough of Miles' complaints, and on February 9 the General sounded off:

> I have already paid you compliments most fulsome, but I cannot make you a Brigadier General, nor can I advise a new department for your special command, nor can I modify my opinions founded on a more comprehensive survey of the northern frontier than

---

[109] Miles to Sherman, Jan. 8, 1878. Sherman Papers, Lby. of Cong.

even you have made. I advise you to do nothing rash, but leave to
time to accomplish much that you now think can be done by you
exclusively.

Wishing to avert any chance of a confrontation with Britain,
Sherman continued by warning Miles not to campaign north of
the Missouri River, and cautioned "most undoubtedly, were
you without the positive orders of the Government here in
Washington to cross the *British Line* on the theory that the
Canadian authorities are not acting in good faith, you would
endanger the high reputation you now possess."[110]

By summer Miles' thoughts were not entirely centered on
Sitting Bull's Sioux. He assembled a small expedition ostensibly
to establish a wagon route and telegraph line West of Tongue
River Cantonment (soon to be renamed Fort Keogh), but
primarily to visit the wonders of Yellowstone Park. Ten officers,
four civilians, five women, three children and 110 soldiers set
out—among them Mrs. Miles and little Cecelia. They travelled
up the Yellowstone to the mouth of the Rosebud, then up that
stream, visiting the scene of Custer's defeat. When the party
reached Yellowstone Park, their vacation soon turned into
serious business; Miles received word that a party of renegade
Bannocks from Howard's Department of the Columbia were
raiding through the Park, bound on a Nez Perce style flight to
Canada. Hurrying the non-combatants to Fort Ellis, Miles led 75
soldiers on a forced march to cover the two passes at the eastern
edge of the Park. Lieutenant H.K. Bailey and 40 men were
stationed at Boulder Pass; Miles and the remainder of the force,
with 75 Crow allies, took position at Clarks Fork Pass.

On September 3 the Bannock camp was spotted near the
rugged gorge of Clarks Fork. Miles' men attacked at 4 a.m. of
September 4; 11 Bannocks were killed and 31 captured with over
200 horses. Military casualties were light but included capable
Captain Andrew S. Bennett, 5th Infantry killed; one soldier was
wounded, the interpreter and a Crow scout killed. After turning
the captured Bannock over to Lt. Col. George P. Buell and a
column from Fort Custer, Miles recalled the civilians and
continued his interrupted vacation, followed by a leisurely return
to Tongue River.

[110]Sherman to Miles, Feb. 9, 1878. *Ibid.*

In the following months, Miles became increasingly preoccupied with Sitting Bull, many of whose followers made repeated incursions into U.S. territory from their Canadian refuge. Despite Sherman's warnings, he still hoped to lead a campaign to the border. At the same time he continued to lobby for promotion and overall control of the troops in Montana, an ambition seconded by Governor B.F. Potts. Miles did not hesitate to besmirch his rivals—one example being his unreasonable assertion that North Carolina-born Col. Gibbon had manifested "copperhead proclivities" during Reconstruction. The Colonel spent the winter of 1878 through March of the following year in Washington, D.C. as one member of an Equipment Board re-evaluating Army uniforms, arms and accoutrements. By the end of his stay he had once again managed to have a run-in with Sherman. In a letter of March 9, after giving a litany of his past accomplishments, Miles forthrightly requested the creation and command of a District of Montana; he strongly objected to the assignment of Colonel Thomas H. Ruger's 18th Infantry to Montana; Ruger ranked him. The thoroughly frustrated Sherman wrote Sheridan:

> I have told him plainly that I know no way to satisfy his ambitions but to surrender to him absolute power over the whole Army, with President & Congress thrown in. . . He wants to remain on the Equipment Board, and at the same time to command all of Terry's troops, to advance north of the British line, drive back Sitting Bull & Co., and if necessary follow them across the Border as Mackenzie did on the Mexican Border.[111]

Miles regarded Sherman's outright rejection of his requests as "the severest injury that has been done me by any official or friend."[112] He returned to Fort Keogh a chastened, if not humble subordinate.

Miles did, to a degree, succeed in his desire for action when in the summer of 1879 Terry authorized him to move north to counter Sioux incursions in pursuit of buffalo. His troops from Forts Keogh and Custer consisted of seven companies of the 2nd

[111]Sherman to Sheridan, March 9, 1879. Sheridan Papers, Lby. of Cong.; quoted in Robert M. Utley, *Frontier Regulars 1866-1891*, New York, 1973, p. 286.
[112]Miles to Sherman, March 10, 1879. Sherman Papers, Lby. of Cong.

Cavalry and seven mounted companies of the 5th Infantry, some 676 officers and men, plus 143 Indian scouts. Accompanied by his ever-present Adjutant General, Captain Frank Baldwin, Miles rode out of Fort Keogh at 6 a.m. on July 5, and arrived just after sunset the next evening at the camp of Lt. Col. Whistler's mounted infantry and Maj. E.M. Baker's squadron of the 2nd Cavalry. En route to Fort Peck on the Missouri River, the column was increased by another 2nd Cavalry squadron commanded by Maj. David S. Gordon.

By July 12, "with his usual energy,"[113] Miles had crossed his entire command to the north side of the Missouri aboard the steamers *Sherman* and *Rosebud*. Correspondent John F. Finerty noted that "Miles was beginning to show the effect of his arduous campaigns in the deeper lines of his manly face and the occasional sprinkle of gray in his closely cut hair."[114] The troops moved out along the right bank of the Milk River on July 15—Miles keeping in touch with his various battalions by signal, employing the heliostat—an instrument he would make greater use of in his Apache Campaign seven years later.

On July 17 Lt. William Philo Clark, 2nd Cavalry, Miles' Chief of Scouts, unexpectedly encountered a force of 300 Sioux at Beaver Creek. As his Assiniboines and Bannocks fled, Clark attacked with the steadier Crows and Cheyennes and a company each of infantry and cavalry. The hostiles, Sitting Bull himself among them, hotly contested the soldiers and scouts while their families crossed Milk River. Learning of the fight, Miles made a forced march of 20 miles with the main column, arriving just as Clark succeeded in driving the Sioux over the river. Miles' jaded command could contribute little more than a few shells from Major Edmund Rice's Hotchkiss guns. Losses were light—one Crow and one Cheyenne killed, two soldiers of Company C, 2nd Cavalry and one Assiniboine wounded.

Miles followed on the war party's trail to the Canadian border, arriving there on July 22. From July 23 to 29 he had several inconclusive meetings with Major J.M. Walsh, of the Northwest

[113]Oscar F. Long Papers, "Journal of 1879 Expedition," Huntington Library, San Marino, Cal.
[114]John F. Finerty, *Warpath and Bivouac*, Chicago, 1890, p. 322.

Mounted Police, who refused to bring pressure to bear on Sitting Bull to return to reservation life in America. All Miles could do was content himself with the roundup of some 400 "Red River half-breeds," a gypsy-like people who were selling arms and ammunition to the Sioux. At the end of July a telegram from Sherman put an end to the campaign—recalling Miles to the Missouri River. On the return march to Fort Keogh Miles sent off a pessimistic letter to his concerned wife from Fort Peck:

> You had every reason to be anxious for it was a very bungled undertaking, but it has resulted all right, much more successfully than any one anticipated and without serious loss. Whether the government will take advantage of the results gained I do not know, but I have no idea they will. I think the authorities are wrangling among themselves, acting without a proper knowledge of facts and have been entirely ignorant of the situation of affairs. As a result I got the most absurd and senseless orders that could be imagined.[115]

Miles was back at Keogh on August 28, having covered 505.01 miles in the course of the expedition. It would be nearly two more years before Sitting Bull consented to return to American territory, and Miles would not be present to garner the laurels of his strenuous campaigning. But by then he would have his long-coveted star of Brigadier-General.

INDIAN OPERATIONS
1878

The hostiles who had broken away and followed Sitting Bull to the British possessions in 1877, continued hovering in considerable numbers on both sides of the boundary. Reports were received of over four hundred lodges having gone north, in various bands, since the 1st of October preceding; Colonel Miles, with about eight hundred mounted men from Fort Keogh, Montana, started in February for the purpose of finding a large force of Indians then on the south side of the lines; instructions were sent from the War Department not to attack them, however, if they remained north of the Missouri, so the expedi-

[115] Miles to Mrs. Miles, Fort Peck, Montana, August 9, 1879.

tion was recalled under these conditions. On April 2nd the United States Indian Agent at Fort Peck, hearing of the approach of a small force of troops under Lieutenant Frank D. Baldwin, Fifth Infantry, requested that officer to visit the agency, where small parties of well armed hostiles had been coming in constantly, professing a desire to cease hostilities, demanding food, making violent demonstrations when refused, and threatening the agent by firing over his head. Lieutenant Baldwin proceeded to the agency, leaving his troops on the south side of the river, and about April 25th, he received the surrender of a small band, five or six of whom were warriors.

Hostile Bannock Indians from the Department of the Columbia proceeded eastward over the Nez Perces trail of the previous year, stealing stock on the way; Captain J. Egan,[116] with Troop K, Second Cavalry proceeded up the Madison River, in the direction of Henry's Lake, and on August 27th, struck a Bannock Camp and captured fifty-six head of stock.

Hearing of the approach of the Bannocks Colonel Miles with one hundred men of the Fifth Infantry, and a band of thirty-five Crow scouts hastened to intercept the hostiles. A small party under command of Lieutenant William P. Clark,[117] Second Cavalry, was detached by Colonel Miles to make a detour, and on the 29th and 30th of August, struck parties of Bannocks, inflicting some damage in each case, Colonel Miles continued up Clarks Fork of the Yellowstone and on September 4th surprised a camp of Bannocks on Clarks Fork, Montana, killed 11 Indians, and captured thirty-one, together with two hundred horses and mules; Captain Bennett[118] Fifth Infantry was killed, also the interpreter and one Indian scout; one enlisted man was wounded, but prisoners who had escaped from this fight when recaptured in an engagement on Sept. 12th on a tributary of Snake River, Wyoming, by Lieutenant Bishop,[119] Fifth Cavalry, reported that they had lost twenty-eight killed in the fight on Clarks Fork, September 4th.

[116] Capt. James Egan, a native of Ireland who worked his way up through the ranks.
[117] 1st Lt. William Philo Clark (USMA 1868), scholarly and capable, he was an officer with a deep interest in Indian culture.
[118] Capt. Andrew S. Bennett, shot through the chest as he led the attack.
[119] 2nd Lt. Hoel S. Bishop (USMA 1873).

1879

Many depredations having been recently committed by Indians in the vicinity of the Missouri and Yellowstone Rivers, it was ascertained that large numbers of hostiles, half-breeds and foreign Indians from British Columbia including the Indians under Sitting Bull were roaming upon United States Territory, south of the boundary line. From a number of reliable persons who had seen the main hostile camp, this was estimated at not less than five thousand Indians of whom two thousand were warriors, with twelve thousand horses. Half-breed Indians had also been trading with the hostiles and furnishing them with ammunition, so in July Colonel Miles was sent from Fort Keogh with a strong force to break up their Camp, separate the doubtful Indians from those avowedly hostile and force the foreign Indians to return north of the boundary.

Colonel Miles' force consisted of seven companies, Fifth Infantry, seven troops Second Cavalry, a detachment of artillery and some friendly Indian and white scouts. At Fort Peck he was joined by two companies of the Sixth Infantry and his entire command then numbered 33 officers, six hundred and forty-three enlisted men and one hundred and forty-three Indian and white scouts.

The hostiles consisted of the Uncapapas under Sitting Bull, the Minniconjous under Black Eagle, the Sans/Arcs under Spotted Eagle and the Ogallalas under Big Road and Broad Tail.

Colonel Miles reported that the depredations of the hostiles had resulted in the killing of not less than twenty men and the stealing of three hundred head of stock, all of which had been taken to the hostile camp.

As a preliminary step the Yanktonnais camp of about three or four hundred lodges were first moved to the south side of the Missouri about June 23rd.

On July 17th, the advance guard of Colonel Miles' column, consisting of a troop of the Second Cavalry, a company of the Fifth Infantry, and about fifty Indian scouts, commanded by Lieutenant Clark, 2nd Cavalry, had a sharp fight with from three to four hundred Indians, between Beaver and Frenchmen's Creek; the Indians were pursued for twelve miles, when the advance became surrounded; Colonel Miles moved forward rapidly and the hostiles fled north of Milk River, several of the enemy were killed and a large amount of property abandoned; two enlisted men and one Indian scout were wounded and three Indian scouts killed. Sitting Bull himself was present in this engagement.

On July 31, Colonel Miles reported that the main hostile camp had retreated north, across the boundary, to Wood Mountain; the column followed and halted on the main trail at the British line, whence it returned to Milk River.

Attention was then turned to the camps of the half-breeds who had formed a cordon of outposts around the main hostile camp, furnishing the latter with the supplies of war. On Aug. 4th, Captain Ovenshine Fifth Infantry,[120] with a portion of Colonel Miles' Command, arrested a band of half-breeds on Porcupine Creek capturing one hundred and forty-three carts and one hundred and ninety-three horses. On August 5, four camps of half-breeds were arrested numbering three hundred and eight carts. On August 8, Colonel Miles reported the total number of half-breeds arrested by various detachments eight hundred and twenty-nine, with six hundred and sixty-five carts. On August 14, Lieutenant Colonel Whistler,[121] Fifth Infantry, with part of Colonel Miles' command, captured a band of fifty-seven Indians with one hundred ponies, who had left the Rosebud Agency and were in the act of crossing the Missouri River, near Poplar Creek on their way to join Sitting Bull in the north.

General Terry in his annual report for 1879, extracts and embodies in his report from Colonel Miles' report a narrative of his operations and says:

> The value of the results obtained by Colonel Miles can hardly be overestimated. The hostile Sioux who in 1876, found an asylum in British Territory, had been permitted by the Dominion Government to repair all the losses of arms, horses and equipments which they suffered in the campaign of that year, and to completely prepare themselves again for war. Made bold by the knowledge that they possessed close at hand a secure refuge in foreign soil, to

[120]Capt. Samuel Ovenshine, who had served with the 5th Infantry since 1861.
[121]Lt. Col. Joseph N.G. Whistler (USMA 1846) an old soldier, veteran of the Mexican and Civil Wars, with a brevet of Brigadier General in the latter.

which they could retreat in case they should meet a force with which they could not cope, they'had invaded our territory almost as a body, and had covered with marauding parties the country between the boundary and the Yellowstone River, and from Fort Logan on the west nearly to Fort Buford on the east. Horses and cattle had been stolen. Settlers had been murdered by them, and I regret to say that I know of no adequate efforts on the part of the Dominion Govenment to fulfill the obligations which that government assumed when it gave to these people a refuge from the military forces operating against them—of no adequate efforts to prevent this armed invasion of the territory of a friendly neighbor. Now it is believed that not a hostile Sioux remains south of the boundary, and, to quote again the language of Colonel Miles, "This extensive country has been again cleared of hostile Indians and the scattered settlers and travellers in it are as free from molestation as in the States of Kansas and Minnesota."

Colonel Miles clearly and accurately comprehending the purposes of the government, and the objects sought to be accomplished, and conforming in all respects to the instructions which he had received, by a most happy union of enterprise and audacity, prudence and foresight, succeeded in obtaining these results without the loss of a single soldier.

Besides the immediate result of his operations in forcing the hostile Indians across the boundary, there is good ground for the belief that a moral effect of even greater importance has been produced—a moral effect that will be lasting and will tend to preserve the peace of the border in succeeding years.

I desire to thank Colonel Miles and his officers and men thus publicly for the exceedingly important service which they have rendered, and I trust that these services will receive a just recognition from higher authority.

General Sheridan in his report for 1879, referring to the foregoing operations says:

The report of General Terry Commanding the Department of Dakota, is comprehensive, and fully describes the operations in his department, and especially the expedition of Colonel Miles and the beneficial effects arising from it, to which I wish to add a just commendation, by saying that Colonel Miles in the organization of his column and in his soldierly bearing, has given satisfaction to his superiors, and inspired confidence in the officers and men under his command.

General Sherman, Commanding the Army, in his report for 1879, referring to the foregoing operations says:

In May last, General Terry, Commanding the Department of Dakota, reported that Indians from Sitting Bull's camp beyond the northern national boundary had followed the buffalo south and were likely to create disorder and commit acts of hostility against Indians and others belonging to our side, and that he knew of no way to put a stop to this annoyance than by organizing a strong column at Fort Keogh, clearing the country, and then establishing a summer camp of moderate size at Poplar Creek Agency, on the Missouri River, but that under existing orders he did not feel justified in adopting this course and asked for instructions. He was promptly notified that there was no objection to temporary operations and a temporary cantonment, but that we were not prepared to build any permanent post in that quarter other than Fort Assinniboine, for which Congress had made an appropriation. General Terry committed this task to Colonel Nelson A. Miles, Commanding District of the Yellowstone, to whose report and to that of General Terry himself, I refer for full details of the whole expedition. It accomplished all that was designed and resulted in the withdrawal north of the boundary of all Hostile Indians, and a better understanding with the Dominion authorities who have charge of the Canadian Indians.

VII

Promoted to General

On March 25, 1880 Colonel Miles was ordered to Washington, D.C. for what became an extended stay. Three months later, at the invitation of General John M. Schofield, Superintendent of the United States Military Academy, he addressed the West Point graduating class. Though Miles welcomed a rest from his field duties, he was not idle; as always he lobbied for promotion—this time the assignment of Chief Signal Officer of the Army, which carried with it the rank of Brigadier General. His old friend and mentor, Major General Winfield Scott Hancock, now Democratic Presidential nominee, came to his assistance, as did the Governors of New York and Massachusetts, Senator Burnside of Rhode Island, and other powerful men. As it was, Hancock narrowly lost the election to James A. Garfield, and on December 15, William B. Hazen received a star and assignment to the position Miles craved.

Miles could take solace however in the fact that on that same December 15 he finally obtained the General's rank he so desired. Acknowledging the promotion on December 18, he received hearty congratulations from Hancock, and some sound advice: "You are in the place that fits you. . . You have a great career before you. It is only necessary to wait for the opportunity. You can afford to be slow! Now is the time for rest, and for study."[122] After an emotional farewell to the 5th Infantry, his command of eleven years, Miles awaited assignment in Washington. In the Spring of 1881 he was ordered to assume command of the Department of Columbia, headquartered at Vancouver Barracks, Washington State.

After a leisurely cross-country trip, the General arrived at his post on August 2, 1881. His department covered some 250,000

---

[122]Hancock to Miles, Dec. 24, 1880. Miles/Cameron Papers, Lby. of Cong.

square miles, not including the newly acquired Alaska Territory
—a vast region, but one with little military challenge. The only
major Indian threat centered on the dissatisfaction of the
Okinagan Chief Moses, whose Columbia Reservation was increasingly infringed upon by white settlers. Miles handled the
sensitive situation with diplomacy and tact, dispatching a delegation to Washington with Captain Baldwin. By 1885 Moses had
agreed to monetary and property concessions and a resettlement
of the Okinagans on the Colville Reservation. While in command
of the Department Miles also did his best to see belated justice
done the Nez Perces.

In 1882, the year his son Sherman was born, Miles made a tour
of inspection to Alaska. Never one to discourage the spread of
Army influence, he was dissatisfied with the Government's
decision to withdraw troops based at Sitka, and leave the
administration—and exploration—of Alaska to the U.S. Navy.
On his own initiative he instigated a series of expeditions that
rank among the most adventurous undertaken by American
military men. In the Summer of 1883 the General dispatched his
aide, 1st Lt. Frederick Schwatka, a scholarly officer with an
Arctic expedition under his belt, to explore and map the Yukon
River. The next summer, Lt. William F. Abercrombie was less
successful in an attempted journey up the Copper River; but in
1885 Lt. Henry T. Allen, with two enlisted men, set forth at
Miles' behest in an epic journey of some 1500 miles. Allen proved
a redoubtable explorer able to successfully overcome obstacles
and setbacks, and at the end of his six months trek produced the
first complete maps of the Copper, Tanana and Koyukuk Rivers.
Through these intrepid subordinates Miles played a key role in
opening up the riches of the vast new territory.

In July 1885, Miles was transferred to the command of the
Department of the Missouri. While enroute to his Fort Leavenworth headquarters, he received orders to report to Lt. Gen.
Sheridan at Chicago, and accompany "Little Phil" on a peace
mission aimed at quelling a threatened outbreak in Indian
Territory. While troops were massed at Fort Reno under Miles'
direction, the generals set about placating the Kiowa, Arapahoe,
Commanche and Cheyenne tribes whose principal complaint
was directed at the encroachment of white cattlemen on their

land. As was often the case, Miles was not unsympathetic to the Indian problem. "They have been grievously wronged," he wrote his wife, "and have very just grounds for complaints. Their affairs have been managed very badly and their reservations overrun by cowboys and lawless white men."[123] Miles' understanding of these tribes, many of whom he had encountered on the battlefield, assisted Sheridan and President Cleveland in averting a war; concessions were made, the troublesome herds excluded from Indian land, and Miles arrived hot, tired and satisfied at Fort Leavenworth on July 28, 1885.

The General did not enjoy the peace of Leavenworth for long; he soon received an appointment that would precipitate the most controversial actions of his military life.

INDIAN OPERATIONS, 1880
(From Colonel Miles' Report)

On the 6th day of February last, a small party of hostiles attacked two hunters on Powder River, twenty miles from its mouth, wounding one of the men (Samuel Stone). The hunters killed one Indian and wounded another.

Sergeant T.B. Glover, Co. "B" Second Cavalry with eight men and eleven Cheyenne Scouts was ordered in pursuit, which resulted in the capture of three of the Indians, one badly wounded, the troops losing one man killed and one wounded.

March 2nd, 4 companies of cavalry under Captain T.B. Dewees was sent out to scout and clear the country of any hostile Indians that might be near the head of Custer, Sunday and the Porcupine Creeks.

During the eve of March 4th reports were received that the hostiles were raiding the settlements along the Yellowstone near the Porcupine; Captain F.D. Baldwin, with companies I and K Fifth Infantry, were at once detached to the scene of their depredations. From reports received from this command it was believed that the Indians were south of the Yellowstone and Captain E.P. Ewers[124] with his Company E, 5th Infantry, was ordered to the Rosebud and Captain S.T. Hamilton,[125] with companies I and B, Second Cavalry, then at the head of Sunday Creek was ordered west to the head of Little Porcupine to co-operate

---

[123] Miles to Mrs. Miles, Fort Reno, Indian Terr., July 18, 1885.
[124] Capt. Ezra P. Ewers, a capable officer who had worked his way up through the ranks.
[125] Capt. Samuel T. Hamilton of Pennsylvania.

with Captain Baldwin's command. On the 9th the trail of a war party
was discovered near Captain Ewers' camp on Grave Yard Creek.
Lieutenant W.S. Miller, 5th Infantry, with a small party of soldiers and
Indian scouts immediately followed on their trail resulting in his
overtaking them about 12 miles on that day, a fight following in which
two Cheyenne scouts and three hostile Indians were killed.

The trail of the escaping Indians was taken up and followed by
Captain Baldwin, when they were again overtaken and skirmished with
near the head of Little Porcupine on the 10th, resulting in the capture of
all the stolen stock in their possession, excepting what they rode away.
All of these troops returned to this post on the 11th, 12th and 13th of
March. Captain J.N. Wheelan,[126] Second Cavalry, with his company
and Lieutenant W.H. Wheeler,[127] Eleventh Infantry, with a detachment of mounted infantry was ordered out to co-operate against this last
band of Indians, but were recalled from the head of the Porcupine.

During the latter part of March the hostiles ran off from near Fort
Custer a large band of ponies belonging to the crow scouts. Captain J.
Meier, Second Cavalry, with his company was ordered in pursuit; the
next day troops from Custer were ordered to follow. Captain E.L.
Huggins,[128] 2nd Cavalry, with his company and scouts, leaving Keogh
to intercept these Indians on the Rosebud, struck the trail, crossing the
Rosebud, going in an easterly direction which was followed persistently
until the hostiles were overtaken on a branch of O'Fallon Creek; an
engagement following resulting in all of their stock and five Indians
being captured.

Lieutenant J.H. Coale,[129] 2nd Cavalry, with his company and Crow
scouts from Custer, overtook Captain Huggins at Tongue River and
participated in the capture of these Indians. Our losses in the affair was
one soldier killed.

May 27th, two men of the Bismark and Keogh stage line were killed
by Indians at Beaver Station, twenty miles east of Little Missouri, three
companies of cavalry and one of infantry under Major Guido Ilges[130]
were dispatched to that point.

On or about July 11th a driver on the same line was killed by Indians
between Pennel and O'Fallon Stations, Lieutenant J.C.F. Tillson,[131]

[126]Capt. James N. Wheelan would retire in 1906 as Colonel of the 2nd Cavalry.
[127]2nd Lt. William H. Wheeler (USMA 1874).
[128]Capt. Eli L. Huggins, awarded the Medal of Honor for this actions.
[129]1st Lt. John H. Coale.
[130]Maj. Guido Ilges, a native of Prussia.
[131]2nd Lt. John Charles Fremont Tillson (USMA 1878).

Fifth Infantry, was sent in pursuit of this party of Indians. He followed them to the Missouri River.

These movements of troops with other scouts of less importance have been successful in ridding this district of thieving and hostile bands of Indians.

About one thousand Indians who for the past three years sought and found refuge on British soil have come in and surrendered as prisoners of war, turning over to the government their arms and ponies. The latter have been sold, with the exception of two to a family; the proceeds expended in the purchase of domestic stock for their benefit.

The Cheyennes and Sioux who surrendered in 1877, and February 1879, are cultivating the soil, producing all that is necessary to sustain them and nothing can be more gratifying than the rapid strides these Indians are making towards peaceful and industrious modes of life.

In his annual report for 1880, General Terry, Commanding Department of Dakota, in referring to the most important events which have taken place in the Department during the past year mentions: "The surrender of a large body of the hostile Sioux to Colonel Miles the commanding officer at Fort Keogh," and says:

After Colonel Miles' very successful movement against the hostile Sioux in 1879, I hoped and expected that they would remain in the British Possessions and that in the future we should be free from the annoyances to which we had been subjected by them. These hopes and expectations have been disappointed. Driven by necessity to follow the herd of buffalo they soon recrossed the boundary, and in greater or smaller numbers they have been on our side ever since. Raids by small parties into the valley of the Yellowstone, and the contiguous regions have been frequent, but they have been successfully and gallantly met by Colonel Miles, and the troops under his command. Recently a change seems to have taken place in the sentiments of these Indians; a large number of them having come into Fort Keogh and surrendered themselves as prisoners of war; in all 1030 Indians. It is believed that a large majority of those still out will surrender before cold weather sets in. To bring about this result Colonel Miles, at his own suggestion, had been directed to notify the different bands that should they not come into Fort Keogh by a specified time they will be pursued by military force, killed, captured, or driven across the border. Colonel Miles is now making preparations to take the field in case it shall become necessary to do so.

ANNUAL REPORT OF GENERAL MILES FOR 1881
Headquarters Department of the Columbia,
Vancouver Barracks, W.T.,
September 29, 1881.

Sir:

In accordance with your communication of the 7th instant, I have the honor to submit the following report:

The important events and movement of troops in this Department during the year preceding the time of my assuming command have been mentioned in reports of my predecessors already forwarded.

On the 2nd of August, ultimo, in accordance with the orders of the President, I assumed command of the geographical Department of the Columbia. Since that time but few changes have been made. Two companies, E and F, Second Infantry, have been ordered from Camp Spokane, W.T., to Fort Coeur d'Alene, I.T.; Company H, Twenty-first Infantry, from Fort Stevens, Oregon, to Vancouver Barracks, W.T., Company M First Cavalry, from Fort Walla Walla, W.T., to Department of Arizona. The present stations of troops are as follows:

First Cavalry

Regimental Headquarters, Troops A, B, E, and K, at Fort Walla Walla, W.T.

Troop D at Fort Lapwai, I.T.

Troop F at Boise Barracks, I.T.

Troop H at Fort Colville, W.T.

Troop L at Fort Klamath, Oregon.

Fourth Artillery

Batteries F and K at Fort Canby, W.T., with detachment guarding Fort Stevens, Oregon.

Second Infantry

Regimental headquarters, companies A, B, G, and I at Fort Coeur d'Alene, I.T.

Companies D, E, F, and K at Camp Spokane, W.T.

Companies C and H at Fort Colville, W.T.

Twenty-First Infantry

Regimental headquarters, companies E, F, G, H, and K, at Vancouver Barracks, W.T.

Company A at Boise Barracks, I.T.

Company C at Forth Klamath, Oregon

Company I at Fort Lapwai, I.T.

Companies B and D at Fort Townsend, W.T.

As far as practicable, I have inspected the posts in this department, and from personal observation am enable to report the troops well instructed, well disciplined, and in fair condition.

I find, however, that this military force has been inadequately supplied, as seen in the condition of barracks, quarters, and transportation.

The troops at several of the posts are not suitably or comfortably sheltered. This condition of affairs seriously affects both the health and efficiency of the command.

I will forward complete estimates of what is required, and trust that a due proportion of the necessary funds and material appropriated may be furnished this Department.

In addition to the usual military duties, the troops have been engaged, and are now employed in constructing military roads from Fort Colville to Spokane Falls, W.T., from Fort Colville to Camp Spokane, W.T., and from Fort Coeur d'Alene, I.T., east towards Fort Missoula, M.T. These routes (some 230 miles in extent) when completed will not only greatly facilitate the movement of troops and supplies, but will be of great value to the public.

The troops are also engaged in establishing military telegraph lines from Spokane Falls, on the Northern Pacific Railroad, to Camp Spokane, W.T.; from Ashland to Fort Klamath, Oregon, and from Port Townsend to Cape Flattery, W.T., adding some 240 miles to the lines of communication. When completed all the military posts in this department, with one exception, will be within telegraphic communication. At the same time the lines are being used for private and commercial purposes, thereby benefiting the citizens of the country.

The troops, at available points, occupy a wide extent of country, the greater portion of which is inhabited by defenseless settlers and numerous tribes of Indians.

The different Indian tribes in this Department are, in the main, in a peaceable condition; most of the semi-civilized are making some progress toward self-support; yet there are vast tracts of country still occupied by bands of nomadic Indians, and between the latter and the remote settlers conflicts of race may be expected. The evils arising from injudicious and illy-defined treaties made with these Indian tribes are becoming apparent, and the constant clashing of interests between the Indians and the miners, ranchmen, and farmers, is almost inevitable, and quite likely to result in open hostilities.

The germs of future Indian disturbances are already noticeable in some localities.

Measures are being taken which, when completed, will better facilitate communication with and concentration of the available force in this department, and at the same time increase the efficiency of the troops and lessen the cost of supplies, the chief aim being to make the limited force (of 1,570 soldiers) of the least expense to the general government, and at the same time give the greatest protection to a people occupying territory (not including Alaska) of 250,000 square miles in extent. When it is remembered that our troops have contended in the past, and doubtless in the future will have to meet, an enemy of superior numbers where the natural obstacles are dense forests, trackless mountains, and almost impassable rivers, the difficulties to be encountered will be easily understood and appreciated.

In this connection I desire to invite especial attention to the weak and defective condition of the companies and regiments of this command, an evil which previals through the entire service.

It must be apparent to every one familiar with the subject that our little Army is defective in organization, and, consequently greatly overworked.

This nation of 50,000,000 of people calls upon its Army for more than double the labor required of any other troops in the world, and the testimony of those who have had the best means of knowing, from the humble frontier settler to the late Chief Magistrate, James A Garfield, and in the words of the latter, is that the Army has been crippled and reduced "below the limit of efficiency and safety," and the people "expect Congress and the Executive to make the Army worthy of a great nation."

By the present system we have a sufficient number of officers and non-commissioned officers, but there is a great necessity for an increase in the number of soldiers in the different companies.

The "skeleton theory" has been found unwise, most expensive, and least effective.

Our Army is requried to be efficient in every kind of military duty, including skilled marksmanship. It must guard our coast defenses and boundary lines, public arsenals, stores and depots; it must protect the lives and property of citizens, scattered over vast territories; and in cases of necessity those living in the populous States.

At the same time the troops are required to perform almost every kind of laborious work, constructing military posts, building roads and telegraph lines, also performing mechanical, clerical, and difficult manual labor.

This has a demoralizing influence upon the spirit of the troops, and causes desertion and other evils of the service.

In cases of emergency the skeleton companies are suddenly gathered up from distant points at great expense, and thrown into engagements, illy prepared for such serious business, and expected to perform the work of well organized and strong commands.

With our present facilities for the government and accommodation of troops, companies of 100 men can easily be maintained, and in every sense better fitted for the service required of them. There would probably be ten per cent added to the yearly appropriation required for pay, food, and clothing of the men; but the efficiency of the Army would, in my judgment, be increased more than one hundred per cent.

I am satisfied that, in my own department, the yearly expenditures now made necessary by the weak condition of the companies and regiments could be greatly lessened.

If the companies were made of proper strength, not only would there be a large saving of the extra military expenses, but there would be greater benefit and security given to the people whose lives and property depend to a greater or less degree upon the protection guaranteed by the physical force of the general government.

I would therefore recommend that the authorized maximum number of enlisted men in the different companies be 100 per company where they are so stationed and employed that the public interest would be benefited thereby.

I would also call attention to the fact of the number of officers who are permanently absent from their respective commands through no fault of theirs, men who have become infirm through long years of hard service, or crippled or permanently disabled in the various wars in which our army has been engaged; also to the number of officers who have grown gray in the service and yet are occupying the subordinate grades of captains, and first and second lieutenants. These facts have a very discouraging influence upon a zealous and faithful body of public servants.

In every branch of business or profession in life, advancement or progress is absolutely essential, and the rule is no less applicable to the military service, and some system that will either promote retirements by commutation of retired pay, limiting the retired list to such number as would be suitable for our kind of service, or universal retirement at a given age, would undoubtedly improve the efficiency of the Army, and it is believed to be very generally desired by the officers of our service.

I enclose the reports of the department staff officers, and invite attention to them for matters of detail in the different branches of the service.

I am, sir, very respectfully, your obedient servant,

NELSON A. MILES,

Brigadier General, U.S.A. Commanding Department.

REPORT OF BRIGADIER GENERAL MILES

Headquarters Department of the Columbia,
Vancouver Barracks, Washington,
September 23, 1882

Sir:

I have the honor to submit the following report of operations in the department during the past year. . .

The principal explorations and reconnaissances made during the year may be mentioned as follows:

Lieutenant Thomas W. Seymon's exploration and examination of the Columbia River, from the line of British Columbia to the mouth of Snake River, Washington Territory was made in January last by means of Indian canoes. Very valuable information of that extensive district of country was obtained, and full reports thereof, with very complete maps, have been forwarded.

The surveys and reconnaissances of the following named officers made during the year have given satisfaction, and the results obtained are valuable for future use.

Second Lieutenant J.F.R. Landis,[132] First Cavalry, surveying route for telegraph line between Forts Klamath, Oregon, and Bidwell, Cal.

Lieutenants T.H. Bradley[133] and Willis Wittich.[134] Twenty-first Infantry, reconnaissance from Fort Townsend, W.T., to Dungeness River.

Captain W.R. Parnell,[135] First Cavalry, reconnaissance through Bruneau and Duck Valleys, Idaho.

Second Lieutenant F.J. Patten,[136] Twenty-first Infantry, surveying route for telegraph line from Fort Spokane to Spokane Falls.

Second Lieutenant William Moffat,[137] Second Infantry, surveying route for road from Fort Colville to Fort Spokane.

---

[132] 2nd Lt. John Fulton Reynolds Landis, 1st Cav. (USMA 1878).

[133] 1st Lt. Thomas H. Bradley, 21st Inf.

[134] 1st Lt. Willis Wittich, 21st Inf. (USMA 1874).

[135] Capt. William R. Parnell, a native of Ireland, awarded the Medal of Honor for bravery at White Bird Canyon in the Nez Perce War.

[136] 1st Lt. Francis J. Patten (USMA 1877).

[137] 2nd Lt. William Moffat, a former Musician.

Captain G.H. Burton,[138] Twenty-first Infantry, reconnaissance of the country bordering on the Sprague River, Oregon.

Captain A.J. Forse,[139] Troop D, First Cavalry, march of instruction from Fort Lapwai to the Lolo Trail, Idaho. Second Lieutenant L.J. Hearn,[140] Twenty-first Infantry, scout from Fort Lapwai to the Lolo Trail.

Lieutenant Colonel Alexander Chambers,[141] Twenty-first Infantry, during the summer has been engaged with a small force of officers and men, clearing a trail for pack animals through the dense forest west of Port Townsend, Washington Territory, with a view of exploring the region of country adjacent to the Olympic Mountains, and between Puget Sound and the coast south of Juan de Fuca Straits. Owing to the inaccessibility of this district and the fact that the surface of the country is covered with a mass of timber and underbrush, this region has up to the present year never been explored. Sufficient progress has been made to enable Colonel Chambers, with a small force, to proceed as far as the West Fork of Dungeness River, and the work will be continued at a favorable time next season.

The extensive reconnaissance made by First Lieutenant H.H. Pierce,[142] Twenty-first Infantry, with First Lieutenant G.B. Backus,[143] First Cavalry, Assistant Surgeon C.F. Wilson, and Topographical Assistant Alfred Downing, is worthy of special mention, the detachment having scouted a section of country between Fort Colville, W.T., and the mouth of Skagit River on Puget Sound, but little known. A portion of the route traversed in this reconnaissance, had never before been passed over by white men.

Lieutenant Pierce's report, with itinerary and map of route traveled, gives a full and most interesting description of that region, comprising additional knowledge obtained of the Indian inhabitants, and the intercourse had by the military with these Indians will have a tendency to promote more friendly relations than has heretofore existed.

The condition of the various tribes of Indians in this department is satisfactory. They are peaceably disposed and are making steady progress toward improvement. They are in better condition to receive

---

[138]Capt. George H. Burton (USMA 1865).

[139]Capt. Albert G. Forse (USMA 1865), killed in action at San Juan Hill in 1898 as Major, 1st Cav.

[140]2nd Lt. Lawrence J. Hearn.

[141]Lt. Col. Alexander Chambers (USMA 1853) a Brigadier General in the Civil War and veteran of many Indian Wars campaigns.

[142]1st Lt. Henry H. Pierce, brevetted Lt. Col. for Civil War service.

[143]1st Lt. George B. Backus (USMA 1875).

the full benefit and share the responsibilities of civil government than is generally supposed; and by giving them the same security of rights of person and property that white people enjoy, and as far as possible the benefits of industrial schools, they will become a producing and self-supporting people, rather than a source of annoyance and expense to the general government.

From personal observation, the reports of inspections made, and the results shown in target contests, I am able to report the troops in this Department as efficient, well instructed, and in good condition for any service.

I would invite special attention to the requirements of Section 9, of Act of Congess, approved September 27, 1850, page 159, of the Revised Statutes which limits the area of the United States military reservation in what is now the States of Oregon, Washington and Idaho Territories.

It is impossible to have the necessary ranges for small arms or artillery on these limited reserves, or to have rifle practice with improved arms without endangering the lives and property of persons occupying adjoining grounds.

Attention is invited to my letter on this subject of February 22, 1882. I recommend the repeal of the Statute, as if affects only this department.

I also recommended the restoration of the Sixty-fifth article of war, which appears in the Army Regulations of 1863, which gave the Colonels Commanding Departments the authority to convene general courts-martial.

The system now in vogue of command being exercised in the name of general officers, not within the limits or jurisdiction of departments, or within reach of communication therewith, in my opinion, is of doubtful legality, and quite likely to result in serious embarrassment to the service, and I believe should be discontinued.

Very respectfully, your obedient servant,
NELSON A. MILES,
Brigadier General Commanding.

The Assistant Adjutant General,
    Military Division of the Pacific, Presidio,
        San Francisco, California.

REPORT OF BRIGADIER GENERAL MILES,
Headquarters Department of the Columbia,
Vancouver Barracks, Washn., Oct. 2, 1884.

Sir:

I have the honor to submit the following brief report of military affairs pertaining to this department for the year ending October 1, 1884.

A condition of desired peace has been maintained during the year, hence little requiring especial mention has occurred beyond the ordinary routine duties of the service.

Within the past four months there has been a change of station of nearly all the troops in this department, the Twenty-first Infantry exchanging with the Fourteenth Infantry from the Department of the Platte, and the troops of the First Cavalry with the Second Cavalry from the Department of Dakota.

Such changes, in my opinion, are highly beneficial to the health of the commands, and while increasing their esprit de corps and efficiency, enlarges their experience and observation in different sections of the country.

I would respectfully recommend, as far as the troops in this department are concerned, that in future they be changed at least once in every four years, and that the distance be not so great as to prevent both infantry and cavalry marching between stations.

The discipline and health of this command has been uniformly good.

All of the military posts save one have been visited during the year by the department commander. The inspections, results of target practice, and all reports from the troops indicate a high order of efficiency.

The general improvement in target practice is commendable, a result obtained by the close attention given this subject by officers and the interest and care taken by enlisted men. The skill that has been acquired in the use of the rifle would render the troops most effective in any future engagement.

The result of the artillery practice of light battery E, First Artillery, with the Hotchkiss revolving cannon, has been most satisfactory. The fact of the cannon being fired from the shoulder of an artillerist seems somewhat novel, yet experience has proved its practicability with the most effective results. Having taken much interest in securing these improved arms for the light battery stationed at Vancouver Barracks, and having had opportunities for observing their utility in the field, I can say that the results of recent practice with these guns confirms my opinion, namely, that they are the most destructive guns against troops of any that have yet been used in the service of our government.

Instructions in signaling and the familiarizing of troops with the use of the appliances has received the attention at all of the posts in this department. Better results would be obtained if more liberal allowances were made for signal apparatus.

Experiments have been made with the heliostat and the most gratifying results obtained.

Captain F.D. Baldwin, Fifth Infantry, assisted by Sergeant Doepke and Private Gilday, Fourteenth Infantry, stationed at Vancouver Barracks, Washington, exchanged messages with Second Lieutenant H.C. Cabell, Jr.,[144] Fourteenth Infantry, assisted by Private Wagner, Second Cavalry, and Private Pipkins, Battery E, First Artillery, stationed on Mount Hood, Oregon, distance 50 miles between instruments used.

Similar results might be obtained by the use of electricity in night signaling.

During winter months the gymnastic drill and exercises have been added to the duties of the garrison at several of the posts, and has contributed very largely to the health, strength and recreation of the several garrisons. I believe a first class gymnasium and amusement room where troops can find beneficial exercise and simple refreshments at slight cost would be largely beneficial to any command.

The principal, and I might say the only serious evil that now prevails in the service is the crime of desertion. The attention that has been given this subject and the simple remedies that have been applied do not appear to check the offense. It can be restrained, in my opinion, by adopting the following measures:

1.   Make the position of a soldier in the Army of the United States such as the young men of the country and veteran soldiers would seek and desire to retain, rather than one that they are too apt to avoid, or after enlisting find not congenial and desert.

2.   Making the offense of desertion a crime of such magnitude as will deter others from attempting it.

3.   Reduce the term of enlistment to three years, and give regimental and company commanders increased facilities for recruiting their commands and ridding the same of worthless and vicious characters when such shall be discovered in the ranks.

As the construction of the Northern Pacific Railway, and other routes of travel has made a very great change in the means of communication in this northwest country, rendering it possible now to move troops and supplies in days the same distance that but a short time ago would have occupied weeks. In view of this, I have as far as practicable discontinued small ineffective posts, and concentrated the troops in larger garrisons, where they will have the advantage of instruction, drill, and discipline, and will be maintained at much less expense.

Forts Walla Walla, Spokane, and Coeur d'Alene have been made the principal posts of this department, where troops are stationed for immediate use in the sections of country most liable to Indian hostility,

[144] 2nd Lt. Henry C. Cabell, Jr. (USMA 1883).

while Vancouver Barracks serves all purposes for the station of a strong reserve force for the entire department. The latter post enjoys unusual facilities in this respect, owing to its near proximity to the center of the system of railway and steamship communication of the Northwest— Portland, Oregon, which, from its geographical location, from its railroad connection, and from its river and ocean service, renders all sections of the country easily accessible. The artillery stations (Forts Canby, Washington, and Stevens, Oregon), commanding the entrance to the Columbia River, are well located and kept in as good condition as limited means will admit.

Fort Canby has a good armament and an effective garrison.

Fort Stevens has a strong armament, but for some years has been without a sufficient garrison, and very deficient in the necessary appropriations needed to maintain it in proper condition for defense.

I would especially invite attention to the defenseless condition of the entrance of Puget Sound. In addition to the very large commercial interests of that great harbor or inland sea, there are national interests required that this important district of country should receive the adequate protection of the general government. Olympia, Tacoma, Seattle, Ports Ludlow, Madison, and Townsend, and the present terminus of the Northern Pacific Railroad on Puget Sound are places of great commercial interest. The Government has reserved important sites for batteries and defensive works at the entrance of Puget Sound; and the most valuable of these, in my opinion, should be occupied and put in proper condition for use. I have ordered a board of experienced artillery officers, after consulting with Captain Powell,[145] Corps of Engineers, to examine these military reserves, and make special report as to their relative importance, and the proper armament, garrison, and work necessary to place them in proper condition for use. When received, this report will be forwarded for consideration of the division commander.

The relations existing between the white population within the geographical limits of this military department and the various Indian tribes during the last year has been received in the main peaceable and friendly. Not a single report has been received at these headquarters of any serious acts of hostility on the part of the Indians. Many complaints have been received from both whites and Indians of trespasses, trivial annoyances, and some acts of violence. The military have used every effort to prevent disturbances of the peace, and to avoid open hostilities, and in this they have met with good success.

Within the last year the difficult and complicated questions concern-

---

[145]Capt. Charles F. Powell (USMA 1867).

ing the Moses and Upper Columbia River Indians have been adjusted by an amicable and equitable settlement or treaty between these Indians and the Government, whereby the Indians surrender a valuable district of country, larger in area than several of the Eastern States, and locate either in severalty or on the Colville Reservation.

The agreement having been confirmed by Congress, I believe it will result most favorably to the Indians and white settlers in that vicinity and to the General Government.

During the past Winter, Spring and Summer, many complaints have been received from the Lower Columbia River Indians, located between the Dalles and Priest's Rapids, and it has been with great difficulty that serious hostilities have been prevented. I have had officers and men engaged in pacifying these Indians who in the main seem well disposed, although by the rapid settlement of the country they have been unjustly deprived in many instances of their cultivated grounds, their salmon fisheries, and other means of subsistence. Numbers of these Indians have been assisted by the military in locating their claims to homesteads under the laws of Congress, and there is a fair prospect that the conflict of interests and hostile feeling between the two elements may soon be eliminated.

During the past year, when not otherwise engaged, and when practicable, troops have made marches of instructions, and scouted and explored remote and unsettled sections of this department. During the summer of 1883, First Lieutenant Frederick Schwatka,[146] Third Cavalry, A.D.C., Assistant Surgeon George F. Wilson, U.S. Army, Topographical Assistant C.A. Homan, and three soldiers, explored the valley of the Yukon River, Alaska, and rendered interesting reports of the country, accompanied by maps and illustrations, which have been forwarded for the information of the Government. This year Second Lieut. W.R. Abercrombie,[147] Second Infantry, A.D.C., continuing the same system of exploration, left these headquarters June 2, accompanied by Assistant Surgeon S.Q. Robinson, U.S. Army, Second Lieutenant V.J. Brumback,[148] Second Infantry, and Mr. C.A. Homan. They reached the mouth of the Copper River, Alaska, June 16, and will attempt explorations of its basin. Should they encounter serious difficulty they will cross over to the headwaters of the Tananah, about 1200 miles in length, and the principal southern tributary of the Yukon River, and examine that country.

[146] 1st Lt. Frederick Schwatka (USMA 1871). He resigned from the Army in 1885 to pursue his writing career.

[147] 1st Lt. William R. Abercrombie.

[148] 2nd Lt. Virgil J. Brumback (USMA 1881).

This region is wholly unknown, and occupied by natives who have never mingled with the whites or civilized races. The object of this small military reconnaissance is to obtain in advance of any Indian hostilities as thorough and complete knowledge of the country and its inhabitants as possible, and to assure the Indians of the friendly disposition of the Government. Lieutenant Abercrombie's instructions were to endeavor to promote peaceable relations with the natives, and under no circumstances to proceed where he could not go peaceably.

The material and supplies furnished by the various staff departments of the Army have been satisfactory during the year.

Inclosed herewith, and respectfully submitted, are the annual reports of the officers of the department staff.

Very respectfully,
Your obedient servant,
NELSON A. MILES,
Brigadier General, U.S. Army,
Commanding.

To the Adjutant General, Division of the Pacific,
Presidio of San Francisco, California.

REPORT OF BRIGADIER GENERAL MILES
Headquarters Department of the Missouri,
Fort Leavenworth, Kansas, Sept. 12, 1885.

Sir:

I have the honor to submit the following report of the condition of military affairs in this department:

On my assuming command of this department pursuant to telegraphic instructions and assignment by the President, I found the troops in Southern New Mexico occupied in guarding that frontier from the incursions of the hostile Apaches from Arizona and Old Mexico, and they are still engaged in this service; the troops of Northern New Mexico and Colorado holding the disaffected and poorly fed Utes of the mountains under restraint and protecting the settlements. In this they have been successful in preserving the peace. The Indians had just grounds for disaffection and complaint; six of their number had been murdered by lawless white men, their reservation overrun, their game destroyed, and their daily allowances of food reduced to one-half pound of beef and one-quarter of a pound of flour per day per Indian. The last difficulty has been for a time overcome by the prompt action of the honorable Secretary of the Interior in the increase of the food allowance. A large body of troops had been massed in Southern Kansas for the protection of the extensive settlements. I also found a large force of troops in the Indian Territory holding in restraint the turbulent, restless tribes of Indians there. In company with the Lieutenant General commanding the Army I visited the Cheyenne and Arapahoe Reservations in the Indian Territory where the condition of affairs might rightly be termed a pandemonium. A very large part of the Indian Territory and Reservations had been leased, fenced, and to some extent stocked with cattle. The Cheyennes and Arapahoes had been, as far as possible, huddled together in disagreeable and unhealthy camps, they were turbulent, disaffected, and on the verge of open hostilities. Two of their prominent men had been murdered, and they were defiant and utterly beyond the control of their agent or his Indian police. They were receiving rations for over 2,000 more Indians than they numbered. Besides the men engaged with the cattle herds there was a large number of white men that had taken advantage of the condition of affairs scattered through the Territory, without any visible or legitimate means of support. This condition of affairs was soon changed. The President revoked the cattle leases, as under the law and the terms of the leases he had a right to do. A very efficient and resolute Army officer, Captain Lee,[149] was placed in charge of the agency, and he now has the Indians under positive control, and is rapidly improving their condition. There will be a saving of more than $100,000 annually in the legitimate issue of rations. One hundred and thirty of the most active and restless of the young men have been enlisted as soldiers, and are now performing good service under the surveillance of competent officers and strong bodies of troops, and in addition to their military duties they will be required to cultivate ground enough to raise all the vegetables needed during the year. The reservation is being rapidly cleared of lawless and unauthorized white men, and peace and confidence have been restored to the settlements in Southern Kansas. The military garrisons in the Territory have been increased, and the large bodies of troops from other departments (with the exception of four troops of the Third Cavalry) returned to their proper stations.

Indian Territory

The object of reserving the Indian Territory as a place where the scattered tribes of Indians from Texas, Missouri, Kansas, and other States and Territories could be congregated and removed from before the advancing settlements was humane and judicious, and it has accomplished its mission. The Indian Territory is now a block in the pathway of civilization. It is preserved to perpetuate a mongrel race far removed from the influence of civilized people; a refuge for the outlaws

[149]Capt. Jesse M. Lee, 9th Inf.

and indolent of whites, blacks, and Mexicans. The vices introduced by these classes are rapidly destroying the Indians by disease. Without courts of justice or public institutions, without roads, bridges, or railways, it is simply a dark blot in the center of the map of the United States. It costs the Government hundreds of thousands of dollars to peaceably maintain from 60,000 to 80,000 Indians there, when the Territory is capable of supporting many millions of enlightened people.

I am convinced that the time has arrived for a change, and I therefore recommend that Congress authorize the President to appoint a commission of three experienced, competent men, empowered to treat with the different tribes; to consider all legal or just claims or titles; to grant to the Indian occupants of the Territory a sufficient quantity of land in severalty required for their wants and support, but not transferable for twenty years; that their title to the remainder be so far extinguished as it may be held in trust or sold by the Government, and a sufficient amount of the proceeds granted them to indemnify them for any interest they may possess in the land; that enough of said proceeds be provided to enable the Indians in the Territory to become self-sustaining. The land not required for Indian occupation to be thrown open for settlement under the same laws and rules as have been applied to the public domain.

Large Indian Reservations

The same recommendations would apply with equal force to nearly every Indian reservation in the United States, and from an extensive experience both east of the Rocky Mountains and on the Pacific coast, I know that the plan is practicable, just, and humane. I have recommended it for years, and have demonstrated, by actual experience, its success. There are, however, several important elements essential to success; first, the officials or commission to treat with the Indians must be men of experience, who understand the Indian methods of reasoning, their tastes and ambitions. They must be men who would inspire absolute confidence in the Indians. They must be practicable men and not theorists, and, what is more, they should be provided with something more than promises. I have seen the best of efforts fail from this cause alone. To successfully treat with Indians the representatives of the Government should be able to assure them that the Government is acting in good faith and for their benefit, and a sufficient sum of money should be appropriated or made subject to the President's order to fulfill any obligation of the Government. The exact terms would vary with various interests and desires of the several tribes. If this method were adopted I am satisfied that it would be perfectly practicable to make any tribe of Indians self-supporting in five years. Their condition would be greatly improved, they would have homes and property of their own, the Government would be relieved of the enormous expenditures of money to maintain the present system, and millions of acres of valuable lands, now lying idle, would be open to settlement.

I recommend that Congress be requested to authorize the enlistment of larger number of Indians as soldiers; I have had them under my command for years, have found them of great value, and have never known one to desert.

Troops in the Department

From the reports and personal inspections, I have found (the troops) efficient, well supplied, and instructed, temperate, and fairly well quartered. The military duty required of them is excessive and laborious. There are enough companies and regiments, but there are not enough men in the ranks, and I renew my recommendations, heretofore made, that the present number of enlisted men authorized be largely increased. One of the principal causes of the great number of desertions in the Army is, in my judgment, attributable to the present defective and very expensive system of recruiting, and I recommend that it be discontinued. The position of the soldier should be such as intelligent Americans would seek, rather than desert. Sufficient extra compensation should be made to induce men to enlist in the various regiments and companies. The officers would then know the kind of men they were getting, and a less number would come from the lower wards of our great cities, and the Government would be spared the great expense of transporting them from 100 to 3,000 miles to their stations. The enlistment should be for three years, and re-enlistment for one year. In this way many of the best soldiers would continue in the service and the worthless characters be discharged. The penalty for intended and actual desertion should be imprisonment for a definite term of years.

One source of disappointment and discouragement to the ambitious and intelligent soldier is the impossibility of obtaining promotion above the grade of that of an enlisted man. As there are but few vacancies other than those filled by graduates from the Military Academy at West Point, it would be well to allow ambitious young men, after five years service, to go before an examining Board, and should their record as soldiers be found perfect, and they be able to pass a rigid examination, then they should be entitled to their discharge with the rank of second lieutenant. It would be a material and social advantage to many worthy young men, and would disseminate military knowledge and experience in the care of troops among the people of the States and Territories.

The following is a brief statement of the most important movements of the troops in this department since the last annual report was forwarded:

Of the seven troops of the Ninth Cavalry which were in the field in the Indian Territory in October last guarding the Oklahoma country, five were returned in that month to their proper stations, the intruders having apparently disbanded; the remaining two (I & L) were directed to remain in the field during the winter—I, stationed at Camp Russell, Indian Territory, and L, at Caldwell, Kansas.

On December 26, 1884, telegraphic information being received from the Commanding Officer, Fort Reno, that about 225 intruders, armed with shot guns and Winchester rifles, had effected their entrance into Oklahoma and had been met by a detachment of soldiers, five troops of the Ninth Cavalry were sent from Forts Hays, Reno, Riley, and Sill to report to Colonel Hatch at Caldwell, Kansas, at which point they arrived in January. Colonel Hatch calling for additional troops, owing to the large number of intruders encountered, twelve companies of infantry from Forts Lyon, Union, Wingate, Gibson, and Reno were directed to report to Colonel Hatch, but before these companies reached their destination the boomers had surrendered, and they were ordered to return, from en route to their respective stations. The boomers were escorted over the line and six troops of cavalry retained in the field to guard the country.

Brigadier General Miles.
An 1880's portrait.
Courtesy, Westminster, Mass.,
Historical Society.

MILES AND STAFF IN ARIZONA
General Miles and his staff at Bowie Station, Arizona, September 8, 1886.
Left to right: Surgeon Leonard Wood, 1st Lt. Robert F. Ames, 1st Lt. Wilber
Wilder, Capt. Henry Lawton, General Miles, Capt. William A. Thompson
Maj. Amos S. Kimball, 2nd Lt. John A. Dapray, 2nd Lt. Charles D. Clay
Courtesy, National Archives.

VIII

Of Apaches in Arizona

In October of 1873, following brilliant service as Commander of the Department of Arizona, Lt. Col. George Crook had been promoted to the rank of Brigadier General. The as yet unproven Miles was one of several colonels "jumped" by Crook; so began years of rivalry and disagreement between the two men. The two were diametric opposites in appearance, deportment and style, and if either man respected the other it was grudgingly. Crook's Civil War career had been capable, but uneven, while Miles' was a succession of victories. Though Crook's post-war service against Paiutes and Apaches was undeniably deserving of commendation, the General's poor showing in the 1876 Campaign reinforced Miles' belief that the "Gray Fox" was vastly overrated. From Crook's standpoint Miles was successful, but pompous, vain, grasping and morally dishonest in his dealings with the Indians. Both men had their loyal followers, though Crook was at an advantage with his Boswell, the intellectually-minded Captain John G. Bourke.

On September 14, 1882 Crook for the second time assumed command of the Department of Arizona, relieving incompetent General Orlando B. Willcox. A graveyard of military careers, physically and professionally, the tortured landscape of New Mexico and Arizona once more became the battlefield on which the Army was challenged by Apache raiders under Natchez, Mangus, Chato and Geronimo. This time Crook based his campaign on the use and employment of Apache scouts drawn from the very tribes he sought to subjugate: five tough companies under the leadership of efficient officers like Captain Emmet Crawford and Lieutenant Charles B. Gatewood.

In the summer of 1883 Crook mounted expeditions into Mexico, whose government had acquiesced to U.S. military

intervention in pursuit of a common enemy. By the spring of
1884, the dogged campaigning paid off when a sullen Geronimo
returned to the San Carlos Reservation. Peace was shortlived
however; in 1885 the Chiricahua Apaches revolted, some fifty
warriors and nearly twice as many noncombatants fleeing across
the border. Among them were Geronimo, Mangus, Chihuahua,
Nana and Natchez. Again, in the summer of 1885, Crook sent his
scouts under Crawford and Captain Wirt Davis in pursuit; but
this time the foray into the rugged Sierra Madres failed. A
frustrated Lieutenant General Sheridan urged the deportation of
all reservation Chiricahua and Warm Springs Apaches from the
Southwest, and was highly critical of the important role given
Indian scouts in the campaign. Governor Ross of New Mexico
and other politicians began lobbying for Miles' appointment in
place of Crook; needless to say "Bearcoat" did not disuade them.

Crook's second expedition into Mexico seemed ready to bear
fruit when in January 1886, Captain Crawford's scouts pinpointed
the hostile band and opened negotiations. The promise of success
ended in tragedy on the 11th when Crawford was attacked and
mortally wounded by Mexican militiamen, seeking booty as well
as Apaches. A shaken Lieutenant Marion Maus was forced to
return to Crook's headquarters at Fort Bowie empty handed, but
with the hope that continued negotiations would be productive.

From March 25 through 27, 1886, General Crook met
personally with the Apache leaders at Cañon de los Embudos in
Sonora, Mexico. They came to an agreement, and Crook
returned to Fort Bowie to telegraph news of his victory, while the
troops escorted their armed prisoners northward. Fate dealt
Crook a cruel blow on March 28 when an unscrupulous trader
sold bottles of mescal to the Apaches—Geronimo, Natchez, 20
warriors, 13 women and six children fled into the night. Though
some 60 Apaches did resume reservation life, the escape of the
most dreaded raider of all, Geronimo, sent Sheridan into a rage.
His condemnation of Crook's methods caused the tired General
to offer his resignation:

> I believe that the plan upon which I have conducted operations is
> the one most likely to prove successful in the end. It may be,
> however, that I am too much wedded to my own views in this

matter, and as I have spent nearly eight years of the hardest work of my life in this Department, I respectfully request that I may now be relieved from its command.[150]

Sheridan agreed; Crook was ordered to the Department of the Platte and Miles to Fort Bowie as his successor.

Soon after Miles' ambulance pulled up to a somber Crook on the afternoon of April 11, 1886, the General began to realize that he had his work cut out for him, that a campaign in the Southwest would be different from any other he had waged. "In many respects this is the most difficult task I have ever undertaken," he wrote Mary, "Still I can only make the best effort possible."[151] Almost immediately he began to follow Sheridan's dictates regarding the use of Army personnel, not Indian scouts, to bring the Apaches to bay. He set about the installation of his pet signal apparatus, the heliograph, on thirty mountain peaks within the zone of operations. Yet as indecisive skirmishes showed, "It will take much time to organize fully such an extensive command and occupy and protect such a vast territory." Furthermore, Miles commented, "A more demoralized and inefficient command I have never known."[152]

On May 5, at Miles' order, a small expedition set out for Mexico under the command of Captain Henry W. Lawton of the 4th Cavalry. With him went young Surgeon Leonard Wood, 55 soldiers, 20 Indian scouts under Tom Horn, and a mule train with 30 civilian packers. Marching south from Fort Huachuca, their four-month campaign would cover some 2,000 miles in a fruitless and exhausting search for an elusive enemy. Miles was increasingly frustrated by his cunning opponents. As he wrote his wife on June 8, "When we think we have the best of the Indians they seem to make some move to slip out. But we will get them in time, in spite of their cunning and activity. . . I get very tired some nights, but the fatigue does not cause me to sleep for the responsibility and care keep me awake."[153]

[150]Crook, George. *Operations Against Apache Indians 1882-1886*. Washington, D.C. 1887. p. 12.
[151]Miles to Mrs. Miles, Fort Bowie, Ariz. Terr., April 11, 1886.
[152]Miles to Mrs. Miles, Nogales, May 8, 1886.
[153]Miles to Mrs. Miles, Calabasas, A.T., June 8, 1886.

Eventually Miles came to favor a deportation of all reservation Apaches as the key to Geronimo's surrender. He had no qualms about exiling the Indians from their homeland:

> Crook's policy was to treat those Indians at the Apache reservation more as conquerors than prisoners. They were allowed to retain all their arms, ammunition and stolen property. They have been petted and, if that policy is continued, they will furnish warriors for the next twenty years, liable to break out and raid the settlements on any drunk.[154]

It was Miles' intention to relocate the Apaches to Indian Territory (Oklahoma), but public opinion led the President and General Sheridan to endorse a relocation to Fort Marion, Florida. Knowing this would result in many deaths from disease, not to mention the trauma of adjusting to a completely different climate and way of life, Miles called the decision "very bad policy and unjust, particularly to the women and children."[155] Yet, on August 29 hundreds of Chiricahua and Warm Springs Apaches were deported, among them most of Crook's former scouts.

On July 13, 33-year-old Lieutenant Charles B. Gatewood, 6th Cavalry, accompanied by the scouts Kayitah and Martine set out to make overtures of peace to Geronimo's band. Another of Miles' gambits, this one was framed in the style of the late Department Commander, General Crook. Enroute, Gatewood met the handful of men still able to follow Captain Lawton and Surgeon Wood on the trail of the Apaches—less than thirty all told. Learning that the hostiles were far to their north, near Fronteras, they pushed rapidly on, narrowly avoiding a detachment of 200 Mexican troops. On August 24, Gatewood contacted Geronimo and Natchez on the Bavispe River; and, while Lawton waited at a distance, set about negotiating a surrender. The news that their families and friends were bound for Florida convinced the fugitives to return to American soil, though Geronimo insisted on a meeting with Miles.

As the wary Apaches headed north with Lawton's column, that officer sent frequent messages to Miles urging him to journey to the border and meet with the Apache leader. Avoiding a near

---

[154]Miles to Mrs. Miles, Hqtrs. Dept. of Ariz., Aug. 4, 1886.
[155]Miles to Mrs. Miles, Wilcox, Ariz., Aug. 27, 1886.

battle with Mexican soldiers, the party passed up the San
Bernardino Valley to Skeleton Canyon, where for five tense days
they awaited the General. Whether he was legitimately preoccupied with the deportation of the reservation Indians, or afraid
to set out for a surrender only to have the Apaches escape and
embarrass him as they had Crook, Miles' delay was nearly fatal to
all Gatewood and Lawton had accomplished. From vague
dispatches sent the Captain, it appears Miles would have preferred
Geronimo and Natchez taken hostage, or even killed rather than
have to talk them into a surrender. The day he left Bowie,
September 2, he wrote his wife,

> I go down this morning to see the hostiles under Geronimo. They
> have said they wanted to see me. I have very little faith in their
> sincerity and do not anticipate any good results. But still there is
> one chance that they may come in, and I feel like exhausting every
> effort to get them in without any more loss of life, if possible.[156]

On September 4 Miles met his foe in Skeleton Canyon, and
confirmed the surrender that Gatewood had made possible. A
recalcitrant Natchez was talked into joining Geronimo by the
Lieutenant, and Miles wasted no time bundling them off to Fort
Bowie in the ambulance he had travelled down in. Once
Geronimo's band was safely at the Fort, Miles almost immediately
sent them on towards a reunion with their families in Florida.
Unfortunately politics intervened when President Cleveland
ordered the Apaches detained in San Antonio, Texas pending
legal proceedings against them. For a month Miles debated the
issue with his superiors until, on October 22, the Indians were
sent on to their original destination. As Miles felt,

> They placed themselves entirely at our mercy, and we were in
> honor bound not to give them up to a mob or the mockery of a
> justice where they could never have received and impartial trial.
> After one of the most vigorous campaigns they surrendered like
> brave men to brave men, and placed themselves at the mercy of the
> government.[157]

It is sadly ironic that although he thus defended his prisoners by

---

[156]Miles to Mrs. Miles, Fort Bowie, Ariz., Sept. 2, 1886.
[157]Miles to Mrs. Miles, Albuquerque, N.M., Oct. 4, 1886.

opposing their removal to Florida, and spared them a civilian trial, in the next decade Miles would campaign against the Apaches' resettlement to healthier Indian Territory, the very place he thought they should go in the first place. By then he was in command of the Division of the Missouri, and could not ignore the anti-Apache sentiments of the citizens within its boundaries. The fate of the Apaches was a bitter one, and Miles showed little of the sympathy he had displayed for the Nez Perces, Sioux and Cheyennes.

Equally reprehensible was Miles' self-centered grab for whatever glory Geronimo's surrender had to offer. "It is a brilliant ending of a difficult problem,"[158] he congratulated himself; but while his capable subordinates Lawton and Wood were rewarded with promotion, the man most responsible for Geronimo's surrender was ignored. Charles Gatewood died in 1896, still a lieutenant, and has only posthumously received the credit due him.

Miles hoped his success against the Apaches would gain him promotion to Major General, and once again solicited letters of commendation from friends and supporters. There were even rumours of a Presidential bid in 1888; but on April 6 of that year George Crook received the promotion Miles coveted, while he was transferred to the Military Division of the Pacific. At his Headquarters in San Francisco Miles could at least take comfort in the fact that he was, by virtue of his assignment, an acting Major General.

THE GERONIMO CAMPAIGN
REPORT OF BRIGADIER GENERAL MILES
Headquarters Department of Arizona,
Albuquerque, New Mexico, Sept. 18, 1886

Sir:

I have the honor to submit my annual report as follows:

After rendering my report of last September, while in the command of the Department of the Missouri, and until assigned to this department, there was nothing of importance coming under my observation requiring especial mention.

[158] Miles to Mrs. Miles, Fort Bowie, Ariz., Sept. 7, 1886.

On the 2nd of April last I received the following despatch:

Washington, D.C. April 2, 1886.

General N.A. Miles,
Fort Leavenworth, Kansas.

Orders of this day assign you to command of Department of Arizona, to relieve General Crook. Instructions will be sent you.

R.C. Drum,
Adjutant General.

And on the fifth of April I received the following instructions:

Headquarters of the Army,
Washington, D.C. April 3, 1886.

General Nelson A. Miles,
Fort Leavenworth, Kansas.

The Lieutenant General directs that on assuming command of the Department of Arizona you fix your headquarters temporarily at or near some point on the Southern Pacific Railroad.

He directs that the greatest care be taken to prevent the spread of hostilities among the friendly Indians in your command, and that the most vigorous operations looking to the destruction or capture of the hostiles be ceaselessly carried on. He does not wish to embarrass you by undertaking at this distance to give specific instruction in relation to operations against the hostiles, but it is deemed advisable to suggest the necessity of making active and prominent use of the regular troops of your command. It is desired that you proceed to Arizona as soon as practicable.

R.C. Drum,
Adjutant General.

With as little delay as practicable, I proceeded to Fort Bowie, Arizona, and assumed command of the Department April 12, 1886.

At that time there was trouble threatened with the Ute Indians in Southern Colorado and with the powerful tribe of Navajos in New Mexico and Arizona. These tribes had been formerly within my control, and I was familiar with the questions in dispute between them and the white settlers.

While en route to Arizona I gave the necessary directions for placing troops in their vicinity, and assigned to Colonel L.P. Bradley,[159] commanding the District of New Mexico, the more immediate responsibility of their supervision. He made such use of his troops, in concert with the measures adopted by the Interior Department, that peace was

---

[159]Col. Luther P. Bradley, 13th Infantry.

preserved. These are powerful tribes, occupying the Rocky Mountain region. The Navajos alone number 20,000 souls. There are 47,000 Indians in this Department, located in sections of a territory 300,000 square miles in extent.

Soon after assuming command of this Department my attention was chiefly turned to the hostile element of the Chiricahua and Warm Springs Indians, whose depredations and atrocities had spread a feeling of insecurity and alarm through all the scattered settlements. A more terror-stricken class of people than the citizens of these Territories I have never found in any section of the country.

Many of the industrial interests—mining, agriculture, and pastoral—had been abandoned, and the troops were much discouraged. During the year the hostile Indians had killed one hundred and forty persons, and an impression seemed to prevail that the natural obstacles were too great to be overcome in the subjugation of this race of most savage mountaineers. One difficult feature of this problem was found to be the small number of the hostiles, and the fact that they roamed over the most rugged mountain region on the continent, embracing an area of 600 miles north and south and 400 miles east and west. In physical excellence and as mountain climbers they probably have no superiors on earth. Their transportation consisted of any animals they could steal, and they subsisted by preying upon herds of cattle and flocks of sheep in the valleys, and by securing their natural food of field-mice, rabbits, seeds, desert fruit, and the substance of mescal and the fruit of the giant cactus, found amid the highest ranges.

The small number of the hostiles necessitated the dispersion of the commands over a vast area of country, to give confidence, security, and protection to the settlements, miners, prospectors, &c., and at the same time placing them where they could be most available to act against these hostiles.

On the 20th of April, I issued the following general order:

(General Field Orders No. 7.)

Headquarters Department of Arizona in the Field,

Fort Bowie, Arizona, April 20, 1886.

The following instructions are issued for the information and guidance of troops serving in the southern portions of Arizona and New Mexico.

The chief object of the troops will be to capture or destroy any band of hostile Apache Indians found in this section of country; and to this end the most vigorous and persistent efforts will be required of all officers and soldiers until the object is accomplished.

To better facilitate this duty, and afford as far as practicable protection to the scattered settlements, the territory is subdivided into districts of observation as shown upon maps furnished by the Department Engineer Officer, and will be placed under commanding officers to be hereafter designated.

Each command will have a sufficient number of troops and the necessary transportation to thoroughly examine the district of country to which it is assigned, and will be expected to keep such section clear of hostile Indians.

The signal detachments will be placed upon the highest peaks and prominent lookouts, to discover any movement of Indians and to transmit messages between the different camps.

The Infantry will be used in hunting through the groups and ranges of mountain, the resorts of the Indians, occupying the important passes in the mountains, guarding supplies, etc.

A sufficient number of reliable Indians will be used as auxiliaries to discover any signs of hostile Indians, and as trailers.

The Cavalry will be used in light scouting parties, with a sufficient force held in readiness at all times to make the most persistent and effective pursuit.

To avoid any advantage the Indians may have by a relay of horses, where a troop or squadron commander is near the hostile Indians he will be justified in dismounting one-half of his command and selecting the lightest and best riders to make pursuit by the most vigorous forced marches, until the strength of all the animals of his command shall have been exhausted.

In this way a command should, under a judicious leader, capture a band of Indians or drive them from 150 to 200 miles in forty-eight hours through a country favorable for cavalry movements; and the horses of the troops will be trained for this purpose.

All commanding officers will make themselves thoroughly familiar with the section of country under their charge, and will use every means to give timely information regarding the movements of hostile Indians to their superiors or others acting in concert with them, in order that fresh troops may intercept the hostiles or take up the pursuit.

Commanding officers are expected to continue a pursuit until capture, or until they are assured a fresh command is on the trail.

All camps and movement of troops will be concealed as far as possible, and every effort will be made at all times by the troops to discover hostile Indians before being seen by them.

To avoid ammunition getting into the hands of the hostile

Indians every cartridge will be rigidly accounted for, and when they are used in the field the empty shells will be effectually destroyed.

Friendly relations will be encouraged between the troops and citizens of the country, and all facilities rendered for the prompt interchange of reliable information regarding the movements of hostile Indians.

Field reports will be made on the 10th, 20th, and 30th of each month, giving the exact location of troops and the strength and condition of commands.

By command of Brigadier General Miles:

Wm. A. Thompson,[160]
Captain 4th Cavalry, A.A.A.G.

The districts of observation were placed under command of experienced officers, and sufficient troops were given to each to enable him to make his district untenable for any hostile bands.

Early in April I decided to make prominent use of the Signal Service, and so notified the Chief Signal Officer of that Bureau, and in answer to my request he furnished me ample men and appliances for making that service most useful and effective.

Each troop of cavalry and company of infantry was fully equipped with the necessary supplies and transportation for effective service.

The hostiles were at that time under Chiefs Geronimo and Natchez, son of Cochise, the hereditary Chief of the Chiricahua Indians. Under the terms of our treaty our troops were allowed to follow a trail of Indians south of the Mexican border, and the Mexican Government being at that time embarrassed by a war with the Yaquis, a powerful race of Indians living in Southern Sonora, had withdrawn nearly all its troops from the border, leaving the people of Sonora in an exposed and almost defenseless condition. I made such disposition of our troops as would give the best protection to our own citizens, and organized an effective force to pursue them when in Old Mexico. For this purpose I selected Captain H.W. Lawton,[161] Fourth Cavalry, an officer who had a brilliant record during the war, whose splendid physique, character, and high attainments as an officer and commander peculiarly fitted him for one of the most difficult undertakings to which an officer could be assigned. He also possessed another element of success in believing that the Indians

---

[160]Capt. William A. Thompson of Maryland.

[161]Capt. Henry Ware Lawton, 4th Cavalry. A lieutenant colonel of Volunteers in the Civil War, he was a huge man, a hard drinker and a tough as nails protege of Col. Ranald S. Mackenzie. As General he was killed in the Philippines on Dec. 19, 1899.

could be out-maneuvered, worn down, and subjugated. His command was comprised of picked Cavalry and Infantry, scouts, guides, etc., with a pack train capable of carrying two months provisions, with the necessary ammunition and medical supplies. Before this command was organized the Indians assumed hostilities, making simultaneous attacks at three points in Central Sonora, from near the Mexican border to 150 miles south of that line.

This raid spread terror throughout that district of Mexico. The hostiles swept northward, and on the 27th of April invaded our territory, passing down the Santa Cruz Valley, stealing stock and killing a few citizens, including the Peck Family. The mother and child were murdered, and a girl of some ten years of age captured, but subsequently recaptured. The father was captured and held for several hours, but by some strange freak was finally released by the Indians. At this point they stuck a section of our country further west than they had appeared in for many years, not however, without opposition. Captain T. Lebo,[162] with his troop, Tenth Cavalry, was quickly on the trail, and after a hot pursuit of 200 miles brought them to bay in the Pinito Mountains, some 30 miles south of the boundary in Sonora. In this rapid march and encounter Captain Lebo displayed his usual energy, good judgment and gallantry, and, although engaging a hostile adversary on grounds of their own choosing and with every natural obstacle against him, he made a good fight, inflicting some loss and sustaining very slight loss to his own command. During the engagement Corporal Scott, a brave soldier, was severely wounded, and lay disabled under a sharp fire of the Indians, and Lieutenant Powhatan H. Clarke,[163] a gallant young officer, distinguished himself by rushing forward and with his own hands and at the risk of his life carried the disabled soldier to a place of safety. A youth thus rescuing a veteran under a severe fire indicates that the days of chivalry have not passed.

After the engagement the Indians continued their retreat, and the trail was soon after taken up by Lieutenant H.C. Benson,[164] Fourth Cavalry, a very enterprising young officer of Captain Lawton's command, who during this entire campaign has rendered most difficult and valuable services. They were then pursued south and west. Their trail was again taken up by Lebo's command and later by Captain Lawton, and they were finally, on May 15, intercepted by the command of

[162] Capt. Thomas C. Lebo of Pennsylvania, a capable and efficient company commander.
[163] 2nd Lt. Powhatan Henry Clarke, 10th Cavalry (USMA 1884). He was awarded the Medal of Honor for saving his black trooper's life, an incident commemorated in one of artist Frederic Remington's illustrations. Clarke drowned in July 1893.
[164] 2nd Lt. Harry C. Benson, 4th Cav. (USMA 1882).

Captain C.A.P. Hatfield,[165] Fourth Cavalry, which had been placed to intercept them east of Santa Cruz, Sonora. The hostiles were completely surprised, Captain Hatfield's command capturing their entire camp equipage and about twenty horses. At this fight the hostiles lost their first deserter, who, having his horse shot under him, crawled into the rocks and continued his retreat for forty-five days, surrendering at Fort Apache, 250 miles north, on the 28th day of June. Unfortunately, while passing west through a deep and narrow cañon, towards Santa Cruz, embarrassed with his captured property and Indian horses, Captain Hatfield's command was attacked by the hostiles and a fight ensued. There were several cases of conspicuous bravery displayed in this fight. The action of Sergeant Samuel H. Craig was most heroic and very worthy of praise. First Sergeant Samuel Adams and Citizen Packer George Bowman, exposed their lives in attempting to rescue John H. Conradi, of that troop, who lay seriously wounded on the ground, but still using his rifle to good effect. This act of bravery and heroism would have been richly rewarded had not the unfortunate soldier received a mortal wound as he was being borne from the field by his devoted comrades.

After Hatfield's fight, Lieutenant R.A. Brown,[166] Fourth Cavalry, an enterprising young officer, with a small command, struck the trail and pursued the hostiles in an easterly direction with good effect. The hostiles then divided, and a part struck north, passing through the Dragoon, Caesura, and Santa Teresa Mountains. While these movements were being conducted, preparations were made to prevent the Indians at the different agencies affording the hostiles any assistance in men, ammunition, or provisions, and on the 3rd day of May I went as far north as Fort Thomas, Arizona, and there met Captain F.E. Pierce,[167] commanding at San Carlos Agency, and Lieutenant Colonel J.F. Wade,[168] commanding at Fort Apache.

Soon after assuming command of the department, I became convinced that there could be no permanent peace or lasting settlement of the chronic condition of warfare that had for centuries afflicted the territories now comprising Arizona and New Mexico and the bordering Mexican States until the hostile Apache Indians then on the war-path were captured or destroyed and those at the agencies entirely removed from

---

[165] Capt. Charles A.P. Hatfield (USMA 1872), brevetted Major for this service.

[166] 2nd Lt. Robert A. Brown (USMA 1885).

[167] Capt. Francis E. Pierce, 8th Inf. a Brevet Brigadier General in the Civil War.

[168] Lt. Col. James Franklin Wade, 10th Cav. Wade was a son of Radical Senator Ben Wade of Ohio, and a distinguished veteran of the Civil War. He would serve as Major General of Volunteers in the Spanish American War.

that mountainous region. The trails they had made in past years showed that their raids had been from the agency through the settlements and back again to that source of evil, and every few years their boys became full-fledged warriors, who, in order to achieve distinction according to traditions and practices of their fathers, were compelled to commit savage acts of devastation.

I then informed Colonel Wade that he should make it his duty not only to prevent any communication between the hostiles and the Indians on his reservation, but that he should exert his utmost energy to bring the camp of Chiricahua, and Warm Springs, who were then not only mounted but still armed, and liable at any time to assume hostilities, entirely under his control, and gain their confidence if possible, but at least to obtain such control over them as would enable him to remove them from the Territory in case he received an order from me to that effect, and furnished him additional troops to accomplish that object. That duty could not have been assigned to a more efficient, judicious, and determined officer.

Captain Pierce, who is by appointment of the President in charge of the civil administration of the San Carlos and White Mountain Indians, and who is a very faithful and efficient officer, fully concurred with me in the importance of the work, and actively co-operated in the enterprise. The matter was kept a secret and every effort was made to bring about the desired result.

I return again to the movements of the hostile Indians, who were now divided into two bands. The one moving north through the Dragoon Mountains was intercepted by Lieutenant L.M. Brett,[169] Second Cavalry, they crossing the Southern Pacific Railroad near Dragoon Summit, thence north to a point west of Fort Grant, Arizona.

In this pursuit Lieutenant Brett displayed great energy and determination. The Indians, going over the roughest mountains, breaking down one set of horses, would abandon them and pass straight over the highest ranges and steal others in the valleys below, while the troops, in order to pursue then, were obliged to send their horses around the impassable mountain heights, and followed the trail on foot, climbing in the ascent and sliding in the descent. He went at one time twenty-six hours without halt, and was without water during eighteen hours in the intense heat of that season. When they were in the mountains west of Fort Grant, Lieutenant L.P. Hunt,[170] Tenth Cavalry, took up the trail,

[169] 1st Lt. Lloyd M. Brett (USMA 1879), a Medal of Honor winner for his service at O'Fallon's Creek, Mont., April 1, 1880.
[170] 1st Lt. Levi P. Hunt (USMA 1870).

and later the pursuit was continued by Lieutenant R.D. Read, Jr.,[171] S.D. Freeman,[172] J.W. Watson,[173] J.B. Hughes,[174] and W.E. Shipp,[175] Tenth Cavalry; Lieutenant A.T. Dean,[176] Fourth Cavalry; and Lieutenant G.W. Ruthers,[177] Eighth Infantry, and Captain S.T. Norvell,[178] Tenth Cavalry, and when near Fort Apache all the horses then in the hands of the hostile raiding party were captured by Captain J.T. Morrison,[179] Tenth Cavalry. The Indians then turned south, and the pursuit was again continued by troops under Captain Allen Smith,[180] Fourth Cavalry; Captain G.C. Doane,[181] Second Cavalry; Lieutenant W.E. Wilder,[182] Fourth Cavalry, and others. They finally recrossed the Mexican boundary.

The other party or band of hostiles were followed west by Lieutenant Brown until the trail was struck by Captain Lawton. They were turned north by the movement of the troops under Captain A.E. Wood,[183] Fourth Cavalry, and Lieutenant William Davis, Jr.,[184] Tenth Cavalry, and then entered our territory again east of Oro Blanco, Arizona.

There the pursuit was taken up by Captain Lebo and Lieutenants Davis and Clarke, Tenth Cavalry, and followed through the Santa Rita, Whetstone, Santa Catalina, and Rincon Mountains.

When in the Catalina Mountains they were attacked by a body of citizens under Messrs. Samaniego and Leatherwood, from Tucson, Arizona, and a boy who had been recently captured by them was recaptured. They were pressed south by Captain Lebo and Lieutenant Davis, Captain Lawton and Lieutenant John Bigelow, Jr.,[185] Tenth Cavalry, and in passing through the Patagonia Mountains they were intercepted by Lieutenant R.D. Walsh,[186] Fourth Cavalry, June 6, with

[171] 1st Lt. Robert D. Read, Jr. (USMA 1877).
[172] 2nd Lt. Samuel D. Freeman (USMA 1883).
[173] 2nd Lt. James W. Watson (USMA 1880).
[174] 2nd Lt. James B. Hughes (USMA 1884).
[175] 2nd Lt. William E. Shipp (USMA 1883) killed at San Juan Hill, Cuba, July 1, 1898.
[176] 2nd Lt. Alexander T. Dean, 4th Cavalry.
[177] 2nd Lt. George W. Ruthers, had worked his way up through the ranks.
[178] Capt. Stevens T. Norvell, had worked his way up through the ranks.
[179] Capt. John T. Morrison.
[180] Capt. Allen Smith had attended the Naval Academy from 1863-66.
[181] Capt. Gustavus C. Doane.
[182] 1st Lt. Wilbur E. Wilder (USMA 1877), awarded the Medal of Honor for rescuing a wounded soldier at Horshoe Canyon, N.M., April 23, 1882.
[183] Capt. Abram E. Wood (USMA 1872).
[184] 1st Lt. William Davis, Jr. of Indiana.
[185] 1st Lt. John Bigelow, Jr. (USMA 1877).
[186] 2nd Lt. Robert D. Walsh (USMA 1883).

a loss of much of their equipments and stock. They were then pursued by Captain Lawton and Captain J.G. MacAdams,[187] Second Cavalry, into Sonora, for the second time. These movements occurred in the districts commanded by Colonels Royall,[188] Shafter,[189] Wade, and Mills,[190] who made excellent dispositions of their troops.

From that time Captain Lawton, with a fresh command, assumed the arduous and difficult task of pursuing them continuously through the broken, mountainous country of Sonora for nearly three months.

In this remarkable pursuit he followed them from one range of mountains to another, over the highest peaks, often 9,000 and 10,000 feet above the level of the sea, and frequently in the depths of the cañons, where the heat in July and August was of tropical intensity.

A portion of the command leading on the trail without rations for five days, three days being the longest continuous period. They subsisted on two or three deer killed by the scouts, and mule meat without salt. The pack trains had been delayed by the roughness of the road and the difficulty in following the trail.

A portion of Captain Lawton's command consisted of picked infantry, a part of the time under command of Lieutenants Henry Johnson Jr.,[191] and C.P. Terrett,[192] Eighth Infantry; Lieutenant H.C. Benson, Fourth Cavalry; Assistant Surgeon Leonard Wood,[193] Lieutenant T.J. Clay,[194] Tenth Infantry; and Lieutenants J.J. Haden,[195] and S.E. Smiley,[196] Eighth Infantry.

These men made marches where it was impossible to move cavalry or pack trains; but their laborious and valuable efforts were crippled by the miserable shoes made at, and furnished from the military prison at Fort Leavenworth, Kansas. The worthless material frequently fell to pieces

[187] Capt. James G. MacAdams, a native of Canada.

[188] Col. William B. Royall, 4th Cav., a crusty old veteran of the Mexican and Civil Wars with years of Indian Wars service.

[189] Col. William R. Shafter, 1st Inf., awarded the Medal of Honor for service at the Battle of Fair Oaks in 1862. Miles would have extensive dealings with Shafter during the Spanish American War.

[190] Major Anson Mills, 10th Cav., famous as the inventor of the Mills belt and web suspension equipment; effective leader of troops in many Indian campaigns.

[191] 1st Lt. Henry Johnson, Jr., 8th Infantry.

[192] 2nd Lt. Colville T. Terrett, worked up through the ranks from private.

[193] Assistant Surgeon Leonard Wood, who began his service in January, 1886. He would be awarded the Medal of Honor for bravery in the Apache campaign, and go on to command the "Rough Riders" in the Spanish American War and attain General's rank.

[194] 1st Lt. Thomas J. Clay of Kentucky.

[195] 1st Lt. John J. Haden (USMA 1877).

[196] 2nd Lt. Samuel E. Smiley (USMA 1885).

in three or four days marching. This not only occassioned unjust expense to the soldiers, but caused them unnecessary and cruel hardship and suffering. His scouts and trailers performed very difficult service, under Leighton Finley,[197] Tenth Cavalry.

The troops suffered somewhat from fever, but fortunately they were very strong men and endured their hardships with commendable fortitude. When on the Yaqui River and in the district of Montezuma, the hostile camp was surprised and attacked by Captain Lawton's command. The Indians escaped among the rocks, but their entire property, with the exception of what they could carry, was captured, including all their horses. They scattered in every direction, but whenever this occurred the troops followed the trail of a single Indian until they came together again. They committed several murders and many depredations in the districts of Sahuaripa, Ures, Montezuma, and Arizpe, in the State of Sonora, Mexico, and moved rapidly north by a march of nearly 300 miles to the vicinity of Fronteras, in Arizpe, District Sonora. Meanwhile the concentration of our troops in the vicinity of the hostile camp, the rapid movement of two troops of cavalry under Lieutenant Colonel George A. Forsyth,[198] Fourth Cavalry, from Fort Huachuca, the movement of Lieutenant James Parker,[199] Fourth Cavalry, with his own and Lieutenant D.N. McDonald's[200] troop, Fourth Cavalry, from Fort Bowie to that point, and the very vigorous and rapid movement of Captain Lawton in following them up from the south, were most threatening to the Indians, and had a most discouraging effect upon them.

During their raids in the United States Territories fourteen persons were reported killed by the hostiles; in their raids through the Mexican States their depredations were still greater.

During the time the hostiles were 300 miles south of the Mexican boundary, and when a temporary peace and security prevailed in our own Territories I turned my attention more particularly to the removal of the Chiricahua and Warm Springs Indians, as their camps have been the place of refuge for the hostiles for years.

In my visit to Fort Apache, the Honorable Secretary of the Interior very kindly sent his Secretary, Mr. L.Q.C. Lamar, Jr., to accompany us. This secured co-operation of that Department, and avoided any conflict

[197] 2nd Lt. Leighton Finley of South Carolina.
[198] Lt. Col. George A. Forsyth, 4th Cav. "Sandy" Forsyth was Sheridan's long-time aide, and is best known for his heroic stand at Beechers Island in 1868.
[199] 1st Lt. James Parker, Regimental Adjutant, 4th Cav. (USMA 1876). Awarded the Medal of Honor for service in the Philippines Insurrection.
[200] 1st Lt. David N. McDonald (USMA 1877).

of opinion or authority. I made a very careful examination into the condition of the Chiricahua and Warm Springs Apaches. I found over four hundred men, women, and children, and a more turbulent and dissipated body of Indians I have never met. Some of them, chiefly women, were industrious. They had raised a little barley, but much of their earnings and crops went for trifles and "tiswin" drunks. Riots and bloodshed were not infrequent.

These people were on paper prisoners of war, yet they had never been disarmed or dismounted, and the stillness of the nights was often broken by the discharge of rifles and pistols in their savage orgies. The indolent and vicious young men and boys were just the material to furnish warriors for the future, and these people, although fed and clothed by the government, had been conspiring against its authority. They had been in communication with the hostiles, and some of them had been plotting an extensive outbreak. Being fully confirmed in opinion that the permanent peace of these Territories required the removal of these tribes from the mountains of Arizona, I sent a delegation of both Chiricahua and Warm Springs Indians to Washington, under charge of Captain Dorst,[201] to confer with the authorities with a view of some location being selected for them where they would no longer be a disturbing element. My first intention was to have them moved to some place east of New Mexico, all their arms taken away, the most of their children scattered through the industrial Indian schools, and should they consent to go peaceably, enough domestic stock, money, and farming utensils given them to make them self-sustaining, and such disposition made of the hostiles as should subsequently be determined upon by the Government as most advisable.

There were ten men sent to Washington, and the number included several of the principal leaders and some of the most dangerous characters. Nothing was accomplished at Washington, and the delegation was ordered back to Arizona. Against this I telegraphed an earnest protest, giving as a reason that if these Indians returned to Arizona, in defiance of the military authorities and the appeals of the people for their removal, outbreaks and disturbances might be expected for the next twenty years; that their presence had been a menace to the peace of this country; and that in my opinion there could be no hardship in retaining a handful of Indians at Carlisle, Penn., until a question involving the lives and property, and peace of the people of this section of the country could be satisfactorily decided.

---

[201]Capt. Joseph H. Dorst, 4th Cav. (USMA 1873).

This had the desired effect of stopping their return—not, however, until they had reached Kansas on their way to Arizona.

They were then independent and defiant, and their return to the mountains about Apache, under the circumstances, would have been worse than the letting loose of that number of wild beasts. I then asked that Captain J.H. Dorst, Fourth Cavalry, who had charge of them, be ordered to report to me, and I also ordered Lieutenant Colonel Wade, commanding at Fort Apache, to report to me at Albuquerque, N. Mexico. The importance of the measure then appeared to me sufficient for taking very decided action.

Captain Dorst was directed to return to Fort Leavenworth and inform those Indians that they could be either friendly treaty Indians or individuals; that they could conform to the wishes of the Government and people, and consent to the peaceable removal of the Indians referred to from these Territories, or they could return and be held responsible for their crime. As the principals had committed scores of murders, and warrents for their arrest were awaiting them—and they could not expect the military to shelter them from the just and legal action of the civil courts—the effect of this plain talk was the absolute submission of the Indians to any disposition the Government might decide to make of them. They agreed to go any place that I might designate, there to wait until such time as the Government should provide them a permanent reservation, and funds, domestic stock, and utensils by which they could become self-sustaining. This was the first step in that direction that promised ultimate success. In the meantime I had directed Colonel Wade to place those tribes near his post at Apache entirely within his control, and in addition to the three troops of cavalry and two companies of infantry then under his command, I ordered one troop from San Carlos, two from Fort Thomas, Arizona, and one from Alma, N. Mexico, to march to Fort Apache.

This important and difficult service Lieutenant Colonel Wade performed with good judgment and decision. He placed the Indian men under guard, and moved the entire camp nearly four hundred persons 100 miles to Holbrook, Arizona, on the Atlantic and Pacific Railroad, and thence by rail, via. Albuquerque, Saint Louis, and Atlanta, to Fort Marion, Florida. This I regard as one of the most difficult duties that can be required of a commanding officer, and it was accomplished with complete success.

While at Fort Apache, July 1st, I learned, from one of the Apaches who left Geronimo's camp after Captain Hatfield's fight, of the weakened condition of the hostiles, and that and other information convinced me that they could not hold out much longer against the zealous and persistent action of the troops, and that they would soon surrender. I selected two Chiricahua Indians from those at Apache, and sent them with Lieutenant C.B. Gatewood,[202] Sixth Cavalry, to Fort Bowie, Arizona, and thence south into Sonora.

The effort of a small party of Indians to get through the lines south of Bowie near the boundary, and their action in not committing any depredations indicated a desire to surrender or get past the troops to the agency. When near Fronteras there was some communication between the Indians and the local authorities regarding terms of peace, but it amounted to nothing, as the Indians would not place themselves in the hands of the Mexicans. During the two days of truce while this matter was being considered, Lieutenant Wilder met two of the Indian women belonging to the hostile camp, and informed them that if they and their people desired to give up they could surrender to the American troops; and when the hostiles withdrew from the vicinity of Fronteras, closely followed by Lawton's command, communication was opened, through means of the two men above referred to, with Lieutenant Gatewood. They were sent forward with a demand for the surrender of the camp. This resulted in their meeting Lieutenant Gatewood, when he rode boldly into their presence, at the risk of his life, and repeated the demand for their surrender. They refused to surrender at once, but they desired to see Captain Lawton, who had pursued them with great pertinacity. Captain Lawton granted the interview, but the Indians asked similar terms and privileges to what they had been given before, and, through the interpreters, sent me two messages and made most urgent appeals to see the department commander. I replied to Captain Lawton that their requests could not be granted, and that he was fully authorized to receive their surrender as prisoners of war to the troops in the field. They were told that the troops were brave and honest men, and that if they threw down their arms and placed themselves at the mercy of the officers they would not be murdered. They promised to surrender to me in person, and for eleven days Captain Lawton's command moved north, Geronimo's and Natchez's camp moving parallel and frequently camping near it. At the request of Captain Lawton I joined his command on the evening of Sept. 3, at Skeleton Cañon, a favorite resort of the Indians in former years, and well suited by name and tradition to witness the closing scenes of such an Indian War.

While en route to join Lawton's command, Geronimo had sent his

---

[202] 1st Lt. Charles B. Gatewood, 6th Cav. (USMA 1877). More than any other man Gatewood deserves the credit of Geronimo's surrender. He died ignored and unhonored in 1896.

own brother, with the interpreter, to Fort Bowie, to see me, and, if not as a hostage, as an assurance of their submission and desire to surrender, and as an earnest of their good faith.

Soon after reaching Lawton's command Geronimo came into our camp and dismounted; then coming forward unarmed, he recounted his grievances and the cause of his leaving the reservation. He stated that he had been abused and assailed by the officials, and that a plot had been laid to take his life by Chatto and Mickey Free, encouraged by one of the officials; that it was a question whether to die on the war-path or be assassinated; that at that time he was cultivating a crop, and if he had not been driven away he would by this time have been in good circumstances. A part of this story I knew to be true. I informed him that Captain Lawton and Lieutenant Gatewood were honorable men, and that I was there to confirm what they had said to them; that though Captain Lawton, with other troops, had followed and fought them incessantly, yet should they throw down their arms and place themselves entirely at our mercy we should certainly not kill them, but that they must surrender absolutely as prisoners of war to the Federal authorities, and rely upon the government to treat them fairly and justly. I informed him that I was removing all Chiricahua and Warm Springs Indians from Arizona, and that they would all be removed from this country at once and for all time. Geronimo replied that he would do whatever I said, obey any order, and bring in his camp early next morning, which he did. Natchez sent in word requesting a pass of twenty days to go to the White Mountains, but this was refused. They had found troops in every valley, and when they saw heliographic communication flashing across every mountain range, Geronimo and others sent word to Natchez that he had better come in at once and surrender. Natchez was wild and suspicious, and evidently feared treachery. He knew that the once noted leader Mangus Colorado had years ago been foully murdered after he had surrendered, and the last hereditary Chief of the hostile Apache hesitated to place himself in the hands of the pale faces. He sent in word that if Geronimo would come out he would return with him. I told Geronimo to go and bring him in, and the two subsequently rode in together, and, dismounting, moved forward, and Natchez formally surrendered his camp. It was then late in the afternoon of September 4, and soon commenced raining in torrents.

Early next morning Natchez's people came in and joined Geronimo's camp, and I immediately started to return to Fort Bowie, distant 65 miles, taking with me Natchez, Geronimo, and four other Indians, reaching there after dark. Captain Lawton following, reached that post three days later. The night before reaching Bowie, three men and three squaws crawled out of Captain Lawton's camp and escaped into the mountains. There was one Mescalero among them, and they have since been trailed towards the Mescalero Agency and it is believed will soon be arrested by the troops. On reaching Fort Bowie the Indians were placed in wagons and sent under heavy guard to Bowie station, thence by rail to El Paso and San Antonio, Texas. Immediately before and after the surrender several official communications were received regarding these Indians, but their surrender was in accordance with measures I had taken and directions given to bring it about months before, and the direct result of the intrepid zeal and indefatigable efforts of the troops in the field. When they surrendered they had not ammunition enough to make another fight. At the time referred to I did not suppose that the Indians who surrendered or were captured would in any marked degree be considered different from those hostile Indians who had in the past surrendered to others and to myself in other parts of the country. It is true that they have committed many grievous offenses, and there are some malicious and vicious looking men and boys in the camp, but Natchez and Geronimo and his brother do not appear to be among the worst. Since the establishment of the Government there have been two methods or policies of dealing with the Indians—one holding them individually responsible for their acts and amenable to the local laws, subject to arrest and punishment; the other, the almost universal policy—where their offenses have assumed the nature of an insurrection —to use the military forces against them as a people, and by the devastations of war and destruction of their property, and imprisonment of the whole tribe or banishment from their native country, to effectually subjugate and punish them as one body. Such men as Natchez and Geronimo occupy the same status as Red Cloud, who led the Fort Fetterman massacre, Chief Joseph, Rain-in-the-Face, Spotted Eagle, Sitting Bull, and thousands of others, many of whom have burned and mutilated their living victims.

In determining what policy it is legal and judicious to pursue regarding these Indians, it may be well not only to consider the course the government has pursued heretofore in its relations with Indians, but also the probable effect which any radical departure from established policies would have upon other Indians that may in the future be in hostility to the Government. Should they be held as prisoners of war and never allowed to return again to the Territories of Arizona, and New Mexico—and there are military reasons why this would be advisable—I would recommend that their children of suitable ages be placed in the various industrial Indian Schools, in order that the rising generation may not suffer from the acts of their fathers, and that their present degraded condition may be materially improved.

Arbitrary and absolute banishment is a severe punishment for any people and its effect upon neighboring tribes has been very salutary heretofore in other parts of the country.

All of the friendly Indians in this department have been kept under control, and the hostile bands have, "by prominent use of the regular troops," been subjugated and are now prisoners.

These gratifying results have been produced by the most laborious and persistent effort on the part of all—officers and men.

The hostiles fought until the bulk of their ammunition was exhausted, pursued for more than 2,000 miles over the most rugged and sterile districts of the Rocky and Sierra Madre Mountain regions, beneath the burning heat of midsummer, until worn down and disheartened, they find no place of safety in our country or Mexico, and finally lay down their arms and sue for mercy from the gallant officers and soldiers, who, despite every hardship and adverse circumstance, have achieved the success their endurance and fortitude so richly deserved.

The above is not the only good work accomplished by the disposition of the troops and a thorough system of communication over the different sections of these vast Territories. The military were thus enabled to give substantial protection to the scattered settlements, and, in addition to this, have removed the whole hostile Apache tribe, who have fought the civilized races for three hundred years, from the Territories of Arizona and New Mexico.

This affords the citizens of these Territories great gratification, and the troops a feeling of relief to know that they are away from this part of the United States.

The results of the military operations during the last four months will I believe, effect a saving for the government of $350,000 per annum, and the benefits to the material interest of these Territories can not well be estimated.

I am under obligation to Governor Luis E. Torres, of Sonora, Mexico, for his most courteous and hearty co-operation. His intelligent and liberal construction of the terms of the compact between the two Governments was of very great assistance to our officers in moving troops and supplies through that portion of the country, and was acquiesced in by other Mexican officials. In fact, every assistance within his personal and official powers was rendered by the Governor to aid in arresting the common enemy that had for many years disturbed the peace of the two Republics.

To Governor E.G. Ross, of New Mexico, and Governor C. Meyer Zulick, of Arizona, as well as Territorial officials under them, I am thankful for their fullest sympathy and support.

To the district commanders, Colonels Grierson,[203] Kautz,[204] Shafter, Bradley, and Royall; Lieutenant Colonels Wade and Morrow;[205] Majors Mills, Beaumont,[206] Van Vliet,[207] and Vance,[208] Captains Tupper,[209] Chaffee, Sprole,[210] and others, I am much indebted for the earnest and judicious use of their troops.

Captain William A. Thompson, Fourth Cavalry, was appointed acting assistant adjutant general in the field, and in that capacity rendered most valuable assistance. His personal knowledge of the country, and his many soldierly qualities have rendered his services most valuable.

Lieutenants Dapray[211] and Stanton[212] have each rendered efficient service in the capacity of aides-de-camp. Reports of the officers of the general staff are hereby inclosed; also roster of the troops.

Major Barber[213] has discharged the important duties of assistant adjutant general with fidelity and intelligence, and I enclose herewith his annual reports; also the report of Col. L.P. Bradley, commanding the District of New Mexico.

Lieutenant Spencer's report and map will show the various trails of the Indians and routes of march of the troops, and other topographical information that will be found of interest, and when fully developed will be of value in the future.

The reports of Lieutenants Drave and Fuller will show the workings of the most interesting and valuable heliographic system that has ever been established. I have made this service useful heretofore, and it

[203] Col. Benjamin H. Grierson, 10th Cav., famous Civil War cavalry general.

[204] Col. August V. Kautz, 8th Inf. (USMA 1852), a Brigadier General in the Civil War and past commander of the Department of Arizona.

[205] Lt. Col. Albert P. Morrow, 6th Cav.

[206] Major Eugene Beauharnais Beaumont, 4th Cav. (USMA 1861), awarded the Medal of Honor for Civil War service.

[207] Major Frederick Van Vliet, 10th Cav.

[208] Maj. Duncan MacArthur Vance, 13th Inf.

[209] Capt. Tullius C. Tupper, 6th Cav.

[210] Capt. Henry W. Sprole, 8th Cav. (USMA 1869, after one month at the Naval Academy).

[211] 2nd Lt. John A. Dapray, 23rd Inf.

[212] 1st Lt. William Stanton, 6th Cav.

[213] Maj. Merritt Barber, 16th Inf.

would be found valuable in any Indian or foreign war. These officers and the intelligent men under them have made good use of the modern scientific appliances, and are entitled to much credit for their important service.

I would invite special attention to the report of Major Kimball,[214] chief quartermaster of this Department. This efficient officer has rendered most important assistance in the thorough organization and equipment of the means of transportation and in the prompt and proper disbursement of the public funds, and Lieutenants Benson, Neall, and Patch are entitled to especial mention for their arduous and efficient service as acting assistant quartermasters.

Captain Weston,[215] chief commissary of subsistence, has through his agents kept the scattered camps well supplied.

I enclose herewith the report of Assistant Surgeon Leonard Wood, who accompanied Captain Lawton's command from the beginning to the end. He not only fulfilled the duties of his profession in his skillful attention to disabled officers and soldiers, but at times performed satisfactorily the duties of a line officer, and during the whole extraordinary march, by his example of physical endurance, greatly encouraged others, having voluntarily made many of the longest and most difficult marches on foot.

I also submit the report of Captain Lawton, who has distinguished himself as a resolute and skillful commander. His report of the operations of his command and account of one of the most remarkable marches ever made will be found valuable and interesting.

On the 19th of April last, soon after assuming command and seeing the wants and necessities of the Department, I addressed a letter to the Adjutant General of the Army (copy enclosed), and I would respectfully invite attention to that important subject. The recommendations contained in that letter are respectfully renewed. So long as the territory adjacent to the international boundary remains as it is now, the greatest temptation is offered and facilities afforded for marauding bands of outlaws, whether composed of Indians or others of a kindred nature, to make forays from the Mexican side of the line or seek refuge there after devastating the settlements on our own soil, renders the military defenses of paramount importance, and fully justifies the extension of the appropriation for defenses between Texas and Mexico, made a few years since, to this line also.

The scattered settlements and vast material interests of these Terri-

[214]Maj. Amos S. Kimball of N.Y.
[215]Capt. John F. Weston of Ky., awarded the Medal of Honor for Civil War service.

tories require that strong military garrisons be maintained at available stations, in order that the lives and property of the citizens, as well as the public interests, may be as secure and well protected here as in other parts of the United States.

Very respectfully, your obedient servant,

NELSON A. MILES,

Brigadier General United States Army.

Commanding Department of Arizona.

The Assistant Adjutant General,

Division of the Pacific, Presidio, San Francisco, California.

In his Annual Report for 1886, Lieutenant General Sheridan commanding the Army refers to the Geronimo Campaign as follows:

In the Department of Arizona hostilities against Geronimo were continued during the Fall by the Department Commander, General Crook, but as the results were unsatisfactory, it became apparent to me in November, 1885, that quiet and peace could not be restored until the Chiricahua and Warm Springs Apaches were removed from Arizona. I communicated this impression to the Secretary of War in a personal interview, and in consequence was directed to proceed to Arizona to consult with Crook on this and kindred subjects growing out of existing hostilities. It was my idea to commence by sending immediately the thirty-three prisoners then at Fort Bowie to Fort Marion, Florida. I reached Fort Bowie on November 29th, where I found General Crook and Captain Crawford, the latter in command of two hundred Indian scouts, many of whom were Chiricahuas, on the eve of starting into Mexico on an expedition against the hostiles. General Crook did not think the time for the removal opportune, and suggested that I obtain Captain Crawford's views. Crawford coincided with Crook, and stated that the removal might effect the conduct of the Indian scouts just going out, in whom both seemed to have great confidence and in deference to their opinions I deemed it best to await a more advantageous time for the accomplishment of this purpose.

During the winter, operations were made principally by Indian scouts under the command of Captain Emmet Crawford, Third Cavalry, and Captain Wirt Davis, Fourth Cavalry. The former came upon the Indians in camp in Mexico, January 10, surprised and routed them without loss to his own troops and no loss to the Indians except their camp equipage, horses, and camp plunder. While occupying the hostile camp negotiations were opened with the hostiles, at their solicitation, with a view to their surrender; but unfortunately Captain Crawford's camp was stolen upon and attacked the next morning by irregular Mexican troops, who claimed to have been seeking the camp of the hostile Indians. In the engagement which ensued Captain Crawford was mortally wounded; three of his men wounded; the Mexicans lost their leader (killed) and four or five men killed and wounded. The loss of Captain Crawford was much to be regretted, as he would, in my opinion, have at that time terminated the cruel and bloody atrocities which continued thereafter for many months. After Captain Crawford's death, Lieutenant Marion P. Maus,[216] First Infantry, came in command and continued the negotiations, which resulted, not in the surrender of the Indians, but in a promise on the part of Geronimo that he would go to a point near the boundary line to meet General Crook. This officer met him about twenty-five miles below San Bernardino, Mexico, and exacted a qualified surrender, which was not approved by the President. While en route to Fort Bowie the Indians, suspicious of treachery, marched in skirmish order so as to prevent any considerable number of their party from being entrapped; but the night succeeding the first day's march, Geronimo became alarmed from idle stories and escaped with twenty of his best men and thirteen women. The balance of his band continued on to Bowie, after which they were sent to Fort Marion, Florida, with the thirty-three previously captured. The understanding when Geronimo and his followers started in to Bowie was, that if they surrendered their lives would be spared and they would be located in some distant part of the country. Fort Marion was selected as the best place to secure these blood-thirsty savages (whose lives were spared not from any consideration for them but as an inducement for the balance of the hostiles to surrender), so that honest and industrious white citizens and their families might be protected and trade and commerce restored to the Territories of Arizona and New Mexico. They could not be put at any military post west of the Missouri River, because the people in the vicinity would not tolerate them, and as the law excludes them from the Indian Territory, removal to that section was out of the question.

After Captain Crawford's last engagement it became a belief in my mind that the Indian scouts could not be wholly depended upon to fight and kill their own people. I think they were faithful so far as to try to capture or to induce the surrender of the hostiles, but they had no wish

---

[216] 1st Lt. Marion P. Maus (USMA 1874) had served with Miles in the Nez Perce Campaign and would later become his aide. He was awarded the Medal of Honor for his part in Capt. Crawford's ill-fated expedition to the Sierra Madre.

to kill their own kindred. That this sentiment was reciprocal was demonstrated by the Indian engagement referred to and others that had occured previously. General Crook seemed, however, wedded to the policy of operating almost exclusively with Indian scouts, and as his experience was of great weight his policy could not well be changed without his removal to another field. To relieve the embarrassment he at once requested such a course, and as at about the time of the surrender and escape of a part of Geronimo's band a change of the geographical commands was necesitated by the death of General Hancock and the retirement of General Pope, General Crook was sent to the Department of the Platte, and General Miles, on my recommendation, assigned to the Department of Arizona, the latter's instructions being as follows:

(Letter of instructions dated Headquarters of the Army, Washington D.C. April 3, 1886.)

General Miles went to work with commendable zeal. His troops followed up the hostiles with vigorous energy, broke up their camps by attack four or five times, and gave them no rest until they surrendered on September 4, under circumstances and conditions, however, that should not, in my judgment, permit their being turned over to the civil authorities for punishment, as was intended by the President. On September 8th, they were started by General Miles to Fort Marion, Florida, without authority, but at a later date stopped at San Antonio till their final disposition could be decided upon.

Previous to the surrender, and early in July, General Miles had visited Fort Apache, near which were located the peaceable Chiricahua and Warm Springs Apaches, some of whom had been General Crook's scouts, and many of whom, before serving in that capacity, had committed the most brutal murders. On July 3, Miles telegraphed that there were strong military reasons for the removal of these Indians from Arizona and asked authority to send a few of the tribe to Washington with reference to another location. From this I judged the time had about arrived for the forcible removal of all the Chiricahua and Warm Springs Apaches to Florida, in accordance with the suggestions I had made before visiting General Crook in November, 1885. I consequently approved General Miles' request, and, the Secretary of War having authorized it, I directed the former to send ten of the Indians to Washington under charge of an officer, with instructions to report them to the Secretary of the Interior. A delegation of leading men was speedily started and shortly after arrived in charge of Captain Dorst.

On the 7th of July General Miles forwarded a communication giving his views relative to the subjugation of the hostiles and the control of the

Apaches, suggesting the advisability of moving the four hundred and forty men, women, and children on the reservation to the Indian Territory &c., on which I endorsed, July 30, as my recommendation, the following:

> Respectfully submitted to the Secretary of War. There are now on the reservation near Fort Apache seventy-one Chiricahua and Warm Springs adult male Indians. These are exclusive of those in this city. It is my belief that if the delegation which is now here goes back to the reservation without having received what they may deem the most satisfactory promises on the part of the Government a large number of those that are now peaceable will endeavor to join Geronimo. I therefore recommend that authority be granted me to direct General Miles to immediately arrest all the male Indians now on the Chiricahua Reservation, near Fort Apache, and send them as prisoners to Fort Marion, Florida; that the delegation now here be sent there also, and that they be held at that point as prisoners of war until the final solution of the Geronimo troubles.

The President called together the Secretary of War, the Secretary of the Interior, and myself, and after discussing the question, the President directed me to send a telegram to General Miles asking him what he thought of the proposition to forcibly arrest all on the reservation and send them to Fort Marion, where they could be joined by the party then in Washington, to which he replied that there would be some advantages, but that some serious objections occurred to him which he would explain fully by letter. The objections contained in his letter were that the delegation went to Washington by authority, with a view of making some permanent arrangement for their future, and that it might be charged the Government had taken advantage of them; that it would be known to all other Indians in the Southwest, and, in future, they might hesitate about sending delegations to Washington, and that it would necessitate a war of extermination against the hostiles then in Old Mexico, in which all would have to be killed. To me the objections of General Miles did not seem sufficiently weighty in the face of the many cogent reasons existing for removal—if removed at all—to some point east of the Missouri River, and I am pleased to say that the President finally authorized them to be sent to Fort Marion, after General Miles on August 20th, had reported that Colonel Wade, commanding Fort Apache, was prepared to accomplish the work.

On the 25th of August I again informed General Miles, in answer to a telegram he had sent to the Interior Department, that no proposition looking to the location of the Chiricahua and Warm Springs Indians west of the Missouri River could be entertained, to which he replied with further recommendations as to establishing them at Fort Union, New Mexico. This was forwarded to the President, who adhered, however, to the decision he had already made, and in consequence the four hundred and forty men, women, and children then at Fort Apache were started for Fort Marion, Florida, where they arrived on September 21st.

REPORT OF BRIGADIER GENERAL MILES

Headquarters Department of Arizona,
Los Angeles, Cal., Sept. 3, 1887.

Sir:

I have the honor to report regarding military affairs and operations in this department during the last year as follows:

Immediately after rendering my last annual report in September last, Lieutenant C.P. Johnson,[217] Tenth Cavalry, with a small detachment, followed the hostile band under Mangus, from Chihuahua, Mexico, north through the Black Range and Mogollons Mountains of New Mexico. The movements of the hostiles and pursuing troops were reported to Colonel Wade, commanding at Fort Apache, who, on October 14, 1886, detailed Captain Chas. L. Cooper,[218] Tenth Cavalry, with 20 men, to intercept the hostiles. When near the Bonito Fork of the Black River, Arizona, Captain Cooper proceeded northeast, and on the 17th struck the trail. Following the trail rapidly on the morning of the 18th, through that exceedingly rugged country, he finally, after a forced march of 30 miles, sighted the Indians, who were just going over the top of a mountain fully 2,000 feet high, the troops being at the bottom. A tiresome and difficult climb of over two hours brought the troops in sight of the Indians, and one of the most remarkable pursuits of Indians by troops ensued, crossing five mountain peaks fully as high as the first, and finally, after a hard chase of 15 miles, the Indians abandoned their stock and took to the mountains. But the troops were vigilant and quick, and one by one all but 3 of the Indians were captured in their hiding places, and the next morning the remaining 3 were secured, completing the capture of the noted Mangus, and 2 warriors, 3 squaws, and 2 large boys capable of bearing arms, 1 girl and 4 children; also 29 mules, 5 ponies, and all their supplies and camp outfit. Thus, Chief Mangus and band, whose whereabouts for so many months remained a mystery, were finally added to the list of captives, and on the

217 2nd Lt. Carter P. Johnson, 10th Cav., worked his way up from Private.
218 Capt. Charles L. Cooper, 10th Cav.

19th Captain Cooper's command returned with the prisoners to Fort Apache, and that ended the terrible depredations which the Chiricahua and Warm Springs Indians had for so many generations instigated. From this point they were sent under guard to Florida, thereby effectually clearing the Territories of Arizona and New Mexico of the whole hostile element.

The expenses of the department were very much reduced in consequence of the cessation of Indian hostilities. There was a large decrease in the number of enlisted Indian scouts, over four hundred being discharged and the reduction of expenses in the Quartermaster's Department was very important. Besides this, the troops belonging to the Departments of Texas and California were returned to their respective commands and the 8th Infantry was removed from this department to the Department of the Platte. In fact, the Aggregate of the military expenditures in this department was thereby reduced at the rate of more than one million dollars per annum. In December, 1886, California, south of the thirty-fifth parallel of north latitude, was added to the Department of Arizona, and headquarters fixed at Los Angeles. In November of last year, Fort Lewis, Colorado, was transferred from this Department to the Department of the Missouri, and in January of this year, Fort Bliss, Texas, to the Department of Texas.

On the night of the 3rd of March, ultimo, a disturbance occurred at Nogales, Arizona, in which two or more officers of the Mexican Army were concerned, the latter crossing over to the American side of the town and engaging in a shooting escapade with certain local civil authorities. Prompt action was taken in the matter, however, by the Mexican authorities under the personal supervision of Governor Torres of Sonora, and not only were the offenders speedily and severely punished, but further difficulties avoided.

Nogales is a dual place, about equally divided between Mexicans and Americans. The town is so situated that the national boundary line runs almost direct through its center, and as it is the gateway to the western portion of Mexico, and disturbances like the one above referred to were liable to occur at any time, with more or less serious consequences, I deemed it expedient, for the protection of our own people and their property, to station Company D, Ninth Infantry, under a judicious and efficient officer, Captain J.M. Lee, in the vicinity of the town. The presence of that command there has had a wholesome effect. Captain Lee has not only maintained courteous and amicable relations with the Mexican officials there, but has preserved perfect order in the vicinity, and the moral effect has been agreeable in every way. Although Nogales is within 60 miles of Fort Huachuca, that fact does not, in my judgment, obviate the necessity for establishing a post there in order to assure the safety of rights and property of our citizens, protect public interests, and at the same time maintain in that locality the dignity of the National Government. There are many places in the country where posts are within 60 miles of each other, and so long as Nogales occupies the place it does on the national boundary there will be more or less necessity, in my judgment, to have the Federal Government represented there by national troops, the same as at El Paso, San Diego, Fort Townsend, Assinniboine, Sault Ste. Marie, Detroit, Buffalo, and other places.

On March 9th last, Second Lieutenant Seward Mott,[219] Tenth Cavalry, who was on duty at San Carlos Reservation, in charge of Indians farming on the Upper Gila River, was shot by a young Indian named Nah-d-z-az, receiving wounds from which he died on the following day at the agency; and thus an intelligent young officer gave up his life while in the performance of duty, endeavoring to benefit a guide wild Indians in peaceful pursuits. The cause of the shooting, as developed in the official inquiry which followed Lieutenant Mott's death, was dissatisfaction with a division of farming land made by that officer and the confinement by him of the father of the murderous Indian for disobedience of his orders and for using threatening language toward him. The murderer, a Tonto Apache Indian, was transferred to the civil authorities of Arizona, to be dealt with by them for his crime.

On June 1, Captain F.E. Pierce, First Infantry, in charge of the Indians on the San Carlos Reservation, telegraphed report of a disturbance that had occurred at that agency. On the evening of May 27th or morning of 28th, five of the enlisted scouts at San Carlos absenting themselves without leave, proceeded to the San Pedro Valley and killed an Indian named Rip, belonging to Chief Chiquito's band. Five other Indians accompanied the scouts and were concerned in the affair, the whole party, with one exception, belong to the same band (San Carlos 1), of which Gon-shay-ce is Chief. On the evening of June 1, the party returned, and the scouts were disarmed by Captain Pierce. Upon their being ordered to the guard-house by that officer, a commotion arose among a number of the band who were standing near by, and who fired several shots, one of which seriously wounded the chief of scouts (Al Sieber). During the excitement that followed this disturbance, the five scouts effected their escape and with their friends disappeared. The party were at once pursued by scouts and a detachment of cavalry from the agency, under Lieutenant J.B. Hughes, Tenth

[219] 2nd Lt. Seward Mott (USMA 1886).

Cavalry. Upon the news of the affair reaching these headquarters, troops from Forts Apache, Bowie, Grant, Huachuca, Lowell, and Thomas were ordered to occupy the country through which the Indians would likely pass, and on June 11th, a detachment of the Tenth Cavalry, under Second Lieutenant Carter P. Johnson, Tenth Cavalry, surprised the camp of the renegades on the crest of the Rincon Mountains, capturing all their property, including horses, from which point the Indians made their way back over the roughest mountains, on foot, to the camps on the San Carlos, closely trailed by the troops, where they surrendered June 19, 21, and 23. The troops were then ordered to return to their proper stations, the five scouts were placed in confinement, and a general court-martial ordered for their trial. During the raid Messrs. Diehl and Grace, two citizens, were killed by the Indians, which will probably be made the subject of judicial investigation by the criminal courts of the Territory. This outbreak was quickly suppressed and the most desirable results attained by the promptness and good judgment displayed by post commanders in putting troops into the field and occupying the accustomed routes of the Indians, and the vigilance and zeal of the troop and detachment commanders, and the rapidity and persistency of their pursuits, especially that of Captains Lawton and Wint, and Lieutenants Johnson and Hughes, thereby making the country practically untenable for hostile Indians.

On June 13 I left my headquarters and preceded by way of Wilcox, Forts Grant and Thomas to San Carlos, to personally inquire into the circumstances attending the disturbance and to direct the movement of the pursuing forces. I returned here on June 29th.

Regarding the condition of affairs on the San Carlos Reservation, I found that from 1,000 to 1,200 Indians had left their camps, abandoned their fields and congregated at a place called Coyote Holes, where they were assuming a most threatening attitude. It was, in my opinion, a serious mistake to locate such a large number of Indians at San Carlos, Arizona, 100 miles from railroad communication, where the cost of depositing supplies for the Indians, as well as for the troops necessary to keep them in check, was enormously great, and besides requiring the Indians to live in a sickly region entirely unsuited to them, and depriving them of the privilege of living in the section where they were born and from which they were ruthlessly removed. I am firmly of the opinion that the best plan, now as then, would be to disperse those Indians as to put 100 or 200 miles or more between the different camps, in order that they might be better controlled, and themselves made peaceful, contented, and prosperous, as recommended in my letter of

June 2 last and report of July 16, copies attached hereto, marked "A".
To avoid disturbing any citizens who now occupy the land that once
belonged to those Indians, or to avoid the necessity of their taking up
any part of the public domain, which they could do if they desired, there
certainly could be no harm in utilizing for that purpose portions of
military reservations no longer required for military purposes, and
which have been already partly abandoned by the military in fact, no
better use could be made of such lands than to convert them into
industrial-school farms for Indians, thereby guiding them in the way of
self-support; at the same time they would be so separated and under such
strict surveillance of military power as to render them perfectly
harmless, and moreover it seems to be now the fixed policy of the
Government after years of careful consideration, to gradually break up
the large Indian camps and reservations, and to locate Indians as far as
practical in small bands and in severalty. The plan suggested by me was
simply the beginning of a measure which was deemed to be strictly in
conformity with the purpose of the Government and the laws of
Congress. There can be no question that those Indians if they were so
disposed, have the legal right to relinquish their tribal relations, declare
their purpose to locate in severalty and avail themselves of the rights and
privileges guaranteed by Congress, but I have no doubt that it would be
more beneficial to the Indians and less embarrassing to the Government
to aid and encourage them in their efforts to peacefully locate on their
native lands or as near as practical in the country available, than to risk
the possibility of an outbreak on the reservation, or to arbitrarily confine
them in a place where they must die by slow degrees. That they are
naturally industrious and capable of sustaining themselves is a fact
beyond question, and abundantly proven by the great amount of work
they have done in the last two years under the supervision of Captain
Pierce. If, however, the same order of things respecting the San Carlos
Reservation shall be continued, it will be necessary to build shelter for
troops on the west side of the reservation, as it has been found necessary
for years to keep troops either there or in the vicinity, and without
adequate shelter, comforts, or conveniences they have been compelled
to endure greater hardships than at any other station in the Department.
Fort Thomas has outlived its importance, if not its utility, is extremely
unhealthful, is only 42 miles from Fort Grant, and badly located. It
should be gradually abandoned and a post located at some point on or
near the western portion of the San Carlos Reservation.

Although the Navajo Indians are under the immediate control of
their agent, and Colonel Grierson, commanding the district, has taken

special interest in their affairs, and his judicious management, resulting from thorough knowledge of that tribe, has been conducted with intelligence and ability, yet it is not unlikely that at some future time a serious disturbance may occur between those Indians and white settlers. This is one of the largest and most powerful tribes of Indians we have to deal with, numbering 20,000 souls, with at least 4,000 men capable of bearing arms, and rich enough to supply themselves with the most improved rifles, with an average of one thousand rounds of ammunition per man. In view of such probable disturbances, requiring the immediate action of a strong body of troops, I recommended that Fort Wingate be enlarged and made a twelve-company post, and one of the cavalry regiments concentrated at that point. . .

Very respectfully, your obedient servant,
NELSON A. MILES,
Brigadier General United States Army, Commanding.

EXTRACT FROM REPORT OF BRIGADIER GENERAL MILES
Headquarters Department of Arizona,
Los Angeles, Cal., Sept. 8, 1888.

. . . There has been no disturbance of the peace worthy of mention in this department within the past year. The slight disturbance reported at San Carlos just prior to the rendering of my last annual report was quickly suppressed by the troops, and the offenders arraigned before military and civil tribunals; one of them is now under sentence of death, and the others are serving sentences of from two to twenty years imprisonment. A feeling of confidence and security prevails throughout the department, and persons may travel in any section unarmed and without fear of molestation by Indians.

Owing to the condition of affairs on the Navajo Reservation, I deemed it advisable to concentrate as much cavalry as possible at the adjacent post, Fort Wingate, the garrison of which now consists of five troops and headquarters of the Sixth Cavalry. It should be enlarged with as little delay as possible to accommodate a regiment of cavalry. The condition of that powerful tribe of Indians may at any time become such as to make necessary the presence of a large military command. Although practically at peace, the Navajos are as well equipped for war as many other tribe of Indians in this country.

In regard to the Indians in the department I deem it necessary to refer especially to the condition of those on the White Mountain Reservation. Although nothing indicates any immediate rupture of the peace, yet the same condition of things that existed there one year ago prevails now— the same threatening elements exist, which will sooner or later lead to serious disturbances in Arizona. The greater my experience with and observation of those Indians the more strongly I am of the opinion expressed in my report of a year ago. The congregating of different tribes of Indians at that place was, in my judgment, a most serious mistake, and from information that has come to me I think it was done in the interests of persons who desired to obtain possession of the Indian land, and for the benefit of speculators and Indian plunderers. It has already caused several Indians wars, resulting in the deaths of hundreds of innocent people and the cost of millions of public money, to say nothing of the destruction of private property. The holding of large tracts of territory remote from civil government and amassing thereon large bodies of disaffected Indians, taken, against their will and entreaties, from the homes which nature had designed for them, has resulted in serious disturbances wherever it has been tried, notably in the Indian Territory, and the great Sioux Reservation. The White Mountain Reservation will not be an exception. Of all the acts of injustice coming under my notice I have never known of one more flagrant than this. To force well-disposed Indians to live in an unhealthy climate, where there is neither shelter nor water fit to drink, is, in my judgment, most unjust and unwise, and a hardship as well to the troops who are required to be stationed in their midst to compel the Indians to die peaceably. When I made recommendation last year concerning the removal of some of the Indians from the San Carlos Reservation to the Fort Verde Reservation opposition was raised to it by some cattle men interested in maintaining a cattle range on part of the Government domain in the Verde Valley, and some of the settlers in that locality were induced, principally in the interest of four men, to sign a petition opposing the transfer, under misapprehension and through false representations. Some of the same persons have subsequently, of their own accord, signed a petition to have the Indians removed as was recommended.

The Mojaves, Yumas, and Tontos are well disposed, and it has been their prayer to every commissioner and prominent official who has visited them to be returned to their native country. Part of them are anxious to be returned to the Colorado River, to join others of their own tribe at Yuma and Mojave, while others desire to go to the vicinity of their former homes on the Fort Verde Reservation. To send them there would not only be an act of humanity, but also one of wise administration. The White Mountain Indians that were formerly forced to the Gila Valley declared that they would rather die than lie there. They were told that they could not have rations if they did not remain, and they said that they would go back to their own country if they had to starve. They did go back and for years they have been making a most heroic struggle to live without receiving rations from the Government. They cut wood and hay for Fort Apache, and I have seen their women go out long distances, cut grass with knives, and pack it on their backs to the posts for small sums of money. To force a people of that intelligence and industry to live in such a place as the Gila Valley is, in my judgment, unjust and cruel. If they were dispersed as recommended by me (which would appear to be in conformity with the policy of the Government as indicated by recent acts of Congress), the danger of serious outbreaks and disturbances in the future would be avoided, and much of that reservation, as large as some of the States, would be thrown open to miners and settlers. The loyalty of the Indians would be preserved, and it would not only be beneficial to the people of Arizona, but would result in great savings to the government.

Attention is also invited to the fact that the ration of food furnished by the Government to the Indians at San Carlos has been reduced, and the reason assigned is the high cost of articles of food there, and they are compelled this year to live on 150,000 pounds of beef and 74,259 pounds of flour less than they received last year. Notwithstanding the hardship to which these Indians have been subjected, they have in the main been peaceable and industrious, and have raised crops to support themselves to some extent, but the patience and forbearance of an Indian are not without limit, and as long as they are compelled to remain in that condition just so long will there be danger of serious outbreak, and it would seem needless to argue that such a condition of things should not be permitted to continue. . .

Very respectfully,
NELSON A. MILES,
Brigadier General, U.S. Army.

1889

Headquarters Division of the Pacific,
San Francisco, Cal., Sept. 16, 1889.

. . .There has been no serious disturbance of the peace nor any occasion for the exercise of troop other than the ordinary duties of Garrison service. . .

(Sgd) NELSON A. MILES,
Brigadier General, U.S. Army.

REPORT OF MAJOR GENERAL MILES

Headquarters Division of the Pacific,
San Francisco, Cal. Aug. 30, 1890.

Sir:

I have the honor to submit my annual report concerning military affairs within the Division of the Pacific:

. . . In the Department of Arizona there has been no general outbreak of Indians, and the different tribes are in the main under fair control. The large Navajo tribe, 20,000 in number, is conspicuously peaceable and prosperous, although there is always some friction and contention between them and the whites living in the adjacent country surrounding their large reservation.

The holding of discontented and disaffected tribes on the San Carlos Reservation, especially along the Gila River, which is unsuited for them and often unhealthy, will always be a source of danger and disturbance. Even the troops stationed near them to enforce their remaining on the reservation have to be changed every few months to preserve their health. As several of the military posts and reservations in that department have been abandoned by the Army, with a view to their being occupied by Indians or converted into industrial schools, I would recommend that such use made of them without delay, and that the Mojave, Tonto, and Yuma Indians now forced to remain in the sickly valley of the Gila be removed thereto.

The San Carlos Indians living along the San Carlos River and the White Mountains (including the Coyoteros) should be located on such suitable and sufficient part of the reservation as may be selected for the purpose, and the remainder of the reservation thrown open for such use as can be made of it by citizens. The posts referred to as being abandoned by the military and available for Indian purposes are Forts Verde, Mojave, McDowell, and Selden. With the large San Carlos Reservation on the north, occupied by tribes of Indians unfriendly to each other and forced to remain there against their will, and the rugged Sierra Madre Mountains of Mexico on the south, affording a refuge for outlaws, neither the lives nor the property of settlers in the intermediate zone can ever be so secure as might be desired.

The tribes would be more easily controlled when separated than when congregated in large numbers, especially in such a region as they are now compelled to occupy. . .

I have the honor to remain, your obedient servant,

NELSON A. MILES,
Major General, U.S. Army.

The Adjutant General of the Army,
Washington, D.C.

MILES WITH STAFF FOLLOWING WOUNDED KNEE
Clean-shaven Miles with Buffalo Bill Cody mounted at far left, Captains
Baldwin and Maus flanking Miles at Pine Ridge Agency following the
Wounded Knee fight. General Carr stands with a soldier
in the right rear of the photo.
Courtesy, National Archives.

General Miles dines with his staff during the crisis at Pine Ridge. The
officer on his right is Captain Marion P. Maus. On the General's left
sits Colonel William R. "Pecos Bill" Shafter of the 24th Infantry.
Courtesy, John M. Carroll Collection

IX

Wounded Knee

Miles' old rival, General Crook, died suddenly in March, 1890. Within a month, Miles was in Washington lobbying for the vacant Major Generalcy, which carried the command of the Military Division of the Missouri, encompassing the Departments of Dakota and of the Platte. Senator John Sherman, pressured by his ambitious nephew-in-law, paid a visit to president Harrison on his behalf, but came away with a pessimistic outlook. He wrote Miles on April 3, "The President recognized the merits of your service, but thought you were if not disobedient, at least a troublesome man to get along with; that instead of acting like Thomas and other favorite Generals of his, obeying orders, you made difficulties."[220] Never one to take no for an answer, Miles went to see the President in person, and on April 6 his efforts bore fruit; the twin stars of a Major General were finally his, and he could write the good news to Mrs. Miles, commenting, "The top round of the ladder gives me more pleasure I think than any of the others."[221]

Having relocated his family from San Francisco to Chicago, Miles installed himself in the Pullman Building, Division Headquarters, making sure that his faithful aides Baldwin and Maus had places on his enlarged staff. They soon had their hands full with a strange and potentially violent situation: the Messiah or Ghost Dance craze of the upper plains Indians.

The mystical fusion of Indian and Christian beliefs prophesizing a return of the slaughtered buffalo and the old way of life, spread from the Paiute medicine man Wovoka to the disenchanted reservation Indians of South Dakota. Wovoka's disciples, Short

[220] Letter of Senator John Sherman to Miles, April 3, 1890. Quoted in Virginia Johnson, *The Unregimented General*, Boston, 1962, p. 262.
[221] Miles to Mrs. Miles, Senate Building, Washington, D.C., April 6, 1890.

Bull and Kicking Bear, found ready ears on the Pine Ridge, Rosebud, Standing Rock and Cheyenne River reservations. At Standing Rock they won the support of the most influential Indian of all, Sitting Bull, and their doctrine, fueled by justifiable anger at the Indian Bureau, was tinged with the threat of rebellion.

Miles had little sympathy with the Indian Bureau or their agents. For years he had advocated Military control of the reservations, and if not a liberal in his sentiments for the Indians, he was well aware of the injustice dealt them on a daily basis:

> We have taken away their land and the white people now have it. The Indians have been half fed or half starved. Neither I nor any other official can assure the Indians that they will receive anything different in the future. They say, and very justly, that they are tired of broken promises.[222]

When he attended a council with the Oglala Little Chief at Pine Ridge Agency on October 27, Miles became as convinced of the serious nature of the Ghost Dance as he was of the incompetence of Agent Daniel F. Royer. It was in response to Royer's hysterical pleas for assistance that on November 17 Miles ordered his old Civil War associate, Brig. Gen. John R. Brooke, to mass troops from his Department of the Platte at the Pine Ridge and Rosebud Agencies. They would work in conjunction with General Ruger, commanding the Department of Dakota.

Miles repeatedly cautioned Brooke to keep his soldiers at a safe remove from the Indian villages, not under any circumstances to get "mixed up" with them. He hoped a show of force would coerce the agitated Sioux and Cheyennes without bloodshed, while pressure could be brought to bear on the Indian Bureau to better the ration issue, and make other concessions. At the same time Miles was convinced that his old nemesis Sitting Bull had to be removed from the scene before he could become the rallying point for the disaffected Indians. On November 24 he authorized "Buffalo Bill" Cody, familiar with the Chief from his days with the Wild West Show, to "secure the person of Sitting Bull." This plan met with the anger and scorn of Standing Rock Agent James

[222]Miles to Mrs. Miles, Rapid City, S.D. Dec. 20, 1890.

McLaughlin, who, with the assistance of Lt. Col. William F. Drum, Commandant of Fort Yates, successfully short-circuited Cody's mission. This tampering with his intentions so outraged Miles that he made a visit to Washington in order to push his plans for Military supervision of the reservations, making free use of the Press in venting his feelings.

On December 11, a week after returning from Washington, Miles set out for Rapid City, South Dakota, from which point he hoped to keep a closer eye on operations. On the fifteenth the arrest of Sitting Bull was undertaken by Agent McLaughlin with tragic results; the unfortunate decision to use Indian Police brought about an armed confrontation in which Sitting Bull and eleven others were killed. From this point the situation went rapidly downhill.

While General Brooke kept the hostile followers of Kicking Bear and Short Bull under a virtual state of siege in their natural "Stronghold," it fell to Lt. Col. Edwin V. Sumner, Jr. of the 8th Cavalry to prevent the Miniconjous of Chief Big Foot from leaving their camp on Cheyenne River and joining the hostiles. It was Miles' intention to have Big Foot and the agitators with him arrested, disarmed and sent to Fort Meade; orders to this effect were sent to Sumner, but, with a more immediate understanding of the situation that officer realized such a move would lead to bloodshed. He kept a more than respectful distance between his troopers and Big Foot's band, and accepted the Chief's pledge to refrain from joining the hostiles in the Stronghold. On the night of December 23, the Miniconjous gave Sumner the slip and headed for Pine Ridge Agency, focal point of the uprising.

Miles had only begun to fume at Sumner's failure, when he received far graver news. On December 29, after confronting Big Foot's people at Pine Ridge, Colonel James W. Forsyth's 7th Cavalry attempted to disarm the village on the banks of Wounded Knee Creek. A fight errupted and when it was over 153 Indians, including Big Foot, were dead and 44 wounded; among the fatalities were 44 women and 18 children. 25 soldiers were killed and 39 wounded. The next day, in attempting to corral fifty hostile Sioux, Colonel Forsyth's eight companies were pinned down near Drexel Mission. Had not Major Guy V. Henry and four troops of the 9th Cavalry arrived, clearing the surrounding ridges of warriors, it seems likely a disaster would have occured. Fearing the worst, Miles headed for Pine Ridge to assume personal command.

Arriving on December 31, the General wasted no time in taking his frustrations out on Colonel Forsyth. He dispatched an angry report of Wounded Knee to Army Commander Schofield, stating, "Large numbers of troops were killed and wounded by fire from their own ranks, and a very large number of women and children killed in addition to the Indian men."[223] In letters to his wife, Miles called Forsyth's actions "abominable" and "criminal," "a useless slaughter of innocent women and children."[224] On January 4, 1891, he relieved the Colonel of command and started an official investigation; nor did Lt. Col. Sumner escape Miles' wrath for his failure to keep Big Foot on Cheyenne River, though by the nature of the tragedy Forsyth bore the brunt of Miles' rage:

> I can only partially account for the singular apathy and neglect of Col. Forsyth upon the theory of his indifference to and contempt for the repeated and urgent warnings and orders received by him from the Division Commander or by his incompetence and entire inexperience in the responsibility of exercising command where judgment and discretion are required.[225]

To this day the culpability of Col. Forsyth in the "massacre" of Wounded Knee is a subject of debate. Although General Schofield, Secretary of War Proctor and President Harrison squelched the investigation, and, indeed, testimony was more favorable to Forsyth than not, Miles went to his grave believing the tragic confrontation to have been avoidable.

The subsequent success Miles had in defusing the crisis shows that had he been present from the outset, a bloodbath need not have occured. With an army of 3500 soldiers, he slowly drew the cordon tighter around the hostiles camped in the valley of White Clay Creek. Implied threat of force, masterful diplomacy and

---

[223] Miles to Schofield, Jan. 2, 1891.
[224] Miles to Mrs. Miles, Pine Ridge, Jan. 20, 1891.
[225] Quoted in *The Papers of the Order of Indian Wars*, ed. John M. Carroll, Old Army Press, 1975, p. 69.

promises of justice and fair treatment fragmented his opposition; incidents of violence, most notably the killing of Lieutenant Casey on January 7, were not allowed to fan the flames. On January 15, Kicking Bear placed his rifle at Miles' feet, and the ill-fated rebellion was ended.

Miles would wage war with the Indian Bureau for much of the following year in an attempt to implement Army control of the reservations. Unfortunately he would not be as successful in this political field as he had been in the military one. Yet it is testimony of his respect for his opponents that this most redoubtable of "Indian fighters" would campaign on their behalf, and that as late as 1920 he would ignore the infirmities of age to seek reparations for the survivors and heirs of Wounded Knee.

REPORT OF MAJOR GENERAL MILES
Headquarters Department of the Missouri,
Chicago, Ill., Sept. 14, 1891.

Sir:

I have the honor to submit the following annual report of military events and recommendations:

On the 1st day of September, 1890, in accordance with the provisions of General Orders, No. 84, Headquarters of the Army, 1890, conveying the President's orders, I relinquished command of the Division of the Pacific to assume the command of the Division of the Missouri, with headquarters at Chicago, Ill., which was done on the 15th day of September, 1890. The division, by the changes incident to the general order above mentioned, was limited to the Departments of the Platte and Dakota. This was again changed by executive order, contained in General Orders, No. 57, dated Headquarters of the Army, July 3, 1891, abolishing the divisions and assigning me to the command of the Department of the Missouri, which embraces the States of Michigan, Wisconsin, Indiana, Illinois, Missouri, Kansas, and Arkansas, and Oklahoma, and the Indian Territories, with headquarters at Chicago, Illinois.

The military events and changes have been so important and unusual since assuming command of the Division of the Missouri that a review of them is herewith submitted. Before arriving in the division I was apprised of the communications going on between the different tribes of Indians in the Western States and Territories, embracing those tribes as far south as the Indian Territory, and west as far as western Nevada, and was also made aware of the threatening condition of affairs then existing.

Condition of the Cheyenne Indians in Montana

While en route to the division headquarters at Chicago, I received information at Fort Keogh, Montana, from Cheyenne Indians I had known for many years, of the distressed condition they were in, particularly the tribe of Northern Cheyennes; their suffering for want of food, their being compelled to kill cattle belonging to the white people to sustain life, and the disaffection then existing, as well as the alarm prevailing among the citizens of that State.

To relieve their immediate wants I sent a telegram to the Adjutant General at Washington stating that the principal trouble with the Cheyenne Indians, whose reservation was south of Fort Keogh, was the result of the Government's failure to provide sufficient food and the means to render them self-supporting; saying when I left there, ten years previous, they had a herd of cattle and were at the time largely self-supporting; that they had been obliged to kill their cattle for food; that they had been on the verge of starvation and were at that time very little better; that when without food, or the means of providing for it, they had been obliged to kill cattle belonging to white men; that there was not the least difficulty in controlling them, but ample means should be appropriated at once to supply them with food and the means to render them self-supporting. At the same time I recommended that funds should also be appropriated to reimburse the white citizens who had been obliged to supply them with food. This telegram resulted in their being granted an additional appropriation of twenty-five thousand dollars, and reasonable appropriations for their necessities.

Cause of Indian Disaffection

The causes that lead to the serious disturbance of the peace in the Northwest last autumn and winter were so remarkable that an explanation of them is necessary in order to comprehend the seriousness of the situation. The Indians assuming the most threatening attitude of hostility were the Cheyennes and Sioux. Their condition may be stated as follows: for several years following their subjugation in 1877, 1878, and 1879 the most dangerous element of the Cheyennes and the Sioux were under military control. Many of them were disarmed and dismounted; their war ponies were sold and the proceeds returned to them in domestic stock, farming utensils, wagons, etc. Many of the Cheyennes, under the charge of military officers, were located on land in accordance with the laws of Congress, but after they were turned over to civil agents, and the vast herds of buffalo and large game had been destroyed, their supplies were insufficient and they were forced to kill cattle belonging to white people to sustain life.

Insufficient Food

The fact that they had not received sufficient food is admitted by the agents and the officers of the Government who have had opportunities of knowing. The majority of the Sioux were under the charge of civil agents, frequently changed and often inexperienced. Many of the tribes became rearmed and remounted. They claimed that the Government had not fulfilled its treaties and had failed to make large enough appropriations for their support; that they had suffered for want of food, and the evidence of this is beyond question and sufficient to satisfy any unprejudiced, intelligent mind. The statements of officers, inspectors, both of the military and the Interior Departments, of agents, of missionaries, and civilians familiar with their condition, leave no room for reasonable doubt that this was one of the principal causes. While statements may be made as to the amount of money that has been expended by the Government to feed the different tribes, the manner of distributing those appropriations will furnish one reason for the deficit.

Failure of Crops

The unfortunate failure of the crops in the plains country during the years of 1889 and 1890 added to the distress and suffering of the Indians, and it was possible for them to raise but very little from the ground for self-supporting; in fact, white settlers have been most unfortunate, and their losses have been serious and universal throughout a large section of that country. They have struggled on from year to year; occasionally they would raise good crops, which they were compelled to sell at low prices, while in the season of drought their labor was almost entirely lost. So serious have been their misfortunes that thousands have left that country within the last few years, passing over the mountains to the Pacific slope or returning to the east of the Missouri and the Mississippi.

The Indians, however, could not migrate from one part of the United States to another; neither could they obtain employment as readily as white people, either upon or beyond the Indian reservations. They must remain in comparative idleness and accept the results of the drought—an insufficient supply of food. This created a feeling of discontent even

among the loyal and well-disposed and added to the feeling of hostility of
the element opposed to every process of civilization.

Disaffection at Standing Rock Agency

Reports forwarded by Brigadier General Ruger, commanding
Department of Dakota, contain the following:

The commanding officer at Fort Yates, N. Dak., under date of
December 7, 1890, at the time the Messiah delusion was approaching a
climax says, in reference to the disaffection of the Sioux Indians at
Standing Rock Agency, that it is due to the following causes:

(1) Failure of the Government to establish an equitable southern
boundary for the Standing Rock Agency Reservation.

(2) Failure of the Government to expend a just proportion of the
money received from the Chicago, Milwaukee and St. Paul Railroad
Company for right of way privileges, for the benefit of the Indians of said
agency. (Official notice was received October 18, 1881, by the Indian
Agent at the Standing Rock Agency, that the said railroad company had
paid the Government, under its agreement with the Sioux Indians, for
right of way privileges, the sum of $13,911. What additional payments,
if any, have been made, by the said railroad company, and what
payments have been made by the Dakota Central Railroad Company,
the records of the agency do not show. In 1883, and again in 1885, the
agent, upon complaints made by the Indians, wrote the Commissioner of
Indian Affairs, making certain recommendations as regards the expenditure of the money received from the said railroad company, but was in
each instance informed that until Congress took action with respect to
the funds referred to nothing could be done. No portion of the money
had been expended up to that time (December, 1890) for the benefit of
the Indians of the agency, and frequent complaints had been made to the
agent by the Indians because they had received no benefits from their
concessions to the said railroad companies).

(3) Failure of the Government to issue the certificates of title to
allotments, as required by Article 6 of the Treaty of 1868.

(4) Failure of the Government to provide the full allowance of seeds
and agricultural implements to Indians engaged in farming, as required
in Article 8, Treaty of 1868.

(5) Failure of the Government to issue to such Indians the full
number of cows and oxen provided in Article 10, Treaty of 1868.

(6) Failure of the Government to provide comfortable dwelling
houses for the Indians, as required in Article 6, Treaty of 1876.

(7) Failure of the Government to issue to the Indians the full ration
stipulated in Article 5, Treaty of 1876. (For the fiscal year beginning
July 1, 1890, the following shortage in the rations were found to exist:

485,275 pounds of beef [gross], 761,212 pounds of corn, 11,937 pounds of coffee, 281,712 pounds of flour, 26,234 pounds of sugar, and 39,852 pounds of beans. Although the obligations of the Government extend no further than furnishing so much of the ration prescribed in Article 5 as may be necessary for the support of the Indians, it would seem that, owing to the almost total failure of crops upon the Standing Rock Reservation for the past four years and the absence of game, the necessity for the issue of the full ration to the Indians here was never greater than at the present time, December, 1890.)

(8) Failure of the Government to issue to the Indians the full amount of annuity supplies to which they are entitled under the provisions of Article 10, Treaty of 1868.

(9) Failure of the Government to have the clothing and other annuity supplies ready for issue on the first day of August of each year. Such supplies have not been ready for issue to the Indians, as a rule, until the winter season is well advanced. (After careful examination at this agency, the commanding officer is convinced that not more than two-thirds of the supplies, provided in Article 10 have been issued there, and the Government has never complied with that provision of Article 10 which requires the supplies enumerated in paragraphs 2, 3, and 4 of said article to be delivered on or before the first day of August of each year. Such supplies for the present fiscal year, beginning July 1, 1890, had not yet reached [December, 1890] the nearest railway station, about 60 miles distant, from which point they must, at this season of the year, be freighted to this agency in wagons. It is now certain that the winter will be well advanced before the Indians at this agency receive their annual allowance of clothing and other annuity supplies.)

(10) Failure of the Government to appropriate money for the payment of the Indians for the ponies taken from them, by the authority of the Government, in 1876.

In conclusion, the commanding officer says:

It, however, appears from the foregoing that the Government has failed to fulfill its obligations, and in order to render the Indians law abiding, peaceful, contented, and prosperous it is strongly recommended that the treaties be prompty and fully carried out, and that the promises made by the Commission in 1889 be faithfully kept.

Disaffection at Pine Ridge Agency

Under date of November 30, 1890, General John R. Brooke, commanding Department of the Platte, after having investigated the cause of disaffection among the Indians, says of those at the Pine Ridge Agency that—

The act of Congress approved February 28, 1877, provides for a

ration whose proportion of different articles of food are fixed for
these Indians, and the act directs that such ration shall be
continued to them, or so much of said ration as may be necessary,
until the Indians are able to support themselves. In 1888 the
annual beef issue authorized by the Commissioner of Indian
Affairs was 5,000,000 pounds. In 1889 the issue was 4,000,000
pounds. There was no decrease in the number of Indians in that
one year to account for this reduction of 1,000,000 pounds of beef.
The attention of the Sioux Commission was called to this fact by
the agent here, and they promised him to reestablish the amount of
5,000,000 pounds. On the strength of this promise the agent issued
on the basis of 5,000,000 pounds. The promise was not redeemed,
and the inevitable deficiency resulted.

In a letter of April 12, 1890, of Mr. Gallager, agent here, to the
Commissioner of Indian Affairs, he states that the monthly issue of
beef at that time is 205,000 pounds, whereas by the treaty the ration
would be 470,000 pounds, a deficiency per month of 265,400
pounds in that called for by the treaty, or a reduction of more than
one-half the proper treaty allowance. The following is an extract
from the reply to this letter, which is dated April 21, 1890: "It is
better to issue half rations all the time than to give them three-
fourths or full rations during two months and none for the balance
of the year." The Commissioner further states in the same letter
that the Interior Department is able to furnish such articles as
shoes, shawls, blankets, ticking, gingham, et cetera, as an
equivalent, in lieu of subsistence, or in lieu of parts of the ration as
fixed by the treaty referred to. The Act of Congress fixing the
ration says: "and for every one hundred rations four pounds of
coffee, eight pounds of sugar, and three pounds of beans, or in lieu
of said articles, the equivalent thereof, in the discretion of the
Commissioner of Indian Affairs, such rations, or so much thereof
as may be necessary, shall be continued." It is thought that when
the Commissioner interprets the words (when the ration only is
spoken of) "or in lieu of said articles, the equivalent thereof," to
mean shoes, shawls, blankets, et cetera, that the Commissioner is
in error, and that the resultant reduction in food is in violation of
the Act of Congress. The enormous reduction in the beef issue at
this agency, which is the principal supply of food, is shown by the
following figures:

In the year 1886 the annual authorized issue was 8,125,000
pounds; in 1889 it was 4,000,000 pounds, a reduction of 4,125,000

pounds in three years, or an average annual reduction of 1,378,333 pounds; or in other words, in that space of time, the beef issue has been reduced largely over one-half, and it is known that there has been no such corresponding reduction in the number of Indians, or advancement in their ability to support themselves, as the land in the vicinity of this agency and adjacent to it is not sufficiently good for agricultural purposes, except by irrigation. I do not consider, however, that these reductions in subsistence are sufficient grounds for the attitude recently assumed by large numbers of these Indians. A part of them who are subject to the same conditions in this respect are not in any wise disaffected, though they deplore the inadequacy of the food supply. The disaffected are those who are under the influence of Kicking Bear and his supporters. The Ghost Dance appears to be a means to an end, viz, to draw under the influence of Kicking Bear and his lieutenants such of the young men as can be won over by means of the excitement of this dance.

In regard to complaints of broken promises General Brooke invited attention to the following statement of American Horse, speaking for himself and voicing the sentiments of four other chiefs present, as embodied in a letter of Indian Agent Royer to the Acting Commissioner of Indian Affairs, dated November 17, 1890, in which the Indian says:

I was speaker for the whole tribe. In a general council I signed the bill (the late Sioux bill) and five hundred and eighty signed with me, the other members of my band drew out and ever since these two parties have been divided. The non-progressive started the Ghost Dance to draw from us. We were made many promises, but have never heard of them since. The Great Father says if we do what he directs it will be to our benefit, but instead of this they are every year cutting down our rations and we do not get enough to keep us from suffering. . . After we signed the bill they took our land and cut down our allowances of food. The Commissioners made us believe that we would get full sacks if we signed the bill, but instead of that our sacks are empty. Our chickens were all stolen; our cattle, some of them were killed. Our crops were entirely lost by being here with the Sioux Commission, and we have never been benefitted one bit by the bill, and in fact, we are worse off than we were before we signed the bill.

We are told if we do as white men we will be better off but we are getting worse off every year. The Commissioners promised the Indians living on Black Pipe and Pass creeks, that if they signed the bill they could remain where they were and draw their rations at this agency, showing them on the map the line, and our people want them here, but they have been ordered to move back to Rose Bud Agency. This is one of the broken promises. The Commission promised to survey the boundary line and appropriate funds for the purpose, but it has not been done. When we were at Washington the President, the Secretary of the Interior and the Commissioner all promised us that we would get the million pounds of beef taken from us, and I heard the bill appropriating the money passed Congress, but we never got the beef. The Commissioner refused to give it to us. American Horse, Fast Thunder and Spotted Horse, were all promised a spring wagon each, but they have never heard anything of it; this is another broken promise.

In reference to the above remarks by American Horse, General Brooke says:

"If these promises were made, and I have no reason to doubt it, there are reasonable grounds for complaint," and—

It is a notable feature that in the division of these Indians into well disposed and disaffected, the former are those called "Progressive" and favored the Sioux bill, and the latter are "Non-Progressive" and were the opponents of the bill. It is impracticable to reduce the complaints of the Indians to details at this time. The records of the Indian Bureau, I believe, from what I hear at this agency, must contain all this matter; more frequent issues, however, should be made, as too long a time elapses from issue to issue, and an Indian does not, or will not, understand the necessity for care in the use of his food; he always eats up his two weeks' supply in ten days or less, and as a consequence, he goes hungry the rest of the time, and it should be noted that by irrigation it is always possible to raise a crop in this section, whereas without irrigation it is almost an impossibility.

In addition to disarming the Indians I would recommend that the broken or deferred promises be made good, that the food of those living in regions where the white man's crops have failed, with its consequent impoverishment, be increased, that this may in time render the Indians "law-abiding and peaceable" and ultimately, I hope, "contented and prosperous." There general remarks apply equally to the Indians of the Rose Bud Agency. It must be borne in mind that the Interior Department in making its issue of beef makes no allowance for loss in weight, an animal weighing one thousand pounds at date of purchase is issued at that weight, regardless of the actual weight, no estimated or actual loss is considered. During the winter months there is a large shrinkage in the amount of meat which comes from the edible part of the animal.

Disaffection at Rosebud Agency

The officer, in compliance with instructions to report upon the status of the Indians at the Rosebud Agency, November 27, 1890, stated that:

Under treaty the United States Government agreed to supply the Rosebud Indians with three pounds of fresh beef per day (in gross weight) for each person. These cattle are usually delivered at the Agency in the month of October, the season of the year when cattle are in the best condition. A calculation is then made, averaging the cattle for the year's issue. The loss in weight in these cattle from October to February is about 35%, or a beef weighing one thousand pounds in October will weigh but 700 gross in February, and dressed, possibly 300 pounds. Two issues are made during the month of one beef to every thirty people, or about ten ounces per man per day.

In October last 3,499,810 pounds of beef were delivered at the Agency with instruction that this supply must be made to last until June 30, 1891, whereas the actual quantity these Indians are entitled to for this period is 4,384,926 pounds. I have also learned there has been quite a heavy reduction in the allowance of sugar and coffee for the year. Up to the time of the taking of the census, 2,700 rations in excess of the actual number of Indians was delivered at the agency for issue, so it is presumed they were well fed up to that time. The total number of Indians belonging to the agency is 5,354. Two Strike, Crow Dog, White Horse, Short Bull and Lance are the leaders of these Indians. They have always been more or less troublesome and in my opinion should be arrested and sent to some military post.

The officer further said:

I have obtained information from a reliable source that the Indians at Rosebud do not now, nor never have received the full treaty ration. The ration of beef issued early in the fall, just after the delivery of cattle, comes nearer the full ration than at any other season of the year. The average ration of beef for the year will not exceed eight ounces per capita.

Another officer reports, under date of November 29, 1890, that the beef ration was cut down ten years ago, that it was again reduced last year, and the allowance has been reduced for the period from October 1,

1890, to June 30, 1891, 900,000 pounds. He further says that Hollow-horn-bear (a prominent Indian) has stated it as his belief that the Ghost Dance, which is popular because it is a feast to which the hungry and starving Indians are attracted, and where they are fed would cease if the people received sufficient rations to live upon. The Indian mentioned asserts, from experience under civil and military administrations at Indian agencies, that if an Army officer was appointed agent at Rosebud and Pine Ridge agencies, and supplied with the treaty allowances of food and goods, the trouble would end in a few days. The last commission promised to see that these Indians were supplied with cows, that they themselves might go into the cattle business, but none have been furnished. Their crops have failed utterly; few receive any money with which to supply the deficiency in food; the cattle are poor and short in weight; the issue by weight is in some cases impracticable, for the camps are more or less remote; but an ingenious mind ought to devise a system by which, even in these cases, a sufficient allowance of beef could be secured in the winter months.

I believe in the canteen or cooperative system, and know of no reason why the Interior Department should not establish stores, supplies, etc., to be sold to the Indians at reasonable prices on an improved army commissary system. We know how even intelligent men allow themselves to be imposed upon by post traders, and I know of cases where the imposition of Indian traders upon staving Indians was impossible of definition; i.e., where a trader charged and received one dollar in good and lawful money for one dozen "hard tack" crackers. I find that cord wood here is bought from Indians at six dollars a cord, one by one as it happens to come in, but the Indian is paid on an order out of the traders store—at traders prices.

Disaffection at Cheyenne River Agency

The commanding officer at Fort Bennett, S. Dak., reports two classes of Indians, one of which is opposed to everything civilized, giving vent to their grievances at every meeting of the Indians on ration day; the other class, comprising a large majority of the Indians of the Reservation, have accepted the situation forced upon them, and have been for years bravely struggling in the effort to reconcile themselves to the ways of civilization and moral progress, with a gratifying degree of success. It is this class whose complaints and grievances demand considerate attention. They claim, in true Indian style, that they only have kept faith in all treaties made with them, and that somehow the treaties when they appeared in print were not in many respects the treaties which they signed.

They complained principally: (1) That the boundaries of the reservation in treaty of 1877 are not what they agreed to and thought they were signing on the paper, and they specially emphasize the point that the line of the western boundary should be a straight line at the Black Hills, instead of as it appears on the maps; (2) that they have never received full recompense for the ponies taken from them in 1876; (3) that the game has been destroyed and driven out of the country by the white people; (4) that their children are taken from them to Eastern schools and kept for years, instead of being educated among them; (5) that when these Eastern graduates return to them with civilized habits, education, and trades, there is no provision made on the reservation for their employment and improvement, to the benefit of themselves and their people; (6) that the agents and employees sent out to them have not all been "good men" and considerate of their (the Indians) interests and welfare; (7) that the issue of their annuity goods is delayed so late in the winter as to cause them much suffering; (8) that they are expected to plow the land and raise grain when the climate will not permit them to reap a crop. They think cattle should be issued to them for breeding purposes, instead of farming implements for useless labor; (9) that the rations issued to them are insufficient in quantity, and frequently (beef and flour) very poor in quality.

Complaints 2, 3, 4, 5, 7, 8, and 9, are well founded and are justified by the facts in each case, No. 9 especially so, and this through no fault or negligence of the agent. The agent makes his annual estimate for sustenance in kind for the number of people borne on his rolls, based on the stipulated ration in treaty of 1877. This estimate is modified or cut down in the Indian Commissioner's Office to meet the requirements of a limited or reduced Congressional appropriation, and when it returns to the agent's hands approved he finds that he has just so many pounds of beef and flour, etc., placed to his credit for the year, without regard to whether they constitute the full number of treaty rations or not. There is no allowance given him for loss by shrinkage, wastage, or other unavoidable loss, and with the very best efforts and care in the distribution throughout the year of this usually reduced allowance, there can not be issued to each Indian his treaty ration, nor enough to properly sustain life.

As a general thing the Indians of this reservation have been compelled to purchase food, according to their means, between ration issues; those having no means of purchase have suffered. The half pound of flour called for by the treaty ration could not be issued in full, and the half pound of corn required has never been issued, nor anything in lieu of it.

In the item of beef but 1 pound was issued instead of the pound and a half called for in the treaty, and during the early spring months, when the cattle on the range are thin and poor, the pound of beef issued to the Indians is but a fraction of the pound issued to him on the agent's return, and under the system of purchase in practice the present fiscal year must necessarily be sold. The agent's purchase of beef supply on the hoof for the year, under contract, is closed in the month of November, from which time he has to herd them the balance of the year as best he can. He is responsible for the weight they show on the scale when fat and in prime. condition, so that a steer weighing 1,200 pounds in the fall must represent 1,200 pounds in April, while in fact it may be but skin, horns, and bones, and weigh scarcely 600 pounds, while he has done his best to care for them during the severity of a Dakota winter. The Indians do not understand why they should be made to suffer all this shrinkage and loss, and it is a useless and humiliating attempt to explain. The agent is not to blame. The Department of Indian Affairs can do only the best it can with a limited and tardy appropriation.

The remedy in the matter of food supply seems to be a sufficient and early appropriation of funds. All contracts for the beef supply should call for delivery when required by the agent. The agent should be allowed a percentage of wastage to cover unavoidable loss in issue by shrinkage and wastage. The Government should bear the loss and not the Indians. In conclusion, the commanding officer remarks that—"This reservation is not agricultural land. The climate makes it a grazing country. The Indians now can raise cattle successfully and care for them in winter. All attempts at general farming must result in failure on account of climatic conditions."

Disaffection of Yanktonnais

Under date of December 6, 1890, the commanding officer at Fort Randall, S. Dak., reports that he witnessed the issue of rations at the Yanktonnais Indian Agency, and that it has been gradually reduced, forcing the Indians to become self-sustaining to some extent. He said they suffered very much the past season on account of drought, failure of crops, etc., and if something is not speedily done these Indians will perish from famine.

The rations issued for seven days were barely enough for two days, and within his knowledge, during eight years service at the post, Indians have been saved from suffering by eating refuse from soldiers' tables. They can get but little from this source now, as there is but one company at the post. The Indians claim that funds received for right of way of crossing at Pipe Stone ($17,000) have not been divided, and that balance of pay due Sully's scouts has not been paid; that the flour mill at the agency has not been used for two years, being out of repair. General Ruger, in forwarding this report says that suffering will befall these Indians unless increase of allowance is provided, and states that these Indians are most worthy.

The commanding officer at Fort Washakie, Wy., under date of November 28, 1890, states that the rations given the Shoshones is insufficient, it consisting only of a half-pound of flour about 14 ounces of beef, yeast powder, salt, and a small quantity of soup.

Reports of Indian Inspectors

An Indian inspector, in reporting to the Secretary of the Interior, under date of April 7, 1890, gives it as his opinion that it is a bad plan and a great injustice to receive beef in Oct. at its full weight and issue it on that basis in January following, the Indians thereby losing over one-third, for which their money has been paid. He calls attention to the fact that the whites are now occupying Sioux Lands secured under treaty made by the Commissioners of 1889, and that the Indians do not get as much as they did before the land was taken.

Under date of November 2, 1890, special United States Indian Agent E.D. Reynolds calls attention of the Commissioner of Indian Affairs to the extremely disaffected and troublesome state of a portion of the Indians on the Rosebud and other Sioux agencies. He says:

> The coming new order of things, as preached to this people during the past seven months, is the return to earth of their fore-fathers, the buffalo, elk, and all other game, the complete restoration of their ancient habits, customs, and power, and the annihilation of the white man. This movement, which some three weeks ago it was supposed had been completely abandoned, while not so openly indulged in, is continually gaining new adherents, and they are daily becoming more threatening and defiant to the authorities. This latter phase of the case may in a measure be attributed to the scant supply of rations, to which my attention has been almost daily called by the Indians, and especially to the reduction in the quantity of beef, as compared to the issues of former years. They killed cows and oxen issued to them for breeding and working purposes, making no secret of doing so, and openly defy arrest. They said that the cattle was issued to them by the Great Father, and that it is their right to do as they please with them. This evil is increasing daily, and if not checked there will be but very few of this class of stock left on the reservation by Spring.
>
> During the past week it was reported to me that two Indians in the Red Leaf camp, on Black Pipe Creek, had killed their cows for a feast at the ghost dance. I sent a policeman to bring them in; they

refused to come. The following day I sent two officers and eight policemen and they returned without the men, reporting that after they arrived at the camp they were surrounded by seventy-five or more Indians, well armed and with plenty of ammunition, and they unanimously agreed that an attempt to arrest the offenders would have resulted in death to the entire posse. On Friday I sent the Chief of Police with an interpreter to explain matters and endeavor to bring the men in. They positively refused to come, and the Chief of Police reports that the matter is beyond the control of the police. This is one case, which could be repeated indefinitely by attempting the arrest of parties guilty of the same offense.

The religious excitement, aggravated by almost starvation, is bearing fruits in this state of insubordination. Indians say they had better die fighting than to die a slow death of starvation, and as the new religion promises their return to earth at the coming of the millenium, they have no great fear of death. To one not accustomed to Indians it is a hard matter to believe the confident assurance with which they look forward to the fulfillment of the prophet's promises. The time first set for the inauguration of the new era was next Spring, but I am reliably informed that it has since, and only lately been advanced to the new moon after the next one, or about Dec. 11. The indications are unmistakable; these Indians have within the past three weeks traded horses and everything else they could trade for arms and ammunition, and all the cash they become possessed of is spent in the same way. One of the traders here reports that Indians within the last two days, have come into his store and offered to sell receipts for wood delivered at the agency, and for which no funds are on hand to pay them, for one-third of their value in cash. When asked what urgent necessity there was for such sacrifice of receipts for less than their face value, they answered that they wanted the cash to buy ammunition.

These are some of the signs of the times, and strongly indicate the working of the Indian mind. To me there appears to be but one remedy (and all here agree with me) unless the old order of things (the Indians controlling the agency) is to be reestablished, and that is a sufficient force of troops to prevent the outbreak which is imminent, and which any one of a dozen unforseen causes may precipitate.

The Messiah Delusion

In this condition of affairs, the Indians, realizing the inevitable, and seeing their numbers gradually diminishing, their strength and power weakening, very naturally prayed to their God for some supernatural power to aid them in the restoration of their former independence and the destruction of their enemies. It was at this stage of affairs, when driven to desperation, they were willing to entertain the pretensions or superstitions of deluded, fanatical people living on the western slope of the Rocky Mountains, whose emissaries first secretly appeared among the Indians prior to 1889. It was not, however, until the autumn of that year that the widespread conspiracy assumed serious character. They first aroused the curiosity of the Indians by some secret method scarcely realized by the savages themselves and persuaded delegations from different tribes of Indians to leave their reservations in November, 1889.

It is remarkable that by concerted action the delegations from the different tribes secretly left the various reservations, some starting from points a thousand miles apart from others, and some traveling 1,400 miles into a country entirely unknown to them, and in which they had never been before. The delegations from the Sioux, Cheyennes, and other tribes, secretly leaving their reservations, met at and traveled through the Arapahoe and Shoshone Reservations in Wyoming, and thence via the Union Pacific they passed into Utah, and were joined by Gros Ventres, Utes, Snakes, Piegans, Bannocks, Pi-Utes, and others, until they came to a large conclave of whites and Indians, near Pyramid Lake in Nevada, where not less than sixteen prominent tribes of Indians were represented. These delegates were then told that "those present were all believers in a new religion," that "they were all oppressed people," that "the whites and Indians were all the same," and that "the Messiah had returned to them." So well was this deception played by men masquerading and personating the Christ that they made these superstitious savages believe that the so-called Christ could speak all languages, that the whites who were not of their faith were to be destroyed, and that all who had faith in the "new religion" would occupy the earth; that the Messiah would cover the earth with dust and would then "renew everything as it used to be and make it better." He told them also that all of their dead would be resurrected; that they were all to come back to earth again, and that as the earth was too small for them and us he would do away with Heaven and make the earth large enough to contain all of them, and that they must tell all the people they meet about those things. He (or they who were personating one being) spoke to them about fighting, and said that was bad and that they must keep from it, that the earth was to be all good hereafter, and they must all be friends to one another. He said that "in the fall of the year (1890) the youth of all the good people would be renewed so that nobody would be more than 40 years old," and that "if they behaved themselves well after this, the youth of every one would be renewed in the spring." He said "if they were all good he would send people among them who could cure all their wounds and sickness by mere touch and that they would live forever." He told them "not to quarrel, nor fight, nor strike each other, nor shoot one another; that the whites and Indians there were to be all one people." He said "if any man disobeyed what he ordered his tribe would be wiped from the face of the earth; that they must believe everything he said, and must not doubt him or say he lied;" that "if they did he would know it; that he would know their thoughts and actions in no matter what part of the world they might be." Indian delegates who have seen the Messiah describe him in different ways, some as an Indian, others as a white man. There were, undoubtedly, several masquerading in the same robes and disguise as one person. They state that the Messiah is the one who taught them various religious ceremonies and to dance what has been termed the "ghost dance" or a sacred dance, clothed in a light garment like a shirt or hunter's frock, which, after being sanctified, was believed to be bullet proof.

It has been learned that delegates from the different tribes were all present when the Messiah appeared or was seen by them at different times, and these all returned to their various reservations, announcing to their relaties and friends what they had learned, fully convinced themselves, and convincing others that what they had seen and heard was true. These talks lasted sometimes for four or five days, and the warriors were initiated in the mysteries of the new faith as taught by the so-called Messiah. The Indians received the words of prophecy from the Messiah with intense enthusiasm, thinking that after years of distress and discouragement their prayers had been heard and that they were about to enter into a life of happiness for which they believed nature had originally intended them. The fanaticism and superstition of these people were taken advantage of by their disaffected and designing leaders to encourage them to assume hostilities towards the Government and white people.

Outbreak Precipitated

Short Bull, one of the Indians who had made the pilgrimage to Nevada, and who had become one of the acknowledged leaders of the hostile element, in a public harangue announced that he would shorten the time for a general uprising, and called upon all the warriors to assemble in what is known as the Mauvaises Terres or Bad Lands, on the

White River, southwest of S. Dak., in November, 1890. Short Bull's speech, interpreted, was as follows:

My friends and relatives: I will soon start this thing in running order. I have told you that this would come to pass in two seasons, but since the whites are interfering so much I will advance the time from what my Father above told me to do so. The time will be shorter. Therefore you must not be afraid of anything. Some of my relations have no ears, so I will have them blown away. Now there will be a tree sprout up, and there all the members of our religion and the tribe must gather together. That will be the place where we will see our relations. But, before this time, we must dance the balance of this moon, at the end of which time the earth will shiver very hard. Whenever this thing occurs I will start the wind to blow. We are the ones who will then see our Fathers, Mothers, and everybody. We the tribe of Indians, are the ones who are living a sacred life. God, our Father, himself has told and commanded and shown me to do these things. Our Father in Heaven has placed a mark at each point of the four winds; first, a clay pipe, which lies at the setting of the sun and represents the Sioux tribe; second, there is a holy arrow lying at the north, which represents the Cheyenne tribe; third, at the rising of the sun there lies hail, representing the Arapahoe tribe; and fourth, there lies a pipe and nice feather at the south, which represents the Crow tribe. My Father has shown me these things, therefore we must continue this dance. There may be soldiers surround you, but pay no attention to them, continue the dance. If the soldiers surround you four deep, three of you on whom I have put holy shirts will sing a song which I have taught you, around them, when some of them will drop dead, then the rest will start to run, but their horses will sink into the earth; the riders will jump from their horses, but they will sink into the earth also; then you can do as you desire with them. Now you must know this, that all the soldiers and that race will be dead; there will be only 5,000 of them left living on the earth. My friends and relations, this is straight and true. Now we must gather at Pass Creek, where the tree is sprouting. There we will go among our dead relations. You must not take any earthly things with you. Then the men must take off all their clothing and the women must do the same. No one shall be ashamed of exposing their persons. My Father above has told us to do this, and we must do as he says. You must not be afraid of anything. Guns are the

only things we are afraid of, but they belong to our Father in
Heaven. He will see that they do no harm. Whatever white men
may tell you do not listen to them. My relations, this is all. I will
now raise my hand up to my Father and close what he has said to
you through me.

This harangue was followed by the movement of some three thousand
Indians from the Rosebud and Pine Ridge Reservations, to that rough,
broken country of high buttes, ravines, and impassable gulches. The
hostile element on the Cheyenne and Standing Rock Agencies were
prepared to join them. As the following of Short Bull and Kicking Bear
moved to the bad lands they looted the homes of hundreds of Indians
who had been trying for years to farm and in part support themselves,
and carried with them many Indians who were peaceably disposed. This
would have been the case on other reservations had not protection been
given to the loyally disposed and decided measures been taken to
suppress the hostile element.

Threatened Hostiles

The leaders who have been constantly and persistently hostile to every
measure of civilization proclaim there could be no better way of helping
the prophecy and hastening the coming of the Messiah than by aiding
any removal of the white people, and to such disaffected, turbulent,
hostile spirits as Sitting Bull, Kicking Bear, Short Bull, and others, this
was the time for action. Nothing could be more gratifying to them, and
the false prophets and medicine men immediately took advantage of the
wretched condition of the Indians, to spread disaffection among the
different tribes.

The runners of Sitting Bull, who for years had been the great War
Chief and the head center of the hostile element, traveled in various
directions, but more especially to the tribes in the northwest, carrying
his messages to get ready for war and to get all the arms and ammunition
possible, and for all the warriors to meet near the Black Hills in the
spring of 1891. He even sent emissaries beyond the boundary line of the
United States to the Indian tribes in the British Possessions, and
promises of support were returned. The first serious disturbance of any
kind was to be signaled for the gathering of all the warriors from the
different tribes.

The Indians had, in the interim of peace, succeeded in getting
together a large amount of ammunition and arms, particularly their
favorite weapon, the Winchester rifle. They were, consequently, far
better prepared to wage a war than at any previous time in their history.
As some of the delegates to the conclave in Nevada were not imbued

with the peaceful teachings of the "Messiah," but were, on the contrary, disappointed, inasmuch as they had hoped to hear him teach some incendiary doctrine, the disaffection spread by Sitting Bull and other like spirits received their hearty support, and the disseminated knowledge to the Indians not strictly conforming to the Messiah's teachings, but more to their own, and the Indians were wrought up to a frenzy of wild excitement.

The above information and much more was gained from various sources chiefly while the division commander was engaged with the Northern Cheyenne Commission, visiting the various Indian reservations during the latter part of October and the early part of November, 1890, and through the department commanders and staff officers ordered to investigate the subject. As the control of Indian affairs was in the hands of Indian agents the military could not and did not take action until the conspiracy and spread over a vast extent of country, and the most serious Indian war of our history was imminent. In fact, the peace of an area of country equal to an Empire was in peril. The States of Nebraska, the two Dakotas, Montana, Wyoming, Colorado, Idaho, and Nevada, and the Territory of Utah, were liable to be overrun by a hungry, wild, mad horde of savages. The old theory that the destruction of vast herds of buffalo had ended Indian wars, is not well-founded. The same country is now covered with domestic cattle and horses and the Indians would have, in what they believed to be a righteous crusade, looted the scattered homes and lived and traveled upon the domestic stock of the settlers. Pillage would have been followed by rapine and devastation.

So general was the alarm of the citizens, the officials of the General Government, the governors of the States, and the press of that part of the country, that all earnestly appealed for aid and protection for the settlers.

Appeals for Troops

In a letter dated October 29, 1890, from P.P. Palmer, Indian agent, Cheyenne River Agency, to the Interior Department, he says of Hump and his following that the best means of preventing an outbreak among the Indians would be to take these leaders entirely out of the reach of their followers.

In a letter dated October 30, 1890, D.F. Royer, Indian agent at Pine Ridge Agency, informs the Commissioner of Indian Affairs that—

Some of the disadvantages originating from this ghost dance is the believers in it defy the law, threaten the police, take their children out of school, and if the police are sent after the children, they simply stand ready to fight before they will give them up.

When an Indian violates any law the first thing they do is to join
the ghost dance, and then they feel safe to defy the police, the law,
and the agent.

And further—

I have carefully studied the matter for nearly six weeks and have
brought all the persuasion through the chiefs to bear on the leaders
that was possible, but without effect, and the only remedy for this
matter is the use of military, and until this is done, you need not
expect any progress from these people; on the other hand, you will
be made to realize that they are tearing down more in a day than
the Government can build up in a month.

In transmitting the reports of Agents Palmer and Royer, the
Secretary of the Interior says: "It may be best to have a force of soldiers
sufficient to arrest and watch these Indians for a time, but if it is
attempted, it should be done with firmness and power so great as would
overwhelm the Indians from the beginning."

Under date of November 12, 1890, the Acting Commissioner of
Indian Affairs, upon receipt of additional reports from the Indian
Agents, says that the agent at Pine Ridge reports "that the craze has
steadily increased until now it has assumed such proportions both in the
number and spirit of adherents that it is entirely beyond the control of
the agent and police force, who are openly defied by the dancers," and as
a means of stopping the dances, the agent suggests sending a body of
troops sufficient to arrest the leaders therein and imprison them and
disarm the balance of the reservation. And on the 13th he transmits a
telegram from Agent Royer, showing that two hundred participants in
the ghost dance, all armed and ready to fight, had overpowered the
Indian police, and that the agency is at the mercy of these "crazy
dancers," and says:

I deem the situation at said agency arising from the ghost dance
as very critical, and believe that an outbreak may occur at any time,
and it does not seem to me to be safe to longer withhold troops from
the agency. I therefore respectfully recommend that the matter be
submitted to the Honorable Secretary of War with the request that
such instructions as may be necessary be given to the proper
military authorities to take such prompt action as the emergency
may be found by them to demand to the end that any outbreak on
the part of the Indians may be averted and the Indians be shown
that the authority of this department and its agent must be
respected and obeyed by them.

Not until the civil agents had lost control of the Indians and declared themselves powerless to preserve peace, and the Indians were in armed hostility and defiant of the civil authorities was a single soldier moved from his garrison to suppress the general revolt. To prevent this threatened murder of the civil agents and employees at the Rosebud and Pine Ridge Agencies and the destruction of the public property at those places, as well as to give protection to and encourage the loyal and peaceful Indians, troops were ordered to those points under command of General Brooke, commanding the Department of the Platte, on November 17, 1890.

Condition of the Troops

A period of several years of peace and inactivity from serious field service had created a feeling of security on the part of the settlers and a degree of confidence on the part of the troops not warranted by the real condition of affiairs. It was found that this period of peace had to some extent, impaired the efficiency of the troops. This was noticeable in the want of proper equipment for field operations, especially in transportation. There was a reasonable amount of transportation for the ordinary post or garrison service, but it was entirely inadequate for field operations. The time to prepare them for active campaign was so short that they were hardly equipped before their services were required in the field. While the danger and alarm was general throughout the settlements and thousands of unfortunate people, whose homes were shattered throughout that vast territory, were sacrificing what little property they had to obtain transportation to move their families out of the country, leaving much of their property uncared for and unprotected the hostile element of the different tribes was gathering strength and hastening the time for a general outbreak. With as little delay as possible troops were being properly prepared for field service and concentrated where their services would be available.

It was the design of the division commander to anticipate the movements of the hostile Indians and arrest or overpower them in detail before they had time to concentrate in one large body, and it was deemed advisable to secure, if possible, the principal leaders and organizers, namely, Sitting Bull, and others, and remove them for a time from that country. To this end authority was given on November 25, 1890, to William F. Cody, a reliable frontiersman, who has had much experience as chief of scouts, and who knew Sitting Bull very well, and had perhaps as much influence over him as any living man, to proceed to the Standing Rock Agency to induce Sitting Bull to come in with him, making such terms as he (Cody) might deem necessary, and if

unsuccesful in this, to arrest him quietly and to remove him quickly
from his camp to the nearest military station. He was authorized to take
a few trusty men with him for that purpose. He proceeded to Fort Yates
on the Standing Rock reservation and received from Lieutenant
Colonel Drum,[226] commanding, the necessary assistance, but his
mission was either suspected or made known to the friends of Sitting
Bull, who deceived him as to his whereabouts. This had the effect of
delaying the arrest for a time.

At this time the division commander proceeded to Washington for
the purpose of laying before the authorities the plans and measures to be
taken to suppress the hostilities should they commence, and to supply
the necessary food to keep the Indians from suffering. Authority was
given to supply the necessary additional food out of the Army appropriations, as a military necessity, and the Secretary of the Interior also
gave authority to issue the rations authorized by Treaty of 1889. In
addition, orders were given directing all the Sioux Agencies to be placed
practically under the control of the military, especially so far as related to
the police and management of the Indians, and the civil agents were
directed to comply with the orders received from the military authorities.
Complying with the terms of the treaty so far as the ration was
concerned went far to retaining the loyalty of a good percentage of the
Indians who might otherwise become involved. This much having been
accomplished active measures were then taken to suppress the hostile
element who were upon the verge of a general outbreak.

Arrest and Death of Sitting Bull

The first measure for the arrest of Sitting Bull having failed, orders
were given on December 10, 1890, directing the commanding officer,
Fort Yates, to make it his personal duty to secure the arrest of Sitting
Bull without delay. Accordingly the commanding officer, Fort Yates,
directed that certain troops of his command under Captain Fechét[227] go
to Sitting Bull's camp and the remainder of the troops be held in
readiness for service. Mr. McLaughlin, the Indian Agent, selected a
body of police (composed of Indians in whom he had confidence), who
were ordered to the camp of Sitting Bull to make the arrest, to be
followed and supported by the troops under Captain Fechét. Had
Sitting Bull submitted to the arrest by the lawful authorities of the
government he would have been unharmed and probably alive today.
Although urged to submit quietly by the men of his own race, clothed

[226]Lt. Col. William F. Drum, 12th Inf.
[227]Capt. Edmond G. Fechét of Michigan, 8th Cav.

with the authority of the government, acting as police, he resisted, and made a determined effort to avoid going with them. In fact, he raised the cry of revolt, which gathered around him a strong force of his followers, numbering something like 75 warriors, who opened fire upon the police, and a desperate fight ensued, in which Sitting Bull and several of his warriors were killed and many wounded; not, however, without serious loss to the brave Indian policemen carrying out the orders of their agent and the officers of the government. Six of their number were killed and others seriously wounded. In fact, the whole number would have been massacred had it not been for the timely arrival of Captain Fechét who quickly made proper disposition of his force, and with his mounted men and one Hotchkiss gun, drove back the warriors surrounding the police and pursued them through the wooded country for several miles. The action of Captain Fechét was gallant, judicious, and praiseworthy, and it had the effect of striking the first and most serious blow to the hostile element, and of totally destroying it on that reservation.

Regarding the death of Sitting Bull, his tragic fate was but the ending of a tragic life. Since the days of Pontiac, Tecumseh and Red Jacket, no Indian has had the power of drawing to him so large a following of his race, and molding and wielding it against the authority of the United States, or of inspiring it with greater animosity against the white race and civilization. In his earlier years he had gained a reputation constantly organizing and leading war and raiding parties; and, although not a hereditary chief, was the recognized head of the disaffected element when the Sioux were at war, and in his person was the exponent of the hostile element around which gathered the young, ambitious warriors of the different tribes, and his death, for which he alone was responsible, was a great relief to the country in which he had been the terror for many years.

His followers who were not killed were pursued by the troops, a portion surrendered at the Standing Rock Agency, the others with the exception of thirty went to the reservation to the south, where they were intercepted and surrendering their arms were taken to Forts Bennett and Sully, where they were kept for several months under military surveillance.

Removal of Hump

The next important event was the removal of Hump, who had become disaffected on the Cheyenne River Reservation, which was accomplished without violence. For several years Captain Ewers, 5th U.S.

Infantry, had had charge of this Chief and his followers, and had gained their confidence and respect. At the request of the division commander, Captain Ewers was ordered from Texas to S. Dak., and directed to put himself in communication with Hump. Hump was regarded as one of the most dangerous Indians in that part of the country. In fact, so formidable was the considered that the civil agents did not think it possible for Captain Ewers to communicate with him. Captian Ewers promptly acted upon his instructions, proceeded to Fort Bennett, and thence, with Lieut. Hale, without troops, 60 miles into the country to Hump's camp. Hump at the time was 20 miles away, and a runner was sent to him. Immediately upon hearing that Captain Ewers was in the vicinity, he came to him, and was told that the division commander desired him to take his people away from the hostiles and bring them to the nearest military post. He replied that "if Gen. Miles sent for him, he would do whatever was desired." He immediately brought his people into Fort Bennett, and complied with all the orders and instructions given him, and subsequently rendered valuable service for peace. Thus an element regarded as among the most dangerous was removed. All except 30 of Hump's following returned with him and Capt. Ewers to Fort Bennett. The remaining thirty broke away and joined Big Foot's band, which with the addition of twenty or thirty that had escaped from Sitting Bull's camp at Standing Rock Agency, increased his following to one hundred and sixteen warriors. Orders were then given for the arrest of this band under Big Foot, which was accomplished by the troops under Lt. Col. Sumner on the 22nd of December, 1890. Under the pretense that they (the Indians) would go to their agency at the mouth of the Cheyenne River, they, on the night of the 23rd of December, eluded the troops and started south toward the Indian rendezvous in the Bad Lands, near White River, about 40 miles west of Pine Ridge Agency.

Disposition of Troops

While this was being done, seven companies of the Seventh Infantry, under Col. Merriam,[228] were placed along the Cheyenne River to restrain the Indians of that reservation and intercept those from Standing Rock, which had a very salutary effect upon the Indians of both reservations. In the meantime, a strong force had been gathered at the Rosebud and Pine Ridge Agencies. Those at the Rosebud were under the command of Lt. Col. Poland,[229] composed of two troops of the Ninth Cavalry and battalions of the Eighth and Twenty-First Infantry; Col. Shafter, with seven companies of the First Infantry controlled the

[228] Col. Henry C. Merriam, 7th Inf., awarded the Medal of Honor for Civil War service.
[229] Lt. Col. John S. Poland, 21 Inf. (USMA 1861).

country to the south and west of the Rosebud Agency, with station at Fort Niobrara; those at Pine Ridge Agency, under the immediate command of General Brooke, were eight troops of the Seventh Cavalry under Col. Forsyth,[230] a battalion of the Ninth Cavalry under Maj. Henry,[231] a battery of the First Artillery under Capt. Capron,[232] a company of the Eighth Infantry, and eight companies of the 2d Infantry, under Col. Wheaton.[233] West from Pine Ridge Agency was stationed a garrison of two companies under Col. Tilford[234] of the Ninth Cavalry; north of that with headquarters at Oelrichs was stationed Lt. Col. Sanford[235] of the Ninth Cavalry, with three troops, one each from the First, Second, and Ninth Cavalry; north of that on the line of the railroad at Buffalo Gap Capt. Welles,[236] with two troops of the Eighth Cavalry and one troop of the Fifth Cavalry was stationed; north of that on the same railroad at Rapid City, Col. Carr[237] of the Sixth Cavalry, with six troops was in command; along the south fork of the Cheyenne River, Lt. Col. Offley,[238] and seven companies of the Seventeenth Infantry was stationed, and to the east of the latter command, Lt. Col. Sumner, with three troops of the Eighth Cavalry, two companies of the Third Infantry, and Lt. Robinson's[239] company of scouts was stationed. Small garrisons were also stationed at Forts Bennett, Meade, and Sully. Most of the force was placed in position between the large hostile camp in the Bad Lands, which had gathered under Short Bull and Kicking Bear, and the scattered settlers endangered by their presence. As the line under Col. Carr was considered the most liable to be brought in contact with the hostile force, the division commander established his temporary headquarters at Rapid City, S. Dak., where this force was in close communication, and from which their movements could be directed with the least delay.

[230]Col. James W. Forsyth, 7th Cav. (USMA 1856) had been a General in the Civil War and Sheridan's longtime Chief of Staff. His Indian Wars experience was limited.

[231]Maj. Guy V. Henry, 9th Cav. (USMA 1861), awarded the Medal of Honor for bravery at Cold Harbor in the Civil War. An ideal officer, he had been badly wounded in the face at the Rosebud in 1876.

[232]Capt. Allyn Capron (USMA 1867). His son, Allyn Jr., would die in the Spanish American War, as a Captain in the "Rough Riders."

[233]Col. Frank Wheaton, 2nd Inf., Brigadier General in the Civil War.

[234]Col. Joseph G. Tilford, 9th Cav. (USMA 1851).

[235]Lt. Col. George B. Sanford.

[236]Capt. Almond B. Welles, 8th Cav.

[237]Col. Eugene A. Carr, 6th Cav. (USMA 1850), Civil War General, Medal of Honor winner, and old frontier soldier.

[238]Lt. Col. Robert H. Offley, 17th Inf.

[239]1st Lt. William W. Robinson, Jr., 7th Cav. (USMA 1869).

Efforts for Peace

Every effort was made by General Brooke in command at Pine Ridge and Rosebud to create dissension in the hostile camp and to induce as many Indians as possible to return to their proper reservations. At the same time, the troops to the west formed a strong cordon which had the effect to gradually force the Indians back to the agency; the object being, if possible, to avoid conflict, although at any time from the 17th day of December, 1890, to the 15th day of January, 1891, the troops could have engaged the Indians and a serious engagement would have been fought. The effect would have been to kill a large number of Indians, costing the lives of many officers and men, and unless complete annihilation resulted, those who escaped would have preyed upon the settlements, and the result might have been a prolonged Indian war.

The fact that the Indians had lost confidence in the Government was a serious embarrassment to the military. They claimed that their lands had been taken and were then occupied by white settlers, which is true; and that they had received no positive guaranty that the terms of the treaty they had made would be carried out. In order to enable the military to win the confidence of the hostiles, the division commander sent the following telegrams:

Rapid City, S. Dak., Dec. 19, 1890.

Senator Dawes,

    Washington, D.C.

    You may be assured of the following facts that cannot be gainsaid:

First.   The forcing process of attempting to make large bodies of Indians self-sustaining when the Government was cutting down their rations and their crops almost a failure is one cause of the difficulty.

Second.   While the Indians were urged and almost forced to sign a treaty presented to them by the commission authorized by Congress, in which they gave up a valuable portion of their reservation which is now occupied by white people, the Government failed to fulfill its part of the compact, and instead of an increase, or even a reasonable supply for their support, they have been compelled to live on half and two-third rations and receive nothing for the surrender of their lands, neither has the Government given any positive assurance that they intend to do any differently with them in the future.

Congress had been in session several weeks, and could if it were disposed in a few hours confirm the treaties that its commissioners have made with these Indians, and appropriate the necessary funds for its fulfillment and thereby give an earnest of their good faith or intention to fulfill their part of the compact.

Such action, in my judgment, is essential to restore confidence with the Indians and give peace and protection to the settlements. If this be done, and the President authorized to place the turbulent and dangerous tribes of Indians under the control of the military, Congress need not enter into details but can safely trust the military authorities to subjugate and govern and in the near future make self-sustaining any or all of the Indian tribes of this country.

Rapid City, S. Dak., Dec. 19, 1890.

Gen. John M. Schofield,

Commanding the Army, Washington, D.C:

Replying to your long telegram, one point is of vital importance: the difficult Indian problem cannot be solved permanently at this end of the line. It requires the fulfillment by Congress of the treaty obligations in which the Indians were entreated and coerced into signing. They signed away a valuable portion of their reservation, and it is now occupied by white people, for which they have received nothing. They understood that ample provision would be made for their support; instead, their supplies have been reduced and much of the time they have been living on half and two-thirds rations. Their crops, as well as the crops of white people, for two years have been almost a total failure. The disaffection is widespread, especially among the Sioux, while the Cheyennes have been on the verge of starvation and were forced to commit depredations to sustain life.

These facts are beyond question, and the evidence is positive and sustained by thousands of witnesses. Serious difficulty has been gathering for years. Congress has been in session several weeks and could in a single hour confirm the treaties and appropriate the necessary funds for their fulfillment, which their commissioners and the highest officials of the Government have guaranteed to these people, and unless the officers of the Army can give some positive assurance that the Government intends to act in good faith with these people the loyal element will be diminished and the hostile element increased. If the Government will give some positive assurance that it will fulfill its part of the understanding with these 20,000 Sioux Indians, they can safely trust the military authorities to subjugate, control, and govern these turbulent people, and I hope that you will ask the Secretary of War and the Chief Executive to bring this matter directly to the attention of Congress.

At the same time the Indians were notified that if they complied with the orders of the military their rights and interests would be protected so far as the military were able to accomplish.

The measures taken were having a most desirable effect upon the hostiles, for it was reported in their camp that Sitting Bull and his immediate following had been killed, that Big Foot had been arrested, and that Hump had returned to his allegiance. This discouraged them and the presence of a strong cordon of troops, gradually forcing them back to the agency without actually coming in contact with them, and the strong influences brought to bear through the aid of friendly Indians from Pine Ridge, caused them to break camp on December 27, 1890, and leave their stronghold, which was a series of natural fortifications, almost inpenetrable, and moved toward the agency by slow marches. The troops under Col. Carr and Lt. Cols. Offley and Sanford were slowly following in communicating and supporting distance. In fact, the fires of the Indians were still burning in their camps behind them when the troops moved in to occupy the same grounds.

Wounded Knee Creek Affair

Although the camp of Big Foot had escaped the troops on the Cheyenne River, the troops on the south were moved so as to prevent him joining the hostile element and orders were given to the troops under Col. Carr, and Gen. Brooke not only to intercept the movement of Big Foot and party but to cause their arrest. This was accomplished by Maj. Whitside[240] on the 28th day of December, 1890, who met Big Foot one and one half miles west of Porcupine Creek and demanded his surrender. The band submitted to it without resistance and moved with the troops 7 miles, where they were directed to camp, which they did in such position as the commanding officer directed. In order that no mistake might be made, and to have sufficient troops on the ground in case of resistance, Col. Forsyth was ordered by Gen. Brooke to join Maj. Whitside with four troops of cavalry, which, with the company of scouts under Lieut. Taylor,[241] made up a force of eight troops of cavalry, one company of scouts, and four pieces of light artillery, a force of 470 fighting men as against 106 warriors then present in Big Foot's band. The scouting party of Big Foot's band was out looking for the hostile camp of Short Bull and Kicking Bear, but as they (Short Bull and Kicking Bear) had been started from the Bad Lands and were moving into Pine Ridge Agency they were returning to Big Foot's band when the fight occurred on the morning of the 29th of December, 1890.

[240] Maj. Samuel M. Whitside, 7th Cav.
[241] 1st Lt. Charles W. Taylor, 9th Cav. (USMA 1879).

It was the intention to order Big Foot's band to the railroad and then send it back to the reservation where it belonged, or out of the country for a time, in order to separate it from the other Indians. As they had not been within a long distance of the hostile camp in the Bad Lands it was deemed advisable to keep them as far away as possible from it.

The unfortunate affair at Wounded Knee Creek December 29th, 1890, in which thirty officers and soldiers and 200 Indians (men, women, and children) were killed or mortally wounded, prolonged the disturbance and made a successful termination more difficult.

A number of Indians that had remained peaceable at the Pine Ridge Agency became greatly alarmed on learning what had befallen the band of Big Foot, and some of the young warriors went to their assistance. These, on returning with the intelligence of what had occurred, caused a general alarm which resulted in some three thousand leaving the camps located about the agency to join the hostiles and assume a threatening attitude.

The Indians from the Bad Lands, under Short Bull and Kicking Bear, would have camped that night (Dec. 29th) within four miles of the agency, but on hearing the news of the Big Foot disaster turned back and assumed a hostile attitude on White Clay Creek about 17 miles from the Pine Ridge Agency. Thus instead of the hostile camp under Short Bull and Kicking Bear camping within a short distance of the agency, the next day, the 30th of December, found the hostile camp augmented to nearly 4,000, and embracing more than a thousand warriors.

Affair at the Mission

On December 30, a small band of Indians came near the Catholic Mission, 4 miles from the military camp at Pine Ridge, and set fire to one of the small buildings. Col. Forsyth, with eight troops of the Seventh Cavalry and one piece of artillery, was ordered by Gen. Brooke to go out and drive them away. He moved out, the Indians falling back before his command with some skirmishing between the two parties until they had proceeded 6 miles from the camp at Pine Ridge. There the camp halted without occupying the commanding hills, and was surrounded by the small force of Indians. Skirmishing between the two parties followed. Col. Forsyth sent back three times for reinforcements, and fortunately Maj. Henry, with four troops of the Ninth Cavalry and one Hotchkiss gun, was in the vicinity, and moved at once at the sound of the guns. Upon arriving on the ground he made proper disposition of his troops by occupying the adjacent hills and drove the Indians away without casualty, thereby reacuing the Seventh Cavalry from its perilous position. The Seventh Cavalry lost one officer (Lieut. Mann,[242] mortally wounded) and one private killed and several wounded.

From all information that could be obtained the Indians engaged in this affair did not number more than 60 or 70 young warriors. For his conduct on that day and the previous day Col. Forsyth was relieved from command.

Result and Other Affairs

These two affairs, namely at Wounded Knee and what is known as the Mission Fight, seriously complicated the situation and increased the difficulty of suppressing the outbreak. On the evening of the 28th of December everything indicated a settlement without a serious loss of life. The result may be summed up in the loss of nearly 200 people, delay in bringing the Indians to terms, and caused 3,000 Indians to be thrown into a condition of hostility with a spirit of animosity, hatred, and revenge. The spirit thus engendered made it more difficult to force back, or restore the confidence of the Indians, and for a time it looked as if the difficulty would be insurmountable.

On December 30, 1890, the wagon train of the Ninth Cavalry was attacked by Indians and was repulsed by the troops guarding it. On January 3, 1891, an attack was made upon Capt. Kerr's[243] troop of the Sixth Cavalry, then in position between Col. Carr and Lieut. Col. Offley, and quickly and handsomely repulsed by that officer and his troops, aided by the prompt support of Maj. Tupper's battalion, followed by Col. Carr. These repulses had a tendency to check the westward movements of the Indians and to hold them in position along White Clay Creek until their intense animosity had to some extent subsided.

Realizing the importance of restoring confidence to those who were not disposed to assume hostilities, the division commander changed positions with Gen. Brooke and directed him to assume the immediate command of the troops encircling the hostile camp, and took station at Pine Ridge, where he could not only communicate directly with the camp but exercise a general supervision over all the commands.

Having a personal knowledge extending over many years of those Indians, most of whose prominent leaders, including Broad Tail, Little Hawk, Kicking Bear, and Short Bull, had surrendered to me on the Yellowstone ten years before, I was enabled to bring them to reason and restore confidence.

---

[242] 1st Lt. James D. Mann, 7th Cav. (USMA 1877).

[243] Capt. John B. Kerr (USMA 1870). Awarded the Medal of Honor for this action.

Fortunately, Congress appropriated funds necessary for complying with the obligations of the Sioux treaty, and the division commander was enabled to assure the Indians that the Government would respect their rights and necessities.

Messengers were immediately sent representing to them the injudicious policy of contending against the authorities, and assuring them that there was only one safe road, and that was toward the agency, to surrender. They were also advised that the powerful commands were so distributed in the immediate vicinity of their camps and at the most important points as to intercept them should they break through the line, but if they would comply with the directions of the division commander, they would be assured of his support in order to obtain their rights and privileges under their treaties with the Government. They were also informed at the same time that unnecessary acts of violence were disapproved by the authorities; and they must decide whether the military should be their friend or their enemy.

While the troops were exercising the utmost vigilance and constant care in enclosing the large camp of Indians, leaving as far as practicable no outlet for them to escape and steadily pressing them back toward Pine Ridge Agency, every effort was made to restore their confidence and compel them to return to their agencies. Fortunately at that time a change had been made in the administration of their affairs. Their supplies of food had been increased and properly distributed, and officers in whom they had confidence, and whom they had known for years, were placed in charge. Capt. Hurst was given general supervision at the Cheyenne River Agency; Capt. Lee at Rosebud Agency; Capt. Ewers was placed in charge of the Cheyennes, and Capts. Pierce and Dougherty[244] in charge of Pine Ridge. Subsequently, Capt. Penney[245] was appointed as acting Indian agent at Pine Ridge.

The Surrender

Under these circumstances, with the assurance of good faith at the agencies and from the Government, and held by strong cordon of troops encircling them, they were gradually pressed back to the agency, and on the 15th of January, moved up White Clay Creek and encamped within easy range of the guns of the large command, under Col. Shafter, stationed at Pine Ridge, the troops under Gen. Brooke following immediately behind them, almost pushing them out of their camps. On the next day they moved farther in and encamped under the guns of the

[244] Capt. William E. Dougherty, 1st Inf., worked his way up from private.
[245] Capt. Charles G. Penney, 6th Inf.

entire command and surrendered their entire force of nearly 4,000 people. The troops were moved into three strong camps of easy communication, occupying the three points of a triangle, with the Indian camp in the center in close proximity to the troops.

While in this position they surrendered nearly 200 rifles, and were complying with every order and instruction given them; yet the information that was frequently received at the time of the finding of the bodies of Indians (men, women, and children) scattered over the prairies, and their knowledge of the number in the hospitals, the wounded in the Indian camp, and the other casualties that had occurred to them, caused a feeling of great distress and animosity throughout the Indian camp. Yet sufficient arms had been surrendered to show their good faith. These arms, together with what had been taken at other places, viz, in the Wounded Knee affair and at the Cheyenne and Standing Rock Reservation, aggregated in all between 600 and 700 guns; more than the Sioux Indians had ever surrendered at any one time before. This was a sufficient guaranty of good faith; but in order to make it doubly sure, and as they had agreed to comply with every direction given them by the division commander, they were informed that he required the persons of Kicking Bear and Short Bull, the two leaders of the hostiles, and at least twenty other warriors of the same class. As they had agreed to comply with every order given them, these men came forward and volunteered to go as hostages for the good faith of their people and as an earnest of their disposition to maintain peace in the future. Those men were placed in wagons and sent 26 miles to the railroad, and thence by rail to Fort Sheridan, Ill., where it was the purpose of the division commander to retain them until such time as it might be necessary to guaranty a permanent peace.

Knowing the Indians had well founded grievances, he requested authority to send 10 men representing the different elements of the Sioux Nation, and chiefly the loyal and well-disposed portion, to Washington, D.C., to enable them to represent their affairs to the authorities, and to tell their own story. This party included some of the best and wisest counselors, the ablest and most loyal friends of the government living upon the Sioux reservations.

Thus ended what at one time threatened to be a serious Indian war, and the frontier was again assured of peace and safety from Indians who a few weeks prior had been a terror to all persons living in that sparsely populated country. Too much credit cannot be given the troops, who endured the hardships and sustained the honor, character, and integrity of the service, risking their lives in their effort to restore peace and tranquility, placing themselves between a most threatening body of savages and the unprotected settlements of the frontier in such a way as to avoid the loss of a single life of any of the settlers, and establishing peace in that country with the least possible delay. In fact the time consumed in solving the most difficult problem was remarkably brief, it being but fourteen days from the time Sitting Bull was arrested to the time the Indians were moving in to surrender, and would have encamped within 4 miles of the agency had not the disaster at Wounded Knee occurred. Notwithstanding this unfortunate affair, the time occupied was only thirty-two days from the time of the arrest of Sitting Bull until the whole camp of four thousand Indians surrendered at Pine Ridge, S. Dak.

Return of Indians to Reservations

The Brules, the most turbulent of the hostile element, were taken by Capt. Lee (in whom they had great confidence and had great reason to respect on account of his thorough justice in the management of their affairs years previously) across the country to the Rosebud Agency, to which they belonged, without escort and during the most intense cold of the winter.

The Cheyenne Indians, who but a few weeks before were regarded as a most dangerous band, were taken by Capt. Ewers, in whom they had not only confidence and respect, but absolute affection, to the north, on one of the most perilous and difficult journeys ever accomplished in this country, a distance of about 300 miles from Pine Ridge, S. Dak., to the mouth of Tongue River, in Montana, traveling in the intense cold of winter in that desolate country, the ground covered in many places with several feet of snow, and this without an escort of troops. They finally reached Fort Keogh without a single loss of life or without an Indian committing a single unlawful act during that long and perilous journey.

During the time of intense excitement, when it seemed that a serious outbreak was imminent, the governors of Nebraska and South Dakota placed troops along the line of settlements, which gave confidence to the settlers and additional protection to those exposed positions.

Although the campaign was short, it was not without serious loss. Two excellent officers were killed and one mortally wounded. Capt. George D. Wallace,[246] Seventh Cavalry, was killed at Wounded Knee Creek, December 29, 1890, and First Lieut. Edward W. Casey,[247] Twenty-second Infantry, a gallant young officer of great promise, was killed January 7, 1891, near Pine Ridge, while making a reconnaissance.

[246]Capt. George D. Wallace (USMA 1872).

[247]1st Lt. Edward W. Casey (USMA 1873) a capable leader of Indian Scouts.

First Lieut. James D. Mann, Seventh Cavalry, was mortally wounded at White Clay Creek, December 30, 1890; First Lieut. Ernest A. Garlington[248] and John C. Gresham,[249] Seventh Cavalry, and John C. Kinzie,[250] Second Infantry, and Second Lieut. Harry L. Hawthorne, Second Artillery, were wounded at Wounded Knee Creek, December 29, 1890. Twenty-eight gallant soldiers were also killed and 38 wounded in the various skirmishes and affairs, some of whom have since died.

End of the Campaign

The troops participating in the campaign were immediately returned to their proper stations; the force at Pine Ridge was gradually reduced; Capt. Pierce, the acting Indian agent at Pine Ridge, was relieved on account of sickness by Capt. Dougherty, in turn relieved at his own request and Capt. Penney appointed. The latter has administered the affairs of that agency with great ability. Additional appropriations have been given for the support of the Indians, and they now receive nearly one-half as much more than they received a year ago.

Notwithstanding the fact that the "volcano has cooled down" the fires of discord still remain. Even while the hostages were at Fort Sheridan they received communications from their friends in the Sioux camps stating that they had not given up the conspiracy of one grand uprising of the Indians, and that the Utes were ready to join the Sioux whenever they were ready to resume hostilities. Communications have been discovered going between the different camps inciting the Indians to hostility, and even now, while this communication is being written, there is a delegation from the Indian Territory absent, ostensibly to visit relatives at the Arapahoe and Shoshone reservations in Wyoming. They have, in fact, gone across the mountains, and are now in the abodes of the supporters of the Messiah delusion near Pyramid Lake in Nevada.

During the months following the serious disturbance of the peace the confidence of all has been restored. Many of the settlers have gone back to their abandoned homes and ranches, and the Indians have resumed their accustomed occupations.

Advantage was taken of the return of troops to locate them in regimental posts, giving regiments to Fort Snelling, Minn.; Fort Keogh, Mont.; Fort Assinniboine, Mont.; Fort Douglas, Utah; Fort Omaha, Nebr.; Fort D.A. Russell, Wyo.; and Fort Sheridan, Ill.; and very strong garrisons of troops at Forts Meade, Niobrara, and Robinson.

[248] 1st Lt. Ernest A. Garlington (USMA 1876), awarded the Medal of Honor for Wounded Knee.
[249] 1st Lt. John C. Gresham (USMA 1876), awarded the Medal of Honor.
[250] 1st Lt. and Adjutant John Kinzie.

Nothing of importance has occurred since the undersigned assumed command of the Department of the Missouri which requires special mention in this report. The affairs of the Indian Territory are gradually adjusting themselves after being in a state of transition for a long time. The days of large holdings of land by the Indians in common will eventually cease and the Indians take up lands in severalty.

World's Columbian Exposition

As we approach nearer the time of the World's Columbian Exposition, the most important affair of the kind that has ever been held in the world, it would seem advisable to take advantage of the occasion to mobilize or assemble what is known as the national guard or State militia. The Constitution has very judiciously and wisely reserved the control of these forces to the various State governments, but as a means to promote the efficiency of the various organizations, it would be well to assemble them under Congressional enactment, with the approval and authority of the various State governments, in one national encampment at least once in a generation.

As there has been no gathering of that magnitude since the armies were dispersed in 1865, I would respectfully recommend that the militia be brought together at this peace jubilee. Most of the members of the national guard, who are engaged in the great industries of the country, will desire to be present at the exposition at some time during its session, and many of them would prefer to come with their organizations, in order to combine with the encampment the benefits of the exposition. It would also be beneficial to the State organizations to be brought together in one national encampment, where they would have the advantage of meeting troops from other states. For instance, those of New England would be placed alongside of those from the Gulf, and those from the Atlantic and interior meet those from the Pacific slope, making one grand encampment of the citizen soldiery of this country, where patriotism and the spirit of emulation would prompt each organization to attain the highest degree of excellence. Such inspections, parades, and field maneuvers as might be beneficial could be executed.

As the General Government makes yearly appropriations for the equipment of the militia I see no reason why it should not provide transportation for assembling it in the encampment above proposed. The reasonable reduction of rates usual in other countries for such movements of troops, and frequently given in this country, would reduce the aggregate cost, say, for ninety thousand State troops and ten thousand Federal troops to $850,000, approximately. For that purpose I would respectfully recommend that Congress be asked to make the necessary appropriation to provide transportation for the troops from their various State capitals to the national encampment at or near the World's Columbian Exposition, Chicago, Ill., and return, and provide authority for the movement of such State organizations, the same to be designated and directed by the governors of the various States interested.

I would also renew the recommendations contained in my annual report of 1889, mentioned on pages 8, 9, and 10, under the heads of "Recommendations" and "Promotion of subordinate officers."

Accompanying this report are three maps and the reports of the staff officers at these headquarters.

I have the honor to remain, very respectfully, your obedient servant,

NELSON A. MILES,
Major-General, Commanding.

The Adjutant General U.S. Army,
Washington, D.C.

MILES AND STAFF, 1891
Major General Miles was commanding the Military Division of the Missouri when this photograph was taken at Fort Sheridan, Illinois.
Courtesy, National Archives

X

General-in-Chief
of the Army

Now that the last great Indian uprising was quelled, Miles' duties assumed a routine nature. In 1891 he made a visit to Mexico with his family and his aide, Captain Maus, officiating at military reviews and banquets. He ensured that the Columbian Exposition in Chicago was not without appropriate soldierly fanfare, and in 1894 he made efficient use of the troops in his Division in supressing labor unrest in the city. In October, 1894, Miles was transferred to command of the Department of the East, with headquarters on Governor's Island, New York Harbor.

Major General John McAllister Schofield had been general-in-chief of the Army since Sheridan's death in 1888. On February 5, 1895 he was given the third star of Lieutenant General, and September 29 of that year he retired. For Nelson Miles this was a day to remember, the end result of his unbridled ambition to get to the top, for now as senior Major General he assumed command of the Army of the United States. Moving his family to Washington, D.C., where he soon occupied a large mansion with private stables on N Street, Miles could at last indulge his preference for the pomp and circumstance of rank. He put the finishing touches on his *Personal Recollections* in 1896, and in May of the following year made an extended tour of Europe, observed the Greco-Turkish War, attended Queen Victoria's Jubilee celebrations, and returned with notes he published as *Military Europe*.

When the USS *Maine* was destroyed by a mysterious explosion in Havana Harbor on February 15, 1898, and popular enthusiasm for war with Spain swept the country, Miles was one of a few old soldiers who spoke out against the war hysteria. As one who had campaigned unsuccessfuly for an expanded Armed Forces, he felt the Regular Army of 2,116 officers and 25,706 men would be hard put to confront an estimated 128,183 Spanish troops. President McKinley and Secretary of War Alger made up for this disparity by calling for volunteers, and soon over one hundred thousand eager but untrained and poorly equipped soldiers were clamoring for an invasion of Cuba. Within weeks, against Miles' advice, the President called for an additional 75,000 volunteers. The General felt that fifty thousand well-trained troops with the Regulars as a core would be far preferable to a mob of undisciplined State troops; he urged rigid camps of instruction for the new soldiers, and suggested a carefully structured campaign with the Island of Puerto Rico the initial goal. All of these ideas were rejected by the Administration. Ordered to Tampa, Florida, where Major General William R. Shafter's expeditionary force was gathered, Miles was flabbergasted and appalled at the confusion, but could only stand by while the army embarked for Cuba on June 14.

The obese, sickly and cautious Shafter managed to over-run Spanish defenses on San Juan Hill and at El Caney in a hard fought battle on July 1. On July 3, Rear Admiral Winfield Scott Schley destroyed the Spanish fleet off Santiago; while on land, Shafter began a tentative siege. Miles had tried to obtain command of the invasion, but had been rebuffed; now, afraid that Shafter was failing to reap the fruits of his victory, the President ordered Miles to Cuba. The general-in-chief left Washington on July 7, sailed from Charleston S.C., and arrived in Cuba on the 11th. He prodded Shafter into pursuing negotiations with the Spanish commander, General Toral, and was present when the Spaniards surrendered on July 15.

Though he had missed participating in the campaign for Cuba, Miles was able to assume control of the subsequent invasion of Puerto Rico. His 19 day campaign was a brilliantly conducted operation, which cost only 3 American dead and 40 wounded. When war ended on August 13, Miles' success was largely eclipsed by popular images of Rough Riders charging up San Juan Hill; Puerto Rico was regarded as a "picnic" by some, an opinion countered by war correspondent Richard Harding Davis, who wrote,

MAJOR GENERAL MILES, 1898
Photograph taken at the time of the Spanish American War.
Courtesy, Massachusetts Commandry, Military Order of the Loyal Legion of the
United States, U.S. Army Military History Institute.

IN THE FIELD DURING THE SPANISH AMERICAN WAR
Miles with his staff. It is unclear whether this photograph was taken in Cuba or Puerto Rico.
Courtesy, Westminster, Mass., Historical Society.

The reason why the Spanish bull gored our men in Cuba and failed to touch them in Porto Rico [sic] was entirely due to the fact that Miles was an expert matador; so it was hardly fair to the Commanding General and the gentlemen under him to send the Porto Rican Campaign down into history as a picnic.[251]

In the weeks following the Spanish surrender Miles was joined in Puerto Rico by his wife, son Sherman and daughter Cecelia. Their holiday on the sunny island was the calm before the political storm brewing between the General on the one hand and Secretary of War Alger, Adjutant General Corbin and President McKinley on the other. Miles believed, and so stated to the press, that his political enemies—Alger and Corbin—had conspired to keep him from exercising field command in Cuba. He claimed credit for negotiating the Spanish surrender at Santiago as ranking officer on the field, a claim with some validity when one examines the vague orders coming from Washington, but ironic in the light of his controversy with General Howard following Chief Joseph's surrender in 1877.

Miles arrived in New York on September 7, 1898, sunburned, thinner and temporarily shorn of his customary white mustache. As the newspapers speculated on the possibility of his being relieved for insubordination, the General embarked on a path of political controversy that would ultimately cost him the sponsorship of his superiors. His charges that "embalmed beef" had been supplied to American troops in Cuba, thereby contributing to an alarmingly high rate of illness and death from disease, may have won him friends in the ranks, but it seemed a gratuitous rocking of the boat to politicians and the public at large. Although war hero and soon to be Vice President Theodore Roosevelt agreed with Miles' charges,[252] he was not about to indulge in muckraking at this point in his political career. Miles found few supporters and made many enemies.

A third star confirmed Miles as Lieutenant General on June 6, 1900, but it was to be his last hurrah. In October of 1902 he embarked on a three month tour of the World. He crossed the Pacific, visiting Hawaii, Guam and the Philippines, where to his credit he displayed an admiration for the Filippino Nationalists

[251]Quoted in Frank Freidel, *The Splendid Little War*, New York, 1958, p. 277.
[252]Letters, Roosevelt to Miles, Jan. 14, 1899, Miles/Cameron Collection, Lby. of Cong.

and an abhorence of those American troops who would commit atrocities against their guerrilla opponents. He traveled to Japan and noted the probability of war between that nation and Russia. In China he saw Canton, Hong-Kong and Peking, where he had an audience with the Dowager Empress, two years following the Boxer Rebellion in the suppression of which American troops played a major role. He journeyed over the Trans-Siberian Railroad to Moscow, noticing the similarities between that vast territory and the American West. St. Petersburg, Paris and England, where he met with King Edward, concluded his travels. On February 1, 1903 he was back at his Washington, D.C. headquarters.

Miles' abrasive relationship with Theodore Roosevelt worsened from the time "Teddy" assumed the Presidency in 1901. The General thought Roosevelt a military upstart and scheming politician, while T.R. labeled his uncooperative Army Commander "a brave peacock." Although Miles gladly accepted the challenge posed by an order that would retire any officer who could not ride 90 miles in 3 days (he covered the distance from Fort Sill to Fort Reno in 9½ hours), he could not escape the legal retirement age of 64.

On August 8, 1903, Miles stepped down from his position of General-in-Chief without the customary ceremony, which was denied him as a purposeful slight from his President and Secretary of War Elihu Root. Unfazed by the obvious insult, the haughty old man walked proudly down the steps of the War Department and into a civilian life he had not known for 42 years. His successor, Lieutenant General S.B.M. Young, would only briefly relish the position, as the creation of the system of Chiefs of Staff we know today diluted the power once enjoyed by Sherman, Sheridan, Schofield and Miles.

REPORT OF MAJOR GENERAL MILES
Headquarters, Department of the Missouri,
Chicago, Ill., September 14, 1892.
Sir:
I have the honor to submit the following report of affairs and operations in this department during the past year. . .

The inspection reports from the different posts show that the troops are in a good state of discipline and efficiency and are properly drilled and instructed.

A tabulated statement of the work done by post lyceums in the department, established in compliance with General Orders, No. 80, Adjutant-General's Office, series of 1891, accompanies this report, which shows that one hundred and thirty-five essays on professional topics were read by officers during the year, followed in many cases by discussion of the subject treated. These essays and the reports of the discussions thereon contain much valuable and interesting information concerning military matters. The work already done clearly demonstrates that these lyceums will be of much value in stimulating professional zeal and ambition.

No Indian disturbances have occurred sufficiently serious to call for the intervention of troops.

The troops in the Indian Territory have been occupied during a considerable part of the year in removing intruders and cattle from the public lands, and in preserving order and protecting town sites during the settlement of the Cheyenne and Arapaho Reservation.

In conformity with the proclamation of the President these lands were thrown open to settlement at noon on the 19th of April, 1892, the Indians having rights thereon having previously selected and been assigned to allotments of land on said reservation. Large numbers of people seeking homes assembled at the boundary line days before the date fixed, and apprehensions were published in the press that serious violence and disturbance of the peace would accompany the opening of this tract in the absence of organized civil government. The Secretary of War, upon request of the Department of the Interior, directed that troops be sent to prevent the occupation of the land opened for settlement before the date assigned, protect the Indian allotments from encroachment, and assist in the enforcement of the rules laid down by the officials of the Land Bureau for the settlement of this tract. These duties were successfully performed, the lands were taken up on the date fixed by the President with little disturbance, and no one was deprived by evasion or violence of an equal opportunity with others to secure a home. Thus a movement which it was feared would be attended by scenes of disorder and outrage was executed peacefully and the rights of all protected. Special credit is due for this result to the careful precautions and skillful management of Col. James F. Wade, Fifth Cavalry, to whose discretion the duties connected with the opening were intrusted, and to the vigilance and good conduct of the troops under his command.

On May 3, 1892, the commanding officer of Fort Reno reported the existence of serious dissatisfaction among the Cheyenne and Arapaho Indians, owing to the deduction for so-called attorney's fees of $67,500 from the moneys due those Indians in payment for that part of their reservation opened to settlement. With a view of learning what grounds, if any, existed for this discontent and of allaying it, if possible, I directed an investigation to be made by Capt. J.M. Lee, Ninth Infantry, assistant to the inspector general of the department. Capt. Lee's thorough and complete report of this investigation was forwarded to the Adjutant-General of the Army on June 27. That report, together with his annual report, herewith forwarded, gives a complete history of that transaction.

I would earnestly renew the recommendation contained in my last annual report, that advantage be taken of the World's Columbian Exposition "to mobilize or assemble what is known as the National Guard or State militia" in connection with a considerable portion of the regular Army. Very few of our younger officers have ever participated or even witnessed the movements of large bodies of troops, and the benefits to be derived from the proposed mobilization are so obvious that I will not enlarge upon them.

A convention of officers of the National Guard assembled in Chicago, October 27, 1891, at which the subject of an encampment of the National Guard to be held in Chicago in the summer of 1893 was carefully and fully considered. The National Guard of the District of Columbia and of thirty-five States and Territories was represented in this convention. It was unanimously resolved by this convention that an encampment of the National Guard of the United States be held in Chicago during the summer of 1893. From the 5th to the 20th of August was fixed as the time for holding the encampment. An examination of the meteorological record kept by the post surgeon at Fort Sheridan shows that the selection of this date was judicious. During the month of May, 1892, there were seventeen rainy days, with a rainfall of 6.51 inches. During June, twenty-one rainy days, with a rainfall of 10.91 inches, and during July ten rainy days, with a fall of 2.54 inches. No outdoor drill was practicable during May or June, and very little in July. In August there were only four rainy days, and the ground was suitable for drill. . .

In view of the great importance of the proposed encampment, and its national character, I would recommend that Congress be asked to appropriate $1,500,000, to be used under direction of the Secretary of

War for transportation, camp expenses, field equipments, and other general and necessary expenses connected with the encampment.

A detachment of 8 soldiers, under command of First Lieut. W.T. May,[253] and afterwards of Second Lieut. Henry J. Hunt,[254] Fifteenth Infantry, has during the year made several successful practice marches upon bicycles, carrying the ordinary equipments and arms of the infantry soldier.

On the 18th day of May, 1892, a dispatch carried by relays of bicycle carriers posted by the American Wheelmen's Association left these headquarters Department of the East in the New York Harbor.

In spite of extremely bad roads and constant rains, the distance, 975 miles, was made in 4 days and 13 hours.

This experiment was the first one of its kind, and the results obtained, under the most adverse and discouraging conditions, prove conclusively that the bicycle will in future prove to be a most valuable auxiliary to military operations, not only for courier service but also for moving organized bodies of men rapidly over the country.

I also renew the recommendations contained in my annual report of 1889, under the heads of "Recommendations," and "Promotion of subordinate officers."

Accompanying this report are the reports of the staff officers at these headquarters.

Very respectfully, your obedient servant,

NELSON A. MILES,
Major-General, Commanding.

The Adjutant-General, U.S. Army
Washington, D.C.

REPORT OF MAJ. GEN. NELSON A. MILES
Headquarters Department of the Missouri,
Chicago, Ill., August 25, 1893.

SIR: I have the honor to submit the following report of affairs in my department since my last, dated September 14, 1892. . .

The following troops were ordered to Chicago, October 19, 1892, to take part in the ceremonies incident to the dedication of the World's Columbian Exposition buildings:

From Fort Leavenworth, Kans., headquarters and band: Twelfth Infantry, Companies H, Seventh; F, Tenth; F, Twelfth; and F, Thirteenth Infantry.

---

[253] 1st Lt. Will Thompson May, 15th Inf. (USMA 1879).
[254] 2nd Lt. Henry Jackson Hunt, Jr., 15th Inf.

From Fort Mackinac, Mich., Company D, Nineteenth Infantry.

From Fort Reno, Okla., headquarters, band, and Troop C, Fifth Cavalry.

From Fort Riley, Kans., Light Batteries A and F, Second, and F, Fourth Artillery.

From Fort Sheridan, Ill, Troops B and K, Seventh Cavalry, Light Battery E, First Artillery, and the Fifteenth Regiment of Infantry.

From Fort Sill, Okla., Troop D, Fifth Cavalry.

From Fort Wayne, Mich., the band and Companies A, E, and G, Nineteenth Infantry.

From Fort Meade, S. Dak., Troop L, Third Cavalry (Indian).

From Fort Snelling, Minn., headquarters, band, and Companies A, E, G, and H, Third Infantry.

From Fort Niobrara, Nebr., the band and Troops F, G, and L (Indian), Sixth Cavalry.

From Fort Omaha, Nebr., headquarters, band, and Companies A, C, D, and F, Second Infantry.

From Fort Robinson, Nebr., Troops A and F, Ninth Cavalry.

From Washington, D.C., the Marine Band and four companies of U.S. Marines.

The operations of these troops while in Chicago were fully explained in my letter dated January 26, 1893, a copy of which accompanies this report.

No serious Indian hostilities have occurred in the department during the year.

As in previous years, the troops in the Indian Territory have been occupied during much of the time in removing trespassers from the public lands, in preserving order in the newly-settled region, and in keeping the peace between hostile factions of the semicivilized Indian tribes. These difficult duties have been performed in a manner which shows good judgment and discretion on the part of the officers and a good state of discipline and faithful service on the part of the troops.

The inspection reports also show that good administration is preserved at the different posts in the department, and that the garrisons are efficient and well disciplined.

I would respectfully recommend that so much of the act of Congress as prohibits the reenlistment of soldiers who have served for ten years, but less than twenty, or who are over thirty-five years of age, be repealed. The effect of this legislation is, in my opinion, injurious to the Army, depriving the Government as it does of many experienced, heroic, and patriotic men, whose presence in the service would from every point of view promote its efficiency and character.

I again renew the recommendations contained in my report for 1889, and referred to in my last report, under the heads of "Recommendations" and "Promotions."

Accompanying this report are the reports of the staff officers at these headquarters; also a tabulated statement of the work done by post-lyceums in the department, established in compliance with General Orders, No. 80, series of 1891, Adjutant-General's Office.

Very respectfully, your obedient servant,

NELSON A. MILES
Major-General, Commanding

The Adjutant General U.S. Army,
Washington, D.C.

Headquarters Department of the Missouri
Chicago, Ill., January 26, 1893.

SIR: I have the honor to submit the following report of my duties in compliance with letter from the Adjutant-General of the Army, dated August 11, 1892, in response to request of Director-General David, dated July 16, 1891, designating me to command such of the regular troops and the National Guard of the several States as might be assembled in Chicago to take part in the dedication of the buildings of the World's Columbian Exposition on October 12 (changed to October 21), 1892.

Brig. Gen. Eugene A. Carr and Maj. Amos S. Kimball were ordered to report to me for duty in connection with the exercises. Maj. Kimball reported August 8, and was directed to make all the necessary arrangements for transporting the troops, for quartering them in the Exposition buildings at Jackson Park, and for supplying them while there. Gen. Carr reported to me on October 17, and was directed to proceed to Jackson Park and assume command of all the United States troops there, and to exercise general supervision of all other troops reporting there. The United States troops ordered to take part were as follows:

Twenty-four companies of infantry, composed of: Headquarters and Companies E, Twelfth; H, Seventh; F, Tenth, and F, Thirteenth Infantry; band and battalion, Nineteenth Infantry; the Fifteenth Regiment; headquarters, band, and battalion, Third Infantry, and headquarters, band, and battalion of the Second Infantry—aggregating 1,399 officers and men.

Ten troops of cavalry, composed of: Headquarters, band and Troops C and D, Fifth Cavalry; Troops B and K, Seventh Cavalry; L, Third Cavalry; band and Troops F, G, and L, Sixth Cavalry, and Troops A and F, Ninth Cavalry—aggregating 625 officers and men.

Four light batteries of Artillery, composed of: Light Batteries E,
First; A and F, Second; and F, Fourth Artillery—aggregating 235
officers and men.

Battalion of marines—aggregating 215 officers and men.

Total number of United States troops and marines, 2,474 officers and
men.

The following National Guard organizations were also sent by their
respective States and were under the command of the governors of their
respective States and the officers designated by them:

Three regiments from Indiana, with a total of 988 officers and men;
one regiment from Missouri, with a total of 522 officers and men; two
regiments from Iowa, with a total of 2,030 officers and men; two
regiments from Wisconsin, with a total of 1,045 officers and men; three
regiments from Minnesota, with a total of 1,536 officers and men; two
regiments from Ohio, with a total of 1,458 officers and men; one
regiment from Michigan, with a total of 724 officers and men; six
regiments from Illinois, with a total of 3,763 officers and men; two
troops Illinois Cavalry, with a total of 100 officers and men; two batteries
Illinois Artillery, with a total of 105 officers and men. Total number of
State troops, 12,271 officers and men.

These troops, both United States and State (except the First and
Second Illinois regiments living in Chicago), were quartered in the
Exposition buildings, being assigned to their respective positions
therein by Maj. Kimball. The United States troops were subsisted by the
commissary department at a cost of 57 cents per day per man.

On October 19, at 4 p.m., the light artillery was drilled at Washington
Park, under the supervision of Maj. E.B. Williston,[255] Third Artillery,
inspector of artillery at these headquarters, in the presence of several
thousand people. Rodney's Battery (F of the Fourth) and Woodruff's
Battery (F of the Second), were first each drilled separately by their
respective captains. The entire battalion, four batteries, was then drilled
by Maj. Randolph,[256] Third Artillery. After the completion of the
artillery drill the cavalry was drilled on the same ground by Col. James
F. Wade, Fifth Cavalry.

The 20th of October was devoted to a civic parade in which the
military were not expected to participate.

The programme for October 21, as arranged by the joint committee
on ceremonies, was as follows: The distinguished guests and officials
were to be conducted by an escort of honor composed of all the mounted

[255] Maj. Edward B. Williston.
[256] Maj. Wallace Randolph.

troops from the Lake Front Park to Washington Park. At Washington Park a review of the infantry troops by the Vice President. Appropriate salutes were also to be fired at stated intervals. The Vice President, guests, and officials were then to proceed to the building of Manufacturers and Liberal Arts, where the oratorial, literary, and musical exercises of the dedication were to take place. . .

The officials and distinguished guests, mounted and in carriages, left the Lake Front Park at 9 o'clock, moving south on Michigan Avenue, conducted by the following mounted escort, under command of Col. James F. Wade, Fifth Cavalry: Troops C, D, and band, Fifth Cavalry: Troop L, Third Cavalry; Troop L and band, Sixth Cavalry, Troops B and K, Seventh Cavalry; Troops A and F, Ninth Cavalry; Light Batteries E, First, A and F, Second Artillery; Troops A and B, Illinois National Guard, and Battery D, Illinois National Guard.

After moving 2⅜ miles to the corner of Michigan Avenue and Twenty-ninth Street, Hon. Levi P. Morton, Vice-President of the United States, accompanied by President Palmer, President Higinbotham, Director-General Davis, and other officials of the Exposition, were received with due honors. The procession then continued its march south on Michigan Avenue, Thirty-fifth Street, and the Grant Boulevard to Washington Park, 3½ miles distant, where the infantry troops had been formed in three brigades in line of masses, and where the Vice-President reviewed the troops from his carriage, which, for that purpose, was placed 75 yards in advance of the line of the other carriages, his position being marked by a large American flag, conspicuously displayed from another carriage just to the right of the Vice President.

Owing to the limited time the "present" in line and the ride around the line were dispensed with in accordance with paragraph 685, Infantry Drill Regulations, U.S. Army.

The troops were put in motion to pass in review at 10:45 a.m., and the rear of the column passed the reviewing point at 11:40 a.m. The column then became the escort of the procession, conducting it through Washington Park, via Midway Plaisance and the Exposition grounds, to the manufacturers building, where 120,000 people had assembled to witness the ceremony. The entire distance marched from Lake Front Park to the manufacturers building in Jackson Park was 8⅞ miles.

Salutes were fired as follows: The salute of the Speaker of the House of Representatives was fired by Woodruff's Battery on Lake Front Park at 9 o'clock, when the procession first moved. The Vice-President's salute was fired by Rodney's Battery in Washington Park on the arrival of the

Vice-President at the south open green in Washington Park. The national salute was fired by Rodney's Battery in Jackson Park as the head of the procession entered the park, and also by the U.S.S. *Michigan*, commanded by Commander Wingate, U.S. Navy.

The U.S. Marine Corps and band took a prominent part in the parade, and also did good service in connection with the troops in furnishing guards and escorts, and the Marine Band, together with the band of the Mexican Republic, sent by President Diaz, played national airs prior to the dedication ceremonies.

All of the troops presented a fine appearance; were well equipped; marched and maneuvered with commendable skill and accuracy, and executed all that was required of them by the committee on ceremonies and the officials appointed to give general directions, with the single exception of one officer. Unfortunately this peaceful celebration was not an exception to the history of military campaigns and battles where heroism, devotion to duty, and honorable service is the general rule, where almost invariably some one, when least expected, fails in the discharge of his duty. It rarely happens, however, as in this case, that it is done deliberately and for a purpose; but I am glad to say that it occurred in only one instance, and by only one officer, to my knowledge.

On October 22 the beautiful and interesting ceremonies of dedicating the State buildings were conducted by many of the governors of the respective States and the distinguished representatives from the States, in which the state troops in many instances took part.

The United States troops returned to their various stations on October 22, in accordance with instructions from Headquarters of the Army, and the state troops also returned to their proper stations on that day.

The programme for the three days' celebration was executed in every particular as arranged and directed by the joint committee on ceremonies and the council of administration. The dedication of this great enterprise was celebrated in an imposing and dignified manner befitting the magnitude of such an important historical event.

Very respectfully, your obedient servant,

NELSON A. MILES,
Major-General, Commanding.

The Adjutant-General U.S. Army,
Washington, D.C.

REPORT OF MAJ. GEN. NELSON A. MILES
Headquarters Department of the Missouri,
Chicago, Ill., September 4, 1894.

. . . The following troops were concentrated in Chicago, Ill., by the orders of the President of the United States, to execute the orders and processes of the United States court to prevent the obstruction of the United States mails, and generally to enforce the faithful execution of the laws of the United States.

From Fort Brady, Mich., Companies B and F Nineteenth Infantry, left that post July 5, and arrived in Chicago the following day.

From Fort Leavenworth, Kans., Companies A, Fifth, H, Seventh; F, Tenth; E, Twelfth; and F, Thirteenth Infantry, left that post July 5, and arrived in Chicago the following day.

From Fort Riley, Kans., Maj. L.T. Morris[257] with Troops C, E, F, and G, Third Cavalry, Maj. W.F. Randolph with Light Batteries A and F, Second, and F, Fourth Artillery, Lieutenant Maxfield[258] with detachment of signal corps, and Assistant Surgeon Quinton with detachment of hospital corps. These troops left Fort Riley on July 8, and arrived in Chicago on the 10th.

From Fort Sheridan, Ill., the Fifteenth Infantry, Troops B and K, Seventh Cavalry, and Light Battery E, First Artillery, with Surgeon Girard and detachment of hospital corps. This command arrived in Chicago at 11 p.m., July 3, 1894.

From Madison Barracks, N.Y., the Ninth Infantry, which arrived in Chicago July 9, 1894.

From Fort Niobrara, Nebr., Col. D.S. Gordon, with Troops A, E, G, and H, Sixth Cavalry, arrived in Chicago July 10, 1894.

The conduct of the troops in restoring order and confidence where mob violence and a reign of terror existed in and near the city of Chicago was marked by great forbearance, fortitude, and excellent discipline, and their presence and action here very greatly contributed to the maintenance of civil law, and, in my opinion, saved this country from a serious rebellion when one had been publicly declared to exist by one most responsible for its existence.

The troops remained in the city fifteen days, and having accomplished the object for which they were brought together, and carried out to the full extent the orders of the President and the Major General Commanding the Army, they were, with the exception of the Ninth Infantry, which returned to the Department of the East, withdrawn to Fort Sheridan, and during the month of August moved to camps Abraham Lincoln and Orrington Lunt, Evanston, and during that time engaged in field maneuvers, which were both interesting and highly beneficial to the service. . .

NELSON A. MILES,
Major General Commanding.

---

[257] Maj. Louis Thompson Morris, 3rd Cav.
[258] 1st Lt. Joseph E. Maxfield.

Report of Maj. Gen. Nelson A. Miles
Headquarters, Department of the East
Governors Island, New York Harbor, August 31, 1895

Sir: I have the honor to submit the following annual report for the information of the Lieutenant-General Commanding the Army:

The last annual report from this department was submitted by Maj. Gen. Oliver O. Howard, who retained command of the department until his retirement, the 8th of November last. Command of the department was assumed by me, under the orders of the President, on the 20th of the same month.

There are now embraced in this command 25 garrisoned posts and 39 posts not garrisoned, the number in the last annual report having been 26 of the former and 38 of the latter. . .

Indians

. . .In September last there were at Mount Vernon Barracks, Ala. a company of Indian soldiers, 43 men; 17 men and 126 women; 18 boys and 2 girls over 12 years of age; 52 boys and 44 girls under 12 years of age—Apache Indians, prisoners of war; and Es-kim-in-sin's band of 8 men, 14 women, 1 boy and 1 girl over 12, and 8 boys and 13 girls under 12—also Apache Indian prisoners of war. All of these except Es-kim-in-sin's band, under instructions of the Secretary of War of September 14, 1894, were sent to Fort Sill, Okla., on October 2. Under instructions of September 17, 1894, Es-kim-in-sin's band was sent to San Carlos, Ariz., November 23. One Indian, Lah-tsi-nasty, was received from the civil authorities November 22 and sent to Fort Sam Houston, Tex., the next day. There are now no Indian prisoners of war remaining in the hands of troops of this department.

While the property of these Indians was en route to Fort Sill and in the hands of the railroads, one carload was totally destroyed and three carloads badly damaged by fire in a railroad freight shed in New Orleans October 28, 1894. I think this loss should be made good to the Indians whose property was destroyed or damaged. Papers in the case have been forwarded for consideration and action of the War Department.

Troops

The instruction and efficiency of all the cavalry in the department is excellent. The instruction of the artillery is much embarrassed by want of modern artillery and artillery material. In the absence of these, the officers have made very creditable efforts to keep their own knowledge and the instruction of their commands abreast of the times. The range finder devised by Lieutenant Lewis, Second Artillery, and the relocator devised by Lieutenant Rafferty, First Artillery, give promise of great utility in artillery firing.

I strongly recommend that all artillery posts be provided with proper "subcalibers" for a sufficient number of the pieces and a good allowance of ammunition for using them in drill and practice. Something of this kind, in view of the expense of the ammunition for the piece itself, would greatly facilitate instruction in practical work and add to its interest and value. Many "subcalibers" are now in use abroad, and some have been devised by our own officers.

Another question is worthy of careful consideration—whether, in training gunners for service to keep our artillery up to the modern standard, it has not become necessary to have a special class of warrant officers or noncommissioned officers, enlisted for ten or more years, to be trained specially at the artillery schools for all the practical work of the artillery in hitting and destroying an object aimed at, whether by seacoast or siege artillery.

The efficiency and instruction of the infantry is in general excellent.

Instruction in calisthenics, gymnastics, and athletics in general among the troops of all arms has been carried on during the past year and will be still further provided for in the coming year as having the greatest usefulness in fitting officers and men for active service.

Arms

All of the infantry in the department and a portion of the artillery have been armed with the new .30 caliber magazine rifle during the past year, which appears to give good satisfaction, except in the sighting of the piece and some other minor points, which will no doubt be corrected.

Discipline

The discipline of the troops is excellent. The report of the Judge-Advocate shows a less number of trials by general courts martial than last year, though there has been a very considerable increase in the strength of the command. The number of trials by garrison and summary courts is larger, but these trials are generally for small offenses.

Consolidated Post Mess

This method of supplying their daily meals is not entirely satisfactory; the company mess is believed in general to be more agreeable to the men and a better arrangement, as under it the company is very much better prepared to handle its ration and to prepare its own food when, by the demands of the service, it is separated from the conveniences of the elaborate cooking outfit of the post mess hall with its experts trained to handle the modern complicated appliances for cooking on a large scale.

Post Libraries

Some provision for post libraries is very much needed. Books in use need occasional rebinding, and at some of the posts no libraries exist. But little additions can be afforded to those now existing unless some provision is made therefor. These important guidelines should be provided for at all posts.

Post Lyceums

The lyceum season for the year has been fairly successful. An abstract of the work accomplished is appended, marked F. There is a tendency among some officers to go outside of professional subjects in essays, which is deprecated.

Report of Department Commander's Inspection of Posts

A copy of my report on the inspection of the southern posts I have visited is attached to this report, marked A.

Coast Defenses

I desire to call special attention to the fact that the defenses of the approaches to the cities of Mobile, Savannah, Charleston, Washington, and Philadelphia are without garrisons, those of the city of New Orleans being in nearly the same condition, and that Sandy Hook, in New York Harbor, though provided with works and guns, is still without a garrison or barracks and quarters to accomodate one.

Staff Departments

The work of the officers of the staff departments at the headquarters of this department has been entirely satisfactory during the past year— efficient and economical. By reason of lack of appropriation a portion of this command was not paid for the month of June last; this deficiency should be met at an early date. The work of these departments will be found in detail in the several reports.

Very respectfully, your obedient servant,

NELSON A. MILES
Major-General, Commanding

The Adjutant-General United States Army,
Washington, D.C.

ANNUAL REPORT OF THE MAJOR-GENERAL COMMANDING THE ARMY
Headquarters of the Army,
Washington, D.C., November 10, 1896

. . .Fortunately, during the year the Army has been called on only to a limited extent to act either against hostile Indians or against bodies of men who are engaged in violating the United States law or international treaty obligations. There have been several lawless bands that have to some extent disturbed the peace along the Rio Grande and the border line between Mexico and the southern border of Arizona and New Mexico. The troops of the Mexican Republic, as well as our own, have been engaged in suppressing such acts of lawlessness as have in a small degree interfered with the peace of the communities on both sides of the border, and arrangements have been made through the Government of Mexico to secure cooperation of the forces of that Republic and our own to this end.

The troops in the Department of the Colorado have been actively engaged, in small detachments, in protecting the settlements against the depredations of a few Indian outlaws. The zeal and judicious disposition and action of the troops have contributed largely to maintaining a condition of peace and security among the sparsely settled districts of that frontier.

The personnel of the Army was never in better condition. The percentage of violations of military discipline has been exceedingly small during the year, and in the main both officers and men have fulfilled all the requirements that could be expected of a patriotic, intelligent, and efficient army.

The standard of enlisted men is constantly improving. The requirements for entering the service are now so exacting that during the last year out of 49,240 applicants only 7,465 were accepted as qualified for service in the Army, showing the care taken in enlistments and the rising standard of requirements. The soldiers are now very largely American born and taken from every section of our country, and very many of the most respected families are represented among them. This condition of affairs has made to a very large degree the elementary schools established for enlisted men under section 1231, Revised Statutes, unnecessary, and now calls for a different class of instruction, more strictly professional. It also emphasizes the need of a different grade of special text-books, and post libraries should be supplied, with suitable books, for those who would use them. Very many of our soldiers, through their Army training to a faithful performance of duty with promptness and accuracy, and the instruction they have received during their service, are engaged in business for themselves or have secured excellent positions in civil life after their discharge, and are among the most valued citizens in the community where they reside. A good post library at every military post is also needed for the use of the officers in the post lyceum work. Through this work a valuable incentive to study and improvement has been provided for the service. It is recommended that post libraries meeting both these needs be provided.

A great improvement has been made in the architecture, durability, and stability of the public buildings that are now occupied by the Army, which contributes largely to the health and comfort of the occupants and is in the end economical. Yet the necessity for changing from the old temporary and rapidly decaying buildings that have heretofore been constructed, many of them on what was formerly known as the Indian frontier, to the more durable and sanitary buildings that are now being constructed requires a large increase of the construction fund, and this, added to the fact that in many cases new posts have to be constructed for the accommodation of batteries of artillery, renders it necessary that large appropriations be made, and I therefore recommend that a liberal appropriation be furnished for the construction and repair of public buildings for the Army. These buildings, once constructed, will serve their purpose indefinitely with ordinary repairs.

During the last year the country has fortunately been free from any serious ourbreak of Indians, and all the different tribes have been in the main peaceable, well disposed, and constantly making some progress toward civilization. I attribute this to three causes. The first, the presence of, and knowledge on the part of the Indians of the strength and efficiency of the military forces that are within reach of all the tribes. The presence of the troops has a wholesome effect in restraining any turbulent element or spirit of disaffection or dissension that may occur among the tribes. The second is the fact that the Indians are receiving more benefits from the General government and a just, intelligent, and judicious administration of their affairs. The third is that many of the most turbulent and heretofore hostile Indian tribes have been under the care and control of experienced, judicious, and conscientious officers of the Army, who have had years of experience with these people, have administered their affairs with intelligence and fidelity, and command the respect and confidence of the Indians. I recommend that the same policy be continued in regard to the management of the Indians.

Most of the infantry, cavalry, and light artillery have engaged in practice marches and field maneuvers during the year, which have been highly beneficial to the service and instructive to both officers and men. Wherever it has been practicable, especially at Fort Riley, Kans., the forces have been concentrated and practical field maneuvers and problems in minor tactics executed with marked intelligence and efficiency.

Very great attention has been paid to the physical improvement of the commands by thorough athletic training through calisthenic and gymnastic exercises, with highly beneficial results in improving the physical condition of the different commands. At all military posts where shelter is needed in winter a suitable gymnasium building—and for cavalry a riding hall—is absolutely essential to the efficiency of the men and the development of their physical condition.

The requirements of the service render it necessary that troops should be stationed in the important fortifications along our 8,000 miles of seacoast and at certain points along the 7,000 miles of our national boundary, to give security to our national interests against a foreign foe and protection to our border from Indians, etc., on both sides of the national boundary; second, that they should be located within available reach of large bodies of Indians who, while apparently peaceful and harmless, require the presence of strong military forces to keep the hostile element subdued and in a condition of safety; third, the location of troops at strategic points in different parts of the country where they can be economically supplied with all the materials required for the necessities of the service, and be on lines of communication where they can be easily concentrated and made available wherever their presence may be required. While it is important that these positions should be judiciously selected, especially for strategic purposes, there will necessarily be influences used to have the troops stationed where they are not required, but are for the benefit of local communities or for some purpose other than national requirements. I therefore most earnestly recommend that no consideration for the location of military posts be entertained except where they are called for by the military authorities and deemed absolutely essential for the national requirements.

Coast Defenses

The question of coast defenses is one of the most important in military affairs, not only as it concerns the military forces, but also as it affects the interests and welfare of the nation. The history of all civilized nations makes it apparent that this important question can not be disregarded without serious danger to the Government and disaster to the welfare of its people, as a large portion of the wealth of the nation, estimated at upward of six billions of property, and a large percentage of the population are concentrated and congregated in the commercial ports of the nation, and as the safety and existence of our entire foreign commerce depend upon well protected harbors and commercial ports, I again call attention to this subject and renew the recommendations that I have heretofore made.

The modern appliances of war are now so entirely different from those of thirty years ago that it has become an imperative necessity to change not only the character and position of the fortifications but the armament as well. Apparently we have nearly reached the limit in the present type of high-power guns, having a power of throwing large armor-piercing projectiles fully 12 miles, and it is believed by the best military authorities that very great improvement in that respect is a question of extreme doubt. The fact that other nations are armed with these most destructive equipments renders it imperative that our ports should be protected by at least an equally efficient class of modern weapons of war. I therefore call attention to my report of last year, and earnestly renew my recommendations on the subject therein contained.

During the years between 1888 and 1895 the appropriations for both guns and fortifications were so limited as to practically paralyze the work for the construction of high-power guns and fortifications for the protection of our coast. It is exceedingly gratifying to acknowledge the fact that the last Congress made more liberal appropriations for both guns and fortifications than it has heretofore done, and the work of manufacturing high-power guns and mortars, as well as the emplacements for such armament, is progressing satisfactorily, and it is of the highest importance that this work should be continued and that liberal and ample appropriations should be made for that purpose during the coming fiscal year.

The change in the appliances of war has been so great that it necessitates the placing of the high-power guns at much farther distances from the great centers of wealth, communication, and commerce, rendering it necessary to build barracks and quarters for the accommodation of the garrisons to man the works, when completed, by the Ordnance and Engineers Corps. I therefore recommend that liberal appropriations be made by the coming Congress for the manufacture of high-power guns and mortars, the construction of emplacements, platforms, and fortifications for the same, and the construction of barracks and quarters for the accommodation of the artillery garrisons that are to man them, and I urge that a sufficient appropriation be made available during the coming fiscal year. . .

An unwise argument has been made against the construction of modern high-power guns, mortars, and the modern appliances of war that it is a danger and a menace to the laboring classes, and in some instances marked protests have been made against such a national policy. The arguments seem scarcely worthy of consideration; yet it is deemed proper to call attention to the fact that these national safeguards are in no sense a menace to any class of our citizens, not even to the humblest individual, but, on the other hand, they are a protection to the life, property, and welfare of all classes, from the highest to the lowest. They protect not only the commercial ports, with their accumulation of public buildings and private dwellings, the commerce, the shipyards, the factory, the foundry, the workshop, but also the savings banks and the cottage. In fact, the destruction of our great commercial and manufacturing cities would be a national disaster far more serious and appalling to the great masses of the laboring population than it would be to any other class of our people.

I also call attention to my report of last year, under the head of "General condition of the Army," in which I refer to the fact that at a time when we had 30,000,000 less population, and proportionately less wealth in public and private interests, the Army was double the strength that it is to-day. The Army was reorganized in 1866, with the available strength of 51,605; in 1869 it was reduced to 35,036, and in 1870 to 32,788. During the great panic following 1873 it was reduced in 1874 to 25,000. There is no significance in that number any more than in any other number that might by chance be selected. Unfortunately, during the long period of serious depression, when the Government was laboring under a great debt and a protracted panic, a theory became crystallized that this number was suitable for this great nation of nearly 80,000,000 population and its constantly increasing wealth and numbers. Hence the Army, which is one of the pillars of the government, the safeguard of the life, property, and liberty of the people, has remained stagnant and crystallized, in the same condition that it was twenty years ago. I again renew my recommendation that a standard be fixed according to the population and wealth of the nation, which, in my judgment, would be judicious, patriotic, and eminently wise, not only for the welfare of the people of the present day, but for all time during the existence of the Republic. I therefore suggest that the enlisted strength of the Army be fixed at one soldier to every 2,000 of population, as the minimum, and the maximum strength not to exceed one soldier to every 1,000 population, the strength to be determined within these limits by the President of the United States according to the necessities and requirements of the nation. . .

Attention is invited to the recommendations of the Adjutant General of the Army in his report to the Secretary of War, under the head of "Clerical duty in the Army," for the relief of a most deserving class of army clerks. I entirely concur in his recommendation, which is sustained by those of Maj. Gen. Wesley Merritt, Brig. Gen. Elwell S. Otis, Brig. Gen. Frank Wheaton, and Brig. Gen. Z.R. Bliss on the same subject in the reports herewith.

I also renew my recommendation of last year concerning the cavalry and light artillery, and the importance of having at least two stations east of the Rocky Mountains and one west, suitable for the accommodation of one regiment of cavalry; also the recommendations made concerning the use of bicycles and motor wagons; and also renew my recommendation concerning the promotion of enlisted men who shall be found competent after thorough examination to the grade of second lieutenant after five years of service.

Official communications upon military subjects form so important a branch of the duties of the officers of the Army, both in garrison and field, and particularly in the supreme hour of battle, that I deemed it advisable to ascertain the attention paid to this subject, especially by the officers who have joined the service since the last great war. Therefore, on the 15th of June last I addressed a circular letter to the officers of the Army, calling for a report direct to me on nine questions therein propounded. The object of this circular was twofold: first, to ascertain the attention given to this subject by officers; and second, to obtain their unbiased and uninfluenced views on the questions contained in the circular. The replies received have shown that the officers of the Army as a body are most attentive to their duties and have given much thought to their profession. The reports have, in the main, been quite satis-factory, aggregating some 10,000 pages. It will require some time to classify and maturely consider them, and I will refer to this subject in a subsequent communication.

Very respectfully, your obedient servant,

NELSON A. MILES,
Major-General Commanding

The Secretary of War

ANNUAL REPORT OF THE MAJOR-GENERAL COMMANDING THE ARMY
Headquarters of the Army,
Washington, October 21, 1897
. . .During the last year there has been, with one exception, a complete change in the stations of the department commanders.

The Army, although inadequate in point of numbers, was never in a higher state of efficiency, both as to the character and qualifications of its officers and intelligence and loyalty of its soldiers. In the report of Major-General Merritt will be noticed the important changes and improvements that have been made along the Atlantic and Gulf coasts, especially in the mounting of modern artillery and the appliances adopted defense of the coasts. In this report Major-General Merritt calls special attention to the report of Colonel Rodgers,[259] inspector of artillery of the department, also to the report of the chief ordnance officer of the department, and in their recommendations concerning the increased efficiency of the artillery service, and especially that the

[259]Col. John I. Rodgers, 5th Artillery (USMA 1861).

artillery soldiers who qualify as gunners and gunnery specialists shall receive proper compensation, I fully concur.

I also concur in the recommendations of Major-General Brooke concerning the necessity for gymnasiums and drill halls, required especially along the line of northern military posts to enable the commands to be properly instructed and exercised during inclement weather or during the winter season; also in his recommendation concerning general service clerks.

The progress that has been made on the Pacific Coast in the establishment of modern batteries of artillery has made it necessary to occupy new ground and to adopt a new system of defense. The very commanding position known formerly as Lime Point has received a portion of its armament, and will soon become a most formidable part of the defense of the harbor of San Francisco. The name of Lime Point has been changed to "Fort Baker," in honor of the distinguished statesman and hero of two wars, Col. Edward Dickinson Baker, who was killed at Balls Bluff, Va., October 21, 1861. It will be noticed by General Shafter's report that very active and earnest work is being done in putting that important harbor in condition of proper defense. The same work is in progress along the Pacific Coast, especially at San Diego, Cal., and will in time be completed at the mouth of Columbia River, Oregon, and also the entrance to Puget Sound, Washington.

Attention is also invited to the report of General Merriam, commanding Department of the Columbia, especially to the importance of a larger garrison at the entrance of the Columbia River, Oregon, and to his report on the condition and necessities of the great Territory of Alaska.

Alaska is in extent eleven times the area of the State of New York. The recent discovery of rich gold fields, together with valuable silver and copper mines, the timber and fishery interests of that Territory, are attracting and will attract a very large population to that region, necessitating a more stable civil government, and also the occupation of important points by military and by naval forces. As all the other Territories have been occupied by military posts, and appropriations have been made for military roads, establishment of telegraph lines, bridging of rivers, and, in fact, aiding and blocking out the way for occupations of the vast territories by citizens, it is deemed but just and advisable that the same liberal spirit should be manifested toward that great and important Territory. . .

In the report of General Otis it will be observed that during the year there has been conflict with the authorities and disturbance of the peace

by the Indians scattered through that portion of the Rocky Mountain
region, but, by judicious management and prompt action of the civil
authorities and military forces, serious disturbances of the peace have
been avoided.

The report of General Coppinger[260] is very complete and quite
important, especially concerning the instruction of troops, practice
marches, and practical instruction in minor tactics. His views concerning the inspection system of the Army are also worthy of notice.

The condition of the Indians is better to-day than it has been for many
years, and during the last year there has been no serious disturbance of
the peace. . .

The demand for the services of the infantry are constantly increasing,
so that that branch of the service is inadequate for the requirements of
the Government, and in addition to this the great Territory of Alaska,
that it is now necessary to occupy with suitable garrisons, makes a
demand for additional infantry imperative, and I recommend that
Congress authorize the addition of five regiments to that arm of the
service.

In 1866 the Army was organized with 54,000 men; and that, in the
judgment of the best military minds and most eminent statesmen of that
day, was the minimum force which this nation should maintain. Owing
to the fact that the Government was burdened with an unusual and
enormous debt, and the depressed financial condition of the country at
that time, caused a reduction to be made from 54,000 to 45,000, and then
later to 30,000, and finally to 25,000 men, and this standard has
remained so long that the impression has become crystallized that such a
number is sufficient for any and all conditions of the country. The
number has no significance whatever as to the requirements and
necessities of the Government. In my opinion, it would be wise and
judicious for Congress to establish a standard limiting the recruiting of
the Army for all future time, unless the conditions of the country should
be other than what can now be anticipated. . .

I again renew the recommendations I have made concerning the
granting of commissions and discharge to meritorious noncommissioned officers after five years' service who shall successfully pass the
required examination, as an encouragement and just recognition of
their merit and services.

The personnel of the Army, as before stated, is in most excellent
condition and is constantly improving. That there is room for much

[260] Brig. Gen. John J. Coppinger, veteran of the Papal Guards and the Civil War, son in law
of James G. Blaine.

improvement in the war material I am equally confident, both in arms, equipment, uniform, and transportation, and such improvements would, in my opinion, promote the efficiency of the service. These, however, are matters of detail, requiring executive action rather than legislative, and will be made the subject of special reports in due time.

The record of the Army for the past one hundred years has been a record of heroic deeds and honorable service. It is at present and will in the future be entitled to the highest regard and generous support of our government and people.

Very respectfully, your obedient servant,

NELSON A. MILES,
Major-General Commanding

Hon. Russell A. Alger,
Secretary of War

ANNUAL REPORT OF THE MAJOR-GENERAL COMMANDING THE ARMY
Headquarters of the Army,
Washington, D.C., November 5, 1898.

. . .The military operations during the year have been extraordinary, unusual, and extensive.

Early in the fiscal year troops were engaged in transporting supplies to citizens in Alaska, and since then in exploring expeditions through that extensive Territory. These expeditions have been under the direction of Lieut. Col. G.M. Randall, Eighth Infantry (now brigadier-general, United States Volunteers); Capt. P.H. Ray,[261] Eighth Infantry (now colonel Third United States Volunteer Infantry); Capt. W.R. Abercrombie, Second Infantry; Capt. E.F. Glenn, Twenty-fifth Infantry; and Capt. W.P. Richardson, Eighth Infantry; and are still under the direction of Captains Abercrombie and Richardson.

Information recently received from one of the most intelligent frontiersmen and explorers in our service, Mr. Luther S. Kelly,[262] who has been with Captain Glenn's command, indicates that they have successfully explored the country and discovered a route from Portage Bay to the Knik River, which, connecting with Lieutenant Castner's trail up the Matanuska River, insures a practicable route entirely through our own territory to the Tanana River. A good pack trail or wagon road can be built from Portage Bay to the Knik, and would be of great service to the enterprising and venturesome prospectors and miners who occupy that region.

[261]Capt. Patrick Henry Ray.
[262]"Yellowstone" Kelly, Miles' old scout from 1877-79.

The War with Spain

At the close of the great Civil War the Government had a million veterans in arms, well equipped for war for that time. The great amount of war material then in the possession of the Government was sold or gradually used up by issue either to the militia of the States or to the regular forces that have been engaged in military operations on the frontier for the last thirty years. The supplies and material that were not sold, but stored, were gradually reduced to the minimum, and the war with Spain found this country with a very small army—25,000 men— with war material sufficient only to equip that force and furnish it with a small amount of ammunition; but the tentage, transportation, and camp equipage was insufficient for any important military operations; in fact, quite an amount of valuable transportation, including ambulances, had been disposed of within the last few years.

Prior to the passage of the joint resolution of Congress, approved April 20, 1898, demanding that the Government of Spain relinquish its authority and government in the Island of Cuba, etc., Congress had appropriated $50,000,000 for the national defense, and in the interim between this time and actual hostilities efforts were made to have furnished material for military operations on a more extensive scale than had been done in former years. This action of Congress was very important, as that time was most opportune and favorable for securing such munitions of war as were absolutely essential to the proper equipping of an army and to the securing of articles not in demand or available in this country at that time, but which are used in modern warfare; and the purchase of smokeless powder, rapid-fire and machine guns, modern rifles, etc., was urged at that time.

Several bills were pending in Congress during the winter of 1897-98 providing for the increase of the Regular Army, which finally resulted in the act, approved April 26, 1898, authorizing an increase in the enlisted strength of the Army to 62,597 men. Congress subsequently authorized the enlistment of 10,000 men "possessing immunity from diseases incident to tropical climates."

On April 9 I recommended the equipment of 50,000 volunteers, and also on April 15 recommended that an additional auxiliary force of 40,000 men be provided for the protection of the coasts and as a reserve. This, with the increase of the Regular Army, and the 10,000 "im-munes," would have given us an effective force of 162,597, which, with an auxiliary force of 50,000 natives, I considered sufficient, and deemed it of the first importance to well equip such force rather than to partly equip a much larger number.

[Copies of the two letters above referred to followed in the report.]

At the commencement of the war the problem was largely a naval one, and until the question of superiority between our Navy and the Spanish navy, or such naval forces as might be furnished by any other European power or combination of powers supporting the Spanish Government, was determined, military operations had to be determined by the success or failure of our naval forces. I was fully convinced that should our Navy prove superior the position of the Spanish army in Cuba would be rendered untenable with a minimum loss of life and treasure to the United States. There were two most serious obstacles to be avoided— one was placing an army on the Island of Cuba before our Navy controlled the Cuban waters; and the other was putting an army on the island at a time when a large number of the men must die from the diseases that have prevailed in that country, according to all statistics, for the last one hundred years. For the latter reason I addressed a letter to the Secretary of War, under date of April 18, 1898, forwarding a communication from Surgeon-General Sternberg regarding the danger of putting an army in Cuba during the sickly season, and at the same time urged the plan of harrassing the Spanish forces and doing the enemy the largest amount of injury during the time necessary for our Navy to demonstrate its superiority—the rainy or sickly season and the time actually required to equip and instruct the volunteer forces with the least possible loss to ourselves. In that letter I also asserted the belief I have entertained from the first, *that we could secure the surrender of the Spanish army in the Island of Cuba without any great sacrifice of life.*

[A copy of the letter referred to followed in the report.]

In order that the volunteers should be equipped as speedily and efficiently as possible soon after the first call for volunteers was made, and that their wants and necessities might be anticipated, the following letter was addressed to the honorable Secretary of War:

Headquarters of the Army,
Washington, D.C., April 26, 1898.

SIR: I regard it of the highest importance that the troops called into service by the President's proclamation be thoroughly equipped, organized, and disciplined for field service. In order that this may be done with the least delay, they ought to be in camp approximately sixty days in their States, as so many of the States have made no provision for their State militia, and not one is fully equipped for field service. After being assembled, organized, and sworn into service of the United States, they will require uniforms, tentage, complete camp equipage, arms, and ammunition, and a full supply of stationery, including blank books and reports for the Quartermaster's, Commissary, Medical, and Ordnance Depart-

ments. They will also require complete equipment of ordnance,
quartermaster's, commissary, and medical supplies, hospital appliances, transportation, including ambulances, stretchers, etc. The
officers and noncommissioned officers will have to be appointed
and properly instructed in their duties and responsibilities and
have some instruction in tactical exercises, guard duties, etc. all of
which is of the highest importance to the efficiency and health of
the command. This preliminary work should be done before the
troops leave their States. While this is being done, the general
officers and staff officers can be appointed and properly instructed,
large camps of instruction can be judiciously selected, ground
rented, and stores collected. At the end of sixty days the regiments,
batteries, and troops can be brigaded and formed into divisions and
corps, and proper commanding generals assigned, and this great
force may be properly equipped, molded, and organized into an
effective army with the least possible delay.

Very respectfully,

NELSON A. MILES,
Major-General Commanding.

The Secretary of War.

Congregating tens of thousands of men, many of whom were not
uniformed, and scarcely any properly equipped, in great camps away
from their States, rendered it difficult for them to be properly supplied
with food, cooking utensils, camp equipage, blankets, tentage, medical
supplies, transportation, etc., and was to a great extent the cause, in my
judgment, of the debilitating effect upon the health and strength of the
men, who were otherwise in good physical condition. The material
necessary to clothe and equip large armies was not even manufactured at
that time, and the consequent condition of the troops for weeks and
months was injurious to the commands in many ways. . .

The regular infantry was ordered, April 15, 1898, to New Orleans,
Mobile, and Tampa, preparatory to an immediate movement to Cuba
should war be declared. This order, however, was partially suspended,
and a part of the regular infantry, with the artillery and cavalry, ordered
to camp at Chickamauga Park. On May 10 the regular artillery and
cavalry were ordered from Chickamauga to Tampa, preparatory to a
movement on Cuba. Later 70,000 men were ordered to move on Cuba,
and commissary stores for ninety days for the men and thirty days' stores
for the animals were ordered to be concentrated at Tampa. None of
these movements on Cuba, however, materialized. The want of proper
equipment and ammunition rendered the movement impracticable.

While troops were being assembled at Tampa, Mobile, New Orleans,

Chickamauga, Washington, and in the different States, an expedition to the Philippine Islands was gathered at San Francisco under the command of Maj. Gen. Wesley Merritt. The command was well organized and as well supplied as it was possible with the means available. The expedition sailed May 25, 1898, was well conducted and eminently successful in every way. Full reports have been submitted by General Merritt and his subordinate officers.

As soon as hostilities were commenced expeditions were immediately organized to give aid and support to the Cubans in the way of supplying them with arms, munitions of war, and supplies, wherever and whenever possible.

A short time before the commencement of the war, there left Washington, from the Bureau of Military Information, two officers, Lieut. A.S. Rowan and Lieut. H.H. Whitney, to attempt the most difficult and dangerous enterprise of ascertaining existing conditions in the islands of Cuba and Puerto Rico, respectively. Their efforts were eminently successful. Both of these officers penetrated the enemy's country and obtained most accurate and valuable information regarding the position of the military and naval forces, the defenses, and the topographical and climatic features of the country, all of which was of great value in subsequent military operations. Lieutenant Rowan left the United States on April 9 and landed April 24 at El Portillo, about 70 miles west of Santiago de Cuba. He went into the interior, met General García, of the Cuban army, and remained with him for a short time, then, together with Brig. Gen. Enrique Collazo and Lieut. Col. Carlos Hernández, of General García's staff, passed up to Manati on the north coast, and on May 4 went in an open boat to Nassau, New Providence, returning to the United States May 13, 1898.

Lieutenant Whitney left Key West May 5 for Puerto Rico, where he arrived the 15th, and after exploring, under disguise, the southern portion of the island, left on June 1, returning to the United States June 9.

The first expedition with arms and supplies for the Cubans was ordered to start from Key West under the direction of Col. R.H. Hall,[263] Fourth Infantry (now brigadier-general, United States Volunteers), but not sent. Later one landed on the coast, under charge of Capt. J.J. O'Connell,[264] First United States Infantry, Lieut. W.M. Crofton,[265] First Infantry, being the first officer to land on Cuban soil after the commencement of hostilities.

---

[263]Col. Robert H. Hall (USMA 1860).

[264]Capt. John J. O'Connell (USMA 1892)

[265]1st Lt. William M. Crofton.

Several expeditions were subsequently made by Col. J.H. Dorst, Lieut. C.P. Johnson, Tenth Cavalry, and others.

Also, a strong expedition was organized, consisting of 5,000 men, under the command of the senior officer then at Tampa, Maj. Gen. W.R. Shafter, the objective point being Tunas, on the south side of Cuba, where it was expected to open communication with the forces under General Gómez and support and cooperate with him in that mountain region (which is a healthful part of Cuba), and also to furnish all the supplies needed by that force. This expedition, when fully prepared, was delayed on account of the movement of Admiral Cervera's fleet from Cape Verde Islands to the waters of the West Indies, and the movement of our troops was suspended awaiting the result of the expected conflict between that fleet and our own.

An important expedition, under Lieut. Col. Dorst, U.S.V., sailed from Key West to the north of Nassau, New Providence; thence directly south, landing at the harbor of Banes, on the north coast of Cuba, which has been held during the war by the Cubans, where he remained five days, landing a steamer load of the munitions of war most needed, including 7,500 rifles, 1,000,000 cartridges, 5,000 uniforms, and other material needed by the 10,000 Cubans under General García.

The following general order was issued on Memorial Day:

Headquarters of the Army,
Adjutant-General's Office,
Washington, May 30, 1898.

After a prolonged period of peace our Army is once more called upon to engage in war in the cause of justice and humanity. To bring the military forces to the highest state of efficiency and most speedily accomplish what is expected should be the earnest effort and call forth the best energies of all its members of whatsoever station.

The laws and regulations which govern military bodies in civilized countries have been developed to their present perfection through the experience of hundreds of years, and the faithful observance of those laws and regulations is essential to the honor and efficiency of the Army.

All authority should be exercised with firmness, equity, and decorum on the part of superiors, and should be respected by implicit obedience and loyal support from subordinates.

Every officer of whatever grade will, so far as may be in his power, guard and preserve the health and welfare of those under his charge. He must labor diligently and zealously to perfect himself and his subordiantes in military drill, instruction, and discipline; and above all, he must constantly endeavor, by precept and example, to maintain the highest character, to foster and stimulate that true soldierly spirit and patriotic devotion to duty which must characterize an effective army. The Major-General Commanding confidently trusts that every officer and soldier in the service of the Republic, each in his proper sphere, will contribute his most zealous efforts to the end that the honor and character of the Army may be preserved untarnished, and its best efforts crowned with success.

This order is given upon a day sacred to the memory of the heroic dead, whose services and sacrifices afford us example and inspiration, and it is expected that all will be fully impressed with the sacred duty imposed upon the Army by the Government of our beloved country.

By command of Major-General Miles:

H.C. CORBIN, Adjutant-General

Definite information having been received that Cervera's fleet had been inclosed in the harbor of Santiago de Cuba by the Navy, orders were given to General Shafter, May 30, 1898, to place his troops on transports and go to the assistance of the Navy in capturing that fleet and harbor. It was expected that the transports engaged at that time would convey some 25,000 men.

I desired to go with this command, and sent the following telegram to the honorable Secretary of War:

Headquarters of the Army,
Tampa, Fla., June 5, 1898.

THE SECRETARY OF WAR, Washington, D.C.:

This expedition has been delayed through no fault of anyone connected with it. It contains the principal part of the Army, which, for intelligence and efficiency, is not excelled by any body of troops on earth. It contains 14 of the best conditioned regiments of volunteers, the last of which arrived this morning. Yet these have never been under fire. Between 30 and 40 per cent are undrilled, and in one regiment over 300 men had never fired a gun. I request ample protection while at sea at all times for this command from the Navy. This enterprise is so important that I desire to go with this army corps, or to immediately organize another and go with it to join this and capture position No. 2. Now that the military is about to be used, I believe that it should be continued with every energy, making the most judicious disposition of it to accomplish the desired result.

MILES,
Major-General Commanding Army.

June 6, the following telegram was received:

WASHINGTON, D.C., June 6, 1898—2:35 p.m.
Major-General MILES, Tampa, Fla.:

The President wants to know the earliest moment you can have an expeditionary force ready to go to Puerto Rico large enough to take and hold island without the force under General Shafter.

R.A. ALGER, Secretary of War.

and reply sent that such an expedition could be ready in ten days.

It was found that many of the steamers were not suitable for transport service, they having been built largely for freight steamers and not equipped for properly conveying troops and munitions of war. The accumulation of the large amount of supplies and war material for the 70,000 men above mentioned at Tampa had crowded that place, and, owing to the absence of depots and facilities for handling that amount of material, occasioned great delay in properly equipping the expedition intended for Santiago. It was, however, supplied, and orders (hereto attached) given for the proper embarkation of the troops, which were ready to sail June 8, 1898. The movement was, however, suspended, owing to the report received that Spanish war vessels had been seen in the Nicholas Channel. The expedition, consisting of 803 officers and 14,935 men, finally sailed on June 14, leaving some 10,000 troops that were expected to move with this expedition, but which could not do so, owing to insufficient transportation.

IN THE FIELD, Tampa, Fla., June 11, 1898.

SIR: Please ascertain whether the following has been attended to in connection with your fleet of transports:

Have commanding officers required their transport officers to make a list of the contents of each ship, where stored, the bulk of such stores, and an estimate of how many wagon loads there are in each vessel? Do the commanding officers of organizations know exactly where their supplies are? Have arrangements been made in order that if so many rations of any kind, ammunition, hospital supplies, etc., should be required, that they would know at once where they can be found? Have transports been supplied with stern anchors to hold them in place and afford a lee for the landing of troops in case of necessity when sea is somewhat rough? What kind of small boats are supplied to each ship for the landing of the troops of that ship? Has a list been made of them and the total number of men they can safely land at one time? Have stores been put upon transports with a view that each organization's should be complete?

The great importance of these details can not be overestimated. In landing, stores intended for one command are liable to be sent to another, and the necessity of having stores that may be needed accessible at once is manifest.

I would suggest that thorough attention be required to every detail in order to insure perfect order in the disembarking of your command.

Respectfully yours,

MILES,
Major-General, Commanding.

GEN. WILLIAM R. SHAFTER
Port Tampa, Fla.

The following dispatch was received June 15:

WASHINGTON, D.C., June 15, 1898.
Major-General MILES, Tampa, Fla.:

Important business required your presence here; report at once. Answer.

R.A. ALGER, Secretary of War.

On June 24, 1898, I submitted a plan of campaign as follows:

Headquarters of the Army,
Washington, D.C., June 24, 1898.

SIR: I have the honor to submit the following:

With the capture of Santiago de Cuba it is expected that we will have several thousand Spanish prisoners; and with the capture of the second objective position (Puerto Rico), now under consideration, it is expected we will add to the number, making, it is hoped, in the aggregate at least 30,000 prisoners.

After the capture of the position next after Santiago de Cuba, it would be, in my judgment, advisable to take some deep-water harbors on the northern coast of Cuba, which would be available, not only for our army, but also for the navy, as safe ports for our transports, supply ships, and naval vessels between Key West and Puerto Rico. It is also important that we should select some point at which to disembark our mounted troops and light artillery, with which our Government is well supplied. We will have in a few weeks upward of 15,000 cavalry. This force, with the light artillery and a small body of infantry, will make a most formidable army corps with which to conduct a campaign in the interior of Cuba.

The most available point, it appears to me, would be the harbor of Neuvitas, which has 28½ feet of water. From there the command could move to Puerto Príncipe, one of the principal cities in the Island of Cuba. Using that as a base, it could move through the rolling country, which is reported to be free from yellow fever, to Morón and Taguayabón, and thence to Villa Clara; or, by a more southern route, from Puerto Príncipe to Ciego de Ávila; thence to Spíritus, and thence to Villa Clara. A road could be built at the rate of 5 miles per day as that army corps marches; also we would find two railroad bases between Puerto Príncipe and Villa Clara.

To move mounted troops over from Florida to Cuba and make this march would undoubtedly consume the time up to nearly the 30th of September.

This army corps would also have the assistance of all the available forces of García and Gómez, and would by that time be occupying practically two-thirds of the Island of Cuba.

If no serious force was encountered this army corps could continue its march to the south side of Havana. If a large force of Spanish troops, sufficient to check its march, was moved to the vicinity of Villa Clara, then the entire army with which we purpose to invade Cuba could be moved between the forces at Villa Clara and Havana, dividing the Spanish forces and defeating them in detail.

I make this suggestion as having three advantages: First, we could employ at reasonable compensation such prisoners as desired occupation in road building; second, we could move into the interior of Cuba our large cavalry command without serious molestation; third, we would be operating during the rainy or sickly season in the most healthful parts of Cuba, practically free from yellow fever, and at the same time be occupying a large portion of the enemy's territory.

If this proposition does not meet with favor, then, after the capture of Santiago de Cuba and other places to the east, we could move the entire force to the west of Havana and conduct the campaign from the deep harbors on that coast. My judgment, however, is decidedly in favor of the first plan of campaign.

Before reaching Villa Clara we would undoubtedly have upwards of 50,000 prisoners, and if we could, by judicious, humane treatment, use them in a way that would be advantageous to themselves as well as to our interests, I think it would be advisable. There would be one great danger in moving them to our own territory and establishing a large camp of prisoners, and that is, that they would bring the germs of disease with them and spread them among our own people, as many Americans would have to be employed on the ships and railroads, together with the guards necessary to control them.

Very respectfully,

NELSON A. MILES
Major-General Commanding.

The Secretary of War.

The main features of the above plan of campaign were submitted in my letters of May 26 and 27.

The following order was received *to organize an expedition for operation against the enemy in Cuba and Puerto Rico:*

Washington, D.C., June 26, 1898.

SIR: By direction of the President an expedition will be organized with the least possible delay, under the immediate command of Major-General Brooke, United States Army, consisting of three divisions taken from the troops best equipped in the First and Third Army Corps and two divisions from the Fourth Army Corps, for movement and operation against the enemy in Cuba and Puerto Rico. The command under Major-General Shafter, or such part thereof as can be spared from the work now in hand, will join the foregoing expedition, and you will command the forces thus united in person.

Transports for this service will be assembled at Tampa with the least possible delay. The naval forces will furnish convoy, and cooperate with you in accomplishing the object in view. You will place yourself in close touch with the senior officer of the Navy in those waters, with the view to harmonious and forceful action.

Estimates will be made by you immediately in the several staff departments for the necessary supplies and subsistence, such estimates to be submitted to the Secretary of War.

For the information of the President, copies of all orders and instructions given by you from time to time will be forwarded on the day of their issue to the Adjutant-General of the Army. Also daily reports of the state and condition of your command will be made to the Secretary of War direct.

It is important that immediate preparation be made for this movement, and, when ready, report to this Department for further instructions.

Very respectfully,

R.A. ALGER,
Secretary of War.

Maj. Gen. NELSON A. MILES,
United States Army, Washington, D.C.

While these movements were in progress the capture of Puerto Rico had already been determined upon and transports were being gathered for an expedition for that purpose. It was my opinion that during the interim before such an expedition could be equipped and organized, it would be advisable to utilize a small portion of the troops then available at Tampa to take the Isle of Pines, off the south coast of Cuba. It was then occupied by a very small force of Spanish troops, and was being used as a base for smuggling supplies to the Island of Cuba. It was advisable, in my opinion, to take the Isle of Pines, as it was a healthful sanitarium, entirely free from yellow fever, swept by the ocean breezes, had a high altitude, and, there being large public buildings on the island, it would have been most suitable for large hospitals and camps of prisoners. I also deemed it advisable to take the deep-water harbor of Nipe, on the north coast of eastern Cuba, in order to make it available for our naval ships and transports in case of hurricanes, which were liable to occur at that season of the year, and also for use as a coaling station.

The yellow fever at this time had broken out in Mississippi, and it was feared it might spread over the Southern States. The safety of the military camps was then a matter of great importance, and after consulting with the best authorities I advised that the troops at Mobile be sent to Mount Vernon, Ala., which has been a refuge for the garrisons on the Gulf for many years; also to Miami, on the east coast of Florida, another place of refuge, and also to Fernandina, Fla., in order to isolate the troops as much as possible from railroad centers, where they would be likely to become infected by the traveling public. I also recommended that a portion of the troops at Chickamauga be sent to Fernandina and also to Puerto Rico, and at the same time suggested that troops be stationed in the Loudoun and Shenandoah valleys, in the vicinity of Antietam, and on Long Island Sound. These recommendations were made in order to avoid overcrowding the larger camps at Chickamauga and Camp Alger.

During this time Lieutenant Rowan had returned from his journey to Cuba, bringing with him to Washington Brigadier-General Collazo and Lieutenant-Colonel Hernández, of General García's staff. He also brought very important information concerning the active operations of the Cubans against the Spanish troops, and the location and strength of the Spanish forces in the eastern part of Cuba, numbering at that time some 31,000 men. The two Cuban officers mentioned accompanied me to Tampa, and Colonel Hernández, having received permission from the Navy Department to be conveyed by a United States vessel to the harbor of Banes, carried the following letter from me to General García:

Headquarters of the Army,
In the Field, Tampa, Fla., June 2, 1898.

DEAR GENERAL: I am very glad to have received your officers, General Enrique Collazo and Lieut. Col. Carlos Hernández, the latter of whom returns to-night with our best wishes for your success.

It would be a very great assistance if you could have as large a force as possible in the vicinity of the harbor of Santiago de Cuba, and communicate any information, by signals, which Colonel Hernández will explain to you, either to our navy or to our army on its arrival, which we hope will be before many days.

It would also assist us very much if you could drive in and harass any Spanish troops near or in Santiago de Cuba, threatening or attacking them at all points, and preventing, by every means, any possible reenforcement coming to that garrison. While this is being done, and before the arrival of our army, if you can seize and hold any commanding position to the east or west of Santiago de Cuba, or both, that would be advantageous for the use of our artillery, it will be exceedingly gratifying to us.

With great respect and best wishes, I remain, very respectfully,
NELSON A. MILES,
Major-General, Commanding United States Army.
Lieutenant-General García, Cuban Army.

This letter was sent in anticipation of the movement of the command under General Shafter, which sailed twelve days later. Colonel Hernández left Key West with it June 2; General García received it June 6, and I received his reply by cable June 9, of which the following is a copy:

Mole St. Nicholas (via Washington), June 9, 1898.
GENERAL MILES,
Commanding United States Army:
[García's reply on June 6 to your letter of June 2:]
Will take measures at once to carry out your recommendation, but concentration of force will require some time. Roads bad and

Cubans scattered. Will march without delay. Santiago de Cuba well fortified with advanced intrenchments, but believe good artillery position can be taken. Spanish force approximate 12,000 between Santiago de Cuba and Guantánamo, 3,000 militia. Will maintain a Cuban force near Holguín to prevent sending reenforcements to Santiago.

[The above given to me by Admiral Sampson to forward to you. ALLEN.]

Also, the following is an extract from a cablegram from Admiral Sampson to the Secretary of the Navy, which was repeated to me at Tampa, June 12, for my information:

Mole St. Nicholas, Haiti.

General Miles's letter received through Colonel Hernández on June 6. García regards his wishes and suggestions as orders, and immediately will take measures to concentrate forces at the points indicated, but he is unable to do so as early as desired on account of his expedition to Banes Port, Cuba, but he will march without delay. All of his subordinates are ordered to assist to disembark the United States troops and to place themselves under orders. Santiago de Cuba well fortified, with advanced intrenchments, but he believes position for artillery can be taken as Miles desires. (Approximate) twelve thousand (12,000) regulars and three thousand (3,000) militia between Santiago and Guantánamo. He has sent force in order to prevent aid going to Santiago from Holguín. Repeats every assurance of good will, and desires to second plans.

SAMPSON

It will be observed that General García regarded my requests as his orders, and promptly took steps to execute the plan of operations. He sent 3,000 men to check any movement of the 12,000 Spaniards stationed at Holguín. A portion of this latter force started to the relief of the garrison at Santiago, but was successfully checked and turned back by Cuban forces under General Feria. General García also sent 2,000 men, under Perez, to oppose the 6,000 Spaniards at Guantánamo, and they were successful in their object. He also sent 1,000 men, under General Ríos, against the 6,000 men at Manzanillo. Of this garrison, 3,500 started to reenforce the garrison at Santiago, and were engaged in no less than 30 combats with the Cubans on their way before reaching Santiago, and would have been stopped had General García's request of June 27 been granted. With an additional force of 5,000 men General García besieged the garrison of Santiago, taking up a strong position on the west side and in close proximity to the harbor, and he afterwards received General Shafter and Admiral Sampson at his camp near that place. He had troops in the rear, as well as on both sides of the garrison at Santiago before the arrival of our troops.

The expedition against Santiago, commanded by Major-General Shafter, landed at Daiquirí and Siboney June 22, 23, and 24. The subsequent movements of the expedition against the garrison of Santiago have been described in the several communications and reports of commanding officers there engaged.

On July 2 the following dispatch was received:

Siboney, via Playa del Este, July 1, 1898.

ADJUTANT-GENERAL's OFFICE, UNITED STATES ARMY,

Washington, D.C.:

Had a very heavy engagement to-day, which lasted from 8 a.m. till sundown. We have carried their outer works and are now in possession of them. There is now about three-quarters of a mile of open country between my lines and city. By morning troops will be intrenched and considerable augmentation of force will be there. General Lawton's division and General Bate's brigade, which have been engaged all day in carying El Caney, which was accomplished at 4 p.m., will be in line and in front of Santiago during the night. I regret to say that our casualties will be above 400. Of these not many are killed.

W.R. SHAFTER, Major-General.

And on the next day, the following dispatch was received:

Playa del Este, July 3, 1898.

THE SECRETARY OF WAR, Washington:

We have the town well invested on the north and east, but with a very thin line. Upon approaching it we find it of such a character and the defenses so strong it will be impossible to carry it by storm with my present force, and I am seriously considering withdrawing about 5 miles and taking up a new position on the high ground between the San Juan River and Siboney, with our left at Sardinero, so as to get our supplies to a large extent by means of the railroad, which we can use, having engines and cars at Siboney. Our losses up to date will aggregate a thousand, but list has not yet been made; but little sickness outside of exhaustion from intense heat and exertion of the battle of the day before yesterday and the almost constant fire which is kept up on the trenches. Wagon road to the rear is kept up with some difficulty on account of rains, but I will be able to use it for the present. General Wheeler[266] is seriously ill, and will probably have to go to the rear to-day. General Young[267] also very ill, confined to his bed. General Hawkins[268] slightly wounded in foot. During sortie enemy made last night, which was handsomely repulsed, the behavior of the regular troops was magnificent. I am urging Admiral Sampson to attempt to force the entrance of the harbor, and will have a consultation with him this morning. He is coming to the front to see me. I have been unable to be out during the heat of the day for four days, but am retaining the command. General García reported he holds the railroad from Santiago to San Luis, and has burned a bridge and removed some rails; also that General Pando has arrived at Palma, and that the French consul with about four hundred French citizens came into his lines yesterday from Santiago. Have directed him to treat them with every courtesy possible.

SHAFTER, Major-General.

11.44 a.m.

To which I cabled the following answer:

Headquarters of the Army,
Washington, D.C., July 3, 1898.
GENERAL SHAFTER, Playa del Este, Cuba:

Accept my hearty congratulations on the record made of magnificent fortitude, gallantry, and sacrifice displayed in the desperate fighting of the troops before Santiago. I realize the hardships, difficulties, and sufferings, and am proud that amid those terrible scenes the troops illustrated such fearless and patriotic devotion to the welfare of our common country and flag. Whatever the results to follow their unsurpassed deeds of valor, the past is already a gratifying chapter of history. I expect to be with you within one week with strong reinforcements.

MILES,
Major-General, Commanding.

Headquarters Fifth Army Corps,
Near Santiago, Playa, July 4, 1898.
Maj. Gen. NELSON A. MILES,
Commanding the Army of the United States, Washington:

I thank you in the name of the gallant men I have the honor to

[266]Maj. Gen. Joseph Wheeler (USMA 1859), former Confederate General.
[267]Maj. Gen. S.B.M. Young, who would replace Miles as Lieutenant General in 1903.
[268]Maj. Gen. Hamilton S. Hawkins.

command for the splendid tribute of praise which you have accorded them. They bore themselves as American soldiers always have. Your telegram will be published at the head of the regiments in the morning. I feel that I am master of the situation and can hold the enemy for any length of time. I am delighted to know that you are coming that you may see for yourself the obstacles which this army had to overcome. My only regret is the great number of gallant souls who have given their lives for our country's cause.

SHAFTER.

The following dispatch was also received from General Shafter:

Headquarters Fifth Army Corps,
Camp Near San Juan River,
Via Haiti, Playa del Este, July 4, 1898

ADJUTANT-GENERAL, Washington:

If Sampson will force an entrance with all his fleet to the upper bay of Santiago we can take the place within a few hours. Under these conditions I believe the town will surrender. If the Army is to take the place I want 15,000 troops speedily, and it is not certain that they can be landed, as it is getting stormy. Sure and speedy way is through the bay. Am now in position to do my part.

SHAFTER, Major-General.

On receipt of these communications it was decided that I should go immediately to Santiago with the reenforcements already en route and that were being moved as rapidly as possible. Before leaving Washington it was my purpose to land sufficient forces on the west side of the harbor of Santiago to either open the entrance to our fleet or enfilade the enemy's line and take their position in reverse. I left Washington on the evening of July 7, arrived at Columbia at 5 p.m. on the 8th; thence took a special train to Charleston, reaching there in time to go on board the fast steamer *Yale*, already loaded with 1,500 troops, and, with the steamer *Columbia* accompanying, arrived opposite the entrance of Santiago Harbor on the morning of July 11. The fleet under command of Admiral Sampson was then bombarding the Spanish position. Before reaching Santiago I prepared the following note to Admiral Sampson and forwarded it to him by Captain Wise, commander of the *Yale*, immediately upon our arrival. Admiral Sampson was then on board the flagship *New York*, in close proximity to the entrance of Santiago Harbor, and in full view of Morro Castle.

Headquarters of the Army, On Board
U.S.S. Yale,
Off Siboney, Cuba, July 11, 1898.

Admiral SAMPSON,

Commanding United States Fleet.

SIR: I desire to land troops from the *Yale*, *Columbia*, and *Duchesse* to the west of the bay of Santiago Harbor, and follow it up with additional troops, moving east against the Spanish troops defending Santiago on the west. I will be glad if you can designate the most available point for disembarking the troops, and render all the assistance practicable to the troops as they move east.

Very respectfully,

NELSON A. MILES,
Major-General, Commanding.

Admiral Sampson immediately came on board the *Yale*. I explained to him the purpose of my presence and told him that I desired the cooperation of the Navy in the plan above stated. He cordially acquiesced in the plan, and offered every assistance of his fleet to cover the debarkation of the troops and also to enfilade the Spanish position with the guns of the ships. When this arrangement had been concluded, I went on shore and opened communication with General Shafter. I asked him if he had sufficient troops on the east side of the harbor of Santiago to maintain his position, and he replied that he had. I then gave directions for General Garretson to disembark all the troops on the *Yale*, *Columbia*, and other transports that were there or expected to arrive, viz, the *Duchesse* and *Rita*, whenever he should receive orders.

On the following morning I rode from Siboney to the headquarters of General Shafter. After consulting with him, he sent a communication to General Toral, saying that the Commanding General of the American Army had arrived in his camp with reenforcements, and that we desired to meet him between the lines at any time agreeable to him. He replied that he would see us at 12 o'clock the following day. That evening I became apprised of the fact that negotiations regarding a surrender had been pending between the commanding general and the Spanish commander, but no definite conclusions had been reached. Before leaving Washington I was aware of the fact that yellow fever had developed among our troops and by this time learned that it had spread so much that there were over a hundred cases, and the medical officers were undecided as to the extent it might cripple the command. This was the most serious feature of the situation, and impressed me with the importance of the fact that prompt action should be taken, and I so informed the authorities by cable, suggesting that it was a case where discretionary authority should be granted.

At the appointed time, accompanied by Brig. Gen. J.C. Gilmore and Lieut. Col. Marion P. Maus, of my staff, Major-General Shafter, two of his staff officers, and Major-General Wheeler, and Lieutenant Wheeler,[269] aide-de-camp, I met the Spanish General, Toral, with two of his staff officers and an interpreter. After some conversation between General Toral and General Shafter, I informed General Toral distinctly that I had left Washington six days before; that it was then the determination of the government that this portion of the Spanish forces must either be destroyed or captured; that I was there with sufficient reenforcements to accomplish that object, and that if this was not the case any number of troops would be brought there as fast as steamers could bring them if it took 50,000 men. I told him that we offered him liberal terms, namely, to return his troops to Spain; and I also pointed out the fact that this was the only way in which his forces could return, they being on an island 3,000 miles away from their own country with no means of succor. He said that under the Spanish law he was not permitted to surrender as long as he had ammunition and food, and that he must maintain the honor of the Spanish arms. My reply was that he had already accomplished that; that he must now surrender or take the consequences, and that I would give him until daylight the next morning to decide. He appealed for longer time, saying it was impossible for him to communicate with his superiors, and upon his request I granted him until 12 o'clock noon.

After thoroughly examining the entire position and riding along the trenches from right to left, I returned to General Shafter's headquarters. Before reaching that point I received the following cablegram from Washington in reply to mine of the evening before:

> Washington, D.C., July 13, 1898
> (Received 2.45 p.m.)

Major-General MILES:

> You may accept surrender by granting parole to officers and men, the officers retaining their side arms. The officers and men after parole to return to Spain, the United States assisting. If not accepted, then assault, unless in your judgment an assault would fail. Consult with Sampson and pursue such course as to the assault as you jointly agree upon. Matter should be settled promptly.
>
> R.A. ALGER,
> Secretary of War.

---

[269] 1st Lt. Joseph Wheeler Jr., 4th Artillery (USMA 1895) son of the General.

This left the matter entirely to my discretion—to accept surrender, order an assault, or withhold the same. I sent the following telegram to Admiral Sampson, again requesting him to be ready to cover the landing of the troops, in accordance with our previous arrangement, and fixing the time at 12 o'clock the following day:

> Headquarters Fifth Army Corps,
> Camp near Santiago de Cuba, July 13, 1898.
>
> Admiral W.T. SAMPSON:
>   Commanding United States Naval Forces,
>   North Atlantic Squadron.
>
> SIR: Please have General Henry's command, now on *Yale*, *Columbia*, and *Duchesse*, ready to disembark at noon to-morrow at Cabanas. Telegraph notification will be sent you at flag station, also at Siboney, when to commence the debarkation.
>
> Very respectfully,
>   NELSON A. MILES,
>   Major-General, Commanding United States Army.

I also sent the following telegrams to General Henry, whom I had placed in command of all the infantry and artillery then on board transports:

> Headquarters of the Army,
> Camp near Santiago, July 13, 1898.
>
> General HENRY, Commanding Division:
>   Have asked Admiral Sampson to be prepared to cover your debarkation at Cabanas to-morrow after 12 noon in case Spaniards to not surrender. Notification will be sent him by telegraph and signal when your troops should go ashore. Make the best use of your troops against the Spanish troops. Avoid surprise or exposing your troops to artillery fire.
>
> MILES, Commanding.

> Headquarters of the Army,
> Camp near Santiago, July 13, 1898.
>
> General HENRY, Siboney, Cuba:
>   Major-General commanding directs me to inform you that all movements against the enemy are suspended until 12 noon to-morrow.
>
> J.C. GILMORE, Brigadier-General.

On the morning of July 14, Admiral Sampson's fleet was in position to cover the landing of the troops from the transports, which were in the rear and in close proximity to the small harbor of Cabanas, about 2½ miles west from the entrance of the harbor of Santiago. The ground between the harbor of Cabañas and the right flank of General Shafter's command on the north side of the Bay of Santiago, a distance of between 6 and 7 miles, had been occupied by a small force of Cuban troops, and it was my purpose to occupy this ground with a strong body of infantry, and with some 24 pieces of artillery, where the latter could easily reach Morro Castle, as well as enfilade the Spanish lines in front of General Lawton's division. The Spanish commander was well aware of our designs, as the position and movements of the fleet had been in full view of the officers commanding his troops, and they had reported to him having seen 57 vessels, some of them loaded with troops, menacing that part of his position.

Before the time, 12 o'clock on July 14, the following letter was received from General Toral:

Santiago de Cuba, July 14, 1898.

HONORED SIR: His excellency the general in chief of the army of the Island of Cuba telegraphs from Havana yesterday at 7 p.m. the following: "Believing the business of such importance as the capitulation of that place should be known and decided upon by the Government of His Majesty, I give you notice that I have sent the conditions of your telegram, asking an immediate answer and enabling you also to show this to the General of the American army to see if he will agree to await the answer of the Government, which can not be as soon as the time which he has decided, as communication by way of Bermuda is more slow than by Key West. In the meanwhile your honor and the General of the American army may agree upon capitulation on the basis of repatriation [returning to Spain]." I have the honor to transmit this to you, in case you may [consider] the foregoing satisfactory, that we may designate persons in representation of himself, who, with those in my name, agree to clauses of the capitulation upon the basis of the return to Spain, accepted already in the beginning by the general in chief of this army.

Awaiting a reply, I am, very respectfully, your servant,

JOSÉ TORAL, etc.

General in Chief of the American Forces.

On meeting General Toral by appointment at 12 o'clock that day under a flag of truce, at the same place as before, he stated that he was prepared to surrender his command, and that such action was approved by Captain-General Blanco, who had authorized him to appoint commissioners to agree upon the clauses of capitulation, which he was prepared to do, but that before final action it was proper that the Government at Madrid should know and approve what was done. He said, however, that he was sure that the Government would not fail to indorse his action. His manner was so sincere and the language of General Blanco so positive, that I felt no hesitancy in accepting it in good faith, and stated that we would accept the surrender, under the condition that the Spanish troops should be repatriated by the United States. General Toral stated that he would surrender all the troops in the department of Santiago de Cuba, many of them from 70 to 100 miles distant and against whom not a shot had been fired; yet the activity of the Cuban troops and their dispositions had been such as to render the Spanish positions exceedingly perilous. This desirable result I regarded as an accomplished fact, and sent the following telegram:

Headquarters Cavalry Division, United States Army,
Before Santiago, Cuba, July 14, 1898—12.55 p.m.
The Secretary of War, Washington, D.C.:

General Toral formally surrendered the troops of his army corps and division of Santiago on the terms and understanding that his troops would be returned to Spain. General Shafter will appoint commissioners to draw up the conditions of arrangement for carrying out the terms of surrender. This is very gratifying, and General Shafter and the officers and men of this command are entitled to great credit for their tenacity, fortitude, and in overcoming almost insuperable obstacles which they have encountered. A portion of the army has been infected with yellow fever, and efforts will be made to separate those who are infected and those free from it, and to keep those which are still on board ship separated from those on shore. Arrangements will be immediately made for carrying out the further instructions of the President and yourself.

Miles,
Major-General, Commanding the Army.

I then informed General Shafter that he could appoint the commissioners.

Headquarters Cavalry Division, United States Army,
Before Santiago, Cuba, July 14, 1898.

Sir: You are authorized to appoint commissioners to draw up articles of capitulation on the terms upon which the Spanish division has surrendered, namely, the Spanish troops will be supplied at the expense of the United States, and assembled at such place as may be available for their embarkation on the arrival of the necessary transportation.

The attention of the commissioners should be called to the importance of the return of the people that have fled from the city of Santiago and supplying them with food.

The sending of supplies into the harbor on the Red Cross ship and other vessels.

The removal of all obstructions to the entrance of the harbor, or notification to the fleet that no obstacle will be placed in the way of their removing such obstructions.

Respectfully,

NELSON A. MILES,
Major-General, Commanding the Army.

Maj. Gen. William R. Shafter,
Commanding United States Forces.

After learning the real condition of our troops and their urgent necessities, I gave the following instructions:

Headquarters Cavalry Division, United States Army,
Before Santiago, Cuba, July 14, 1898.

SIR: The Spanish army having surrendered, the terms of capitulation will be carried into effect with as little delay as practicable, on the understanding that these troops will be returned to Spain at the expense of the United States. You will, with as little delay as practicable, place such troops as are not infected with yellow fever in separate camps and, as soon as practicable, report the number that will be available for service with another expedition. In those organizations which have been infected with yellow fever every effort will be made to improve their sanitary condition and to check the spread of the disease by placing them in as healthy camps as possible.

Respectfully,

NELSON A. MILES
Major-General, Commanding the Army.

Maj. Gen. William R. Shafter,
Commanding United States Forces.

Headquarters Cavalry Division, United States Army,
Before Santiago, Cuba, July 14, 1898.

SIR: For a double reason I think it would be advisable to isolate the troops that have just joined your command in separate camps on healthful ground, so as to keep them, if possible, free from infection by yellow fever. It will also form a strong force to meet any force that might by any possiblility come from Holguín. Make your disposition accordingly.

Respectfully,

NELSON A. MILES,
Major-General, Commanding the Army.

Maj. Gen. William R. Shafter,
Commanding United States Forces.

Headquarters Cavalry Division, United States Army,
Before Santiago, Cuba, July 11, 1898.

SIR: The cavalry division are separated from their horses and have been doing most extraordinary service. If it is possible, I desire to have them separated from the rest of the command, and in time they can be put on board ship and sent to other fields, as I desire to have them remounted as soon as possible.

Very respectfully,

NELSON A. MILES
Major-General, Commanding United States Army.

Maj. Gen. William R. Shafter,
Commanding Fifth Army Corps.

The following telegram was received:

Washington, D.C., July 14, 1898.

Major-General MILES:

The conditions are such, on account of yellow fever, I have ordered all further shipments of troops in Santiago cease. We are now arranging transportation of 25,000 men for Puerto Rico. As soon as matters are settled at Santiago I think you had better return and go direct with the expedition. Yellow fever breaking out in camp at Santiago will, I fear, deprive you of the use of our forces there; however, [that] can be determined later. As soon as Santiago falls, the troops must all be put in camp as comfortable as they can be made, and remain, I suppose, until the fever has had its run. It is the most difficult problem to solve, but we are sure you and General Shafter, with the aid of the surgeons in charge, will do all that can be done. Have ordered two immune regiments to Santiago. They will be colored regiments; seems to me will answer to garrison the places as long as our forces have to remain there.

R.A. ALGER,
Secretary of War.

And answered as follows:

> Headquarters Cavalry Division, United States Army,
> Before Santiago, Cuba, July 14, 1898—1.40 p.m.

Hon. SECRETARY OF WAR,
  Washington, D.C.:

  Your second dispatch received. Have already anticipated in part by giving directions for separating the troops that have been infected and kept the troops that came on the *Yale*, *Columbia*, *Duchesse*, and part of those on the *Comanche* ready to disembark at Cabañias, on the west side, where I had made all arrangements for putting the troops in on that side of the harbor and opening the entrance to the bay in conjunction with Admiral Sampson. I will now keep these troops away from the infected districts and will probably let them go ashore at Guantánamo. Other vessels en route will go into the harbor at Guantánamo. Presume that will be a good rendezvous, at least for the troops coming from Tampa. They could come in on the south side and go into a safe harbor there. Will consult with the Admiral with regard to rendezvousing our troops at Puerto Rico or one of the islands immediately adjacent thereto. Will keep you fully apprised of any important information.

> MILES,
> Major-General, Commanding the Army.

The following telegrams were also sent:

> General Wheeler's Camp, July 14, 1898.

GENERAL HENRY, Siboney, Cuba:
  The enemy have surrendered.

> GILMORE, Brigadier-General.

> General Wheeler's Camp, July 14, 1898.

ADMIRAL SAMPSON,
  The New York, Siboney, Cuba:
  The enemy have surrendered. I will be down to see you soon.

> MILES, Major-General.

I left without delay, returning to General Shafter's headquarters, and thence to Siboney. While en route I became fully apprised of the condition of the troops at the fever hospitals, and recognized the great need of immediate action to relieve the threatened danger of the whole command. I had already given directions on the 11th of July for the destruction of the infected habitations at Siboney and other places, and now ordered the Twenty-fourth Regiment of United States Infantry to the yellow fever hospital to police the grounds and nurse the sick. I moved all of the troops then on board transports to Guantánamo.

There was some delay in the final capitulation, owing to the non-agreement at first between the two commissions as to the disposition of the small arms, but it was finally settled by leaving it to the decision of our Government, upon the recommendation of our commissioners that they should be sent to Spain with the troops.

My chief desire, after being sure of the surrender of the garrison at Santiago, was to relieve our troops as speedily as possible by getting them away from the trenches and malarial grounds upon which they were encamped. Dispatches were received and sent as follows:

Headquarters Fifth Army Corps, July 16, 1898.
General MILES:
    They surrender.

SHAFTER.

Headquarters of the Army, On Board U.S.S. Yale,
Off Siboney, Cuba, July 16, 1898.
General SHAFTER,
    Commanding Fifth Army Corps:
    Congratulate you and the Army again. The troops should change camps almost daily, occupying fresh ground until free from the fever. I should think ground parallel to the railroad, where men could bathe in salt water, would be good ground. All blockhouses or places occupied by the Spanish troops should be burned.

MILES,
Major-General, Commanding.

The following indorsement upon the report of board composed of Colonel Greenleaf,[270] chief surgeon of the Army, Maj. Louis A. LaGarde, surgeon, and Drs. Guiteras and Parker, was transmitted to Major-General Shafter, with the following indorsement:

Headquarters of the Army, On Board U.S.S. Yale,
Off Siboney, Cuba, July 17, 1898.
    Respectfully referred to Major-General Shafter, commanding Fifth Army Corps.
    This sanitary recommendation has been drawn up by Colonel Greenleaf, chief surgeon of the army, after a consultation with the yellow fever experts on duty with the army, and the commanding general directs that it be complied with as far as possible, the main

270 Col. Charles R. Greenleaf.

purpose being the immediate isolation of those affected by the disease of yellow fever from the commands; second, frequent change of camp, and in all cases the selection of fresh ground, uncontaminated with the disease, and in every case, prior to occupation, the ground must be rigidly inspected, and, if necessary, burned over; third, the command must be kept away from all habitations, blockhouses, huts, and shanties of every description that have been occupied by Spanish or Cuban people; fourth, the establishment of guards and a rigid quarantine, to keep all native or Spanish inhabitants out of any of the camps and away from any intercourse of whatever description with the troops. This rule must be thoroughly enforced.

The commanding general further directs that you make daily reports to General Gilmore,[271] Adjutant-General at Army headquarters, of the condition of your command, and any matters of importance, mentioning specifically the number of men affected with yellow fever, and giving the organization to which they belong.

You will also separate your camps, as far as practicable, so that any organization that may be more seriously affected will not contaminate the whole command.

By order of Major-General Miles:

J.C. GILMORE,
Brigadier-General, U.S.V.

Headquarters of the Army,
Playa del Este, July 17, 1898—7 p.m.

General SHAFTER:

What is the condition of your command to-day? Sent you report of medical board, with direction for changing camps, etc. If it is thought more advisable to move troops to fresh camps on the foothills or mountain sides, and surgeons advise, act accordingly.

The *St. Paul* should be unloaded immediately, and every transport unloaded and returned as soon as possible as they are needed.

MILES,
Major-General, Commanding

Siboney, July 17, 1898—8.48 p.m.
(Received July 18, 1898)

General MILES, On Board *Yale:*

Letters and orders in reference to movement of camp received and will be carried out. None is more anxious than myself to get

---

271 Brig. Gen. John Curtis Gilmore, Jr. (USMA 1894).

away from here. It seems, from your orders given me, that you regard my force as a part of your command. Nothing will give me greater pleasure than serving under you, General, and I shall comply with all your requests and directions, but I was told by the Secretary that you were not to supersede me in command here. I will furnish the information called for as to condition of command to Gilmore, Adjutant-General, Army Headquarters.

SHAFTER, Major-General

Headquarters of the Army,
Playa del Este, July 18, 1898.
(Sent about 11.30 a.m.)

General SHAFTER:

Telegram received. Have no desire and have carefully avoided any appearance of superseding you. Your command is a part of the United States Army, which I have the honor to command, having been duly assigned thereto, and directed by the President to go wherever I thought my presence required, and give such general directions as I thought best concerning military matters, and especially directed to go to Santiago for a specific purpose. You will also notice that the order of the Secretary of War of July 13 left the matter to my discretion. I should regret that any event would cause either yourself or any part of your command to cease to be a part of mine.

Very truly, yours,
NELSON A. MILES,
Major-General, Commanding United States Army.

Headquarters of the Army,
Playa del Este, July 18, 1898—12 m.

SECRETARY OF WAR, Washington, D.C.:

Regarding your telegram of yesterday, I think it important to go direct to Pt. Fajardo, Cape de San Juan. All appliances for the expedition should be sent there if not already en route to Santiago.

Tugs, lighters, construction corps, engineer corps under Colonel Black at Tampa, General Stone's boats now at Jacksonville, artillery, cavalry, siege train, and infantry, ample hospital supplies and appliances and ambulances, full transportation for all the organizations, should all be directed to go to Puerto Rico; also officers to establish depots of quartermasters, commissary, and ordnance supplies, and quartermaster's funds to the extent of $100,000 for hire of native transportation and purchase of horses, should be sent.

Troops fron the north have been heretofore sent, and I would suggest that Kiefer's Division, from Miami, Fla. or troops from Texas, Louisiana, Mississippi, Alabama, Georgia, and Florida be sent as a part of the command to Puerto Rico.

Paymasters, with ample funds, should be sent at once to Santiago and Puerto Rico.

A strong, fast, seagoing dispatch boat should also be sent to Puerto Rico.

MILES,

Major-General, Commanding

Headquarters of the Army, On Board U.S.S. *Yale*,

Guantánamo Bay, Cuba, July 20, 1898.

General SHAFTER, Commanding:

As there appears to be a decided increase of yellow fever cases in your present location, a move should be made of the entire command to the highest ground practicable where the disease is not prevalent. In some cases you can send the troops to the mountains.

By command of Major-General Miles:

J.C. GILMORE, Brigadier-General.

The following is an extract from the telegram to the honorable Secretary of War concerning their condition:

Headquarters of the Army, On Board U.S.S. *Yale*,

Guantánamo Bay, July 21, 1898.

SECRETARY OF WAR,

Washington, D.C.:

. . . There is not a single regiment of regulars or volunteers with General Shafter's command that is not infected with yellow fever, from one case in the Eighth Ohio to thirty-six in the Thirty-third Michigan.

After consulting with best medical authorities, it is my opinion that the best mode of ridding the troops of the fever will be as I have directed, namely, the troops to go up as high into the mountains as possible, selecting fresh camps every day. If this does not check the spread of the disease, the only way of saving a large portion of the command will be to put them on transports and ship them to the New England coast, to some point to be designated by the Surgeon-General. . .

MILES,

Major-General, Commanding

Before leaving Siboney I issued the following general field order:

General Field Orders No. 1

Headquarters of the Army,

Siboney, Cuba, July 16, 1898.

The gratifying success of the American arms at Santiago de Cuba and some features of a professional character both important and instructive are hereby announced to the Army.

The declaration of war found our coutry with a small army scattered over a vast territory. The troops composing this army were speedily mobilized at Tampa. Fla. Before it was possible to properly equip a volunteer force strong appeals for aid came from the Navy, which had inclosed in the harbor of Santiago de Cuba an important part of the Spanish fleet. At that time the only efficient fighting force available was the United States Army, and in order to organize a command of sufficient strength the cavalry had to be sent dismounted to Santiago de Cuba with the infantry and artillery.

The expedition thus formed was placed under command of Major-General Shafter. Notwithstanding the limited time to equip and organize an expedition of this character, there was never displayed a nobler spirit of patriotism and fortitude on the part of officers and men going forth to maintain the honor of their country. After encountering the vicissitudes of an ocean voyage, they were obliged to disembark on a foreign shore and immediately engage in an aggressive campaign. Under drenching storms, intense and prostrating heat, within a fever-afflicted district, with little comfort or rest, either by day or night, they pursued their purpose of finding and conquering the enemy. Many of them, trained in the severe experience of the great war, and in frequent campaigns on the western plains, officers and men alike exhibited a great skill, fortitude, and tenacity, with results which have added a new chapter of glory to their country's history. . .

While enduring the hardships and privations of such a campaign, the troops generously shared their scanty food with the 5,000 Cuban patriots in arms and the suffering people who had fled from the besieged city. With the twenty-four regiments and four batteries, the flower of the United States Army, were also three volunteer regiments. These, though unskilled in warfare, yet, inspired with the same spirit, contributed to the victory, suffered hardships, and made sacrifices with the rest. Where all did so well it is impossible, by special mention, to do justice to those who bore conspicuous part. But of certain unusual features mention can not be omitted, namely, the cavalry dismounted fighting and storming works as infantry, and a regiment of colored troops, who having shared equally in the heroism as well as the sacrifices, is now voluntarily engaged in nursing yellow fever patients and burying the dead. The gallantry, patriotism, and sacrifices of the American Army, as illustrated in this brief campaign, will be fully appreciated by a grateful country, and the heroic deeds of those who have fought and fallen in the cause of freedom will ever be cherished in sacred memory and be an inspiration to the living.

By command of Major-General Miles:

J.C. GILMORE,

Brigadier-General, United States Volunteers.

I was anxious to proceed as quickly as possible to the Island of Puerto Rico, and so telegraphed the authorities in Washington. After some delay authority was granted, and I started from Guantánamo on July 21 with 3,415 infantry and artillery, together with two companies of engineers and one company of the Signal Corps, on nine transports, convoyed by Captain Higginson's fleet, consisting of the battle ship *Massachusetts* (flagship) and two smaller vessels. The *Yale* and *Columbia* were armed ships, but being loaded with troops, they were practically only available as transports. The above number includes the men who were sick, of which there were nearly a hundred, which reduced our effective force to about 3,300 men, and with that number we moved on the Island of Puerto Rico, at that time occupied by 8,233 Spanish regulars and 9,107 volunteers.

For several days, I had been anxiously looking for the arrival of tugs, launches, and lighters that had been ordered from Santiago, Washington, and Tampa, but none arrived prior to our departure, although I still hoped to meet them as we moved north through the Windward Passage. As all cablegrams concerning our landing place had passed over foreign cables, and as it was important to deceive the enemy (who, I afterwards learned, were marching to and intrenching the ground we were expected to occupy, at the very time we were taking possession of the southern coast of Puerto Rico), and nonarrival of launches, lighters, etc., the question of successfully disembarking the command became somewhat serious; and, after all hope of receiving any appliances of this kind had disappeared, I considered the advisability of finding a safe harbor and capturing necessary appliances from the enemy. I therefore wrote the following letter to Captain Higginson while at sea:

On Board U.S.S. *Yale*,
En route to Puerto Rico, July 22, 1898.

Sir: Our objective point has been Pt. Fajardo or Cape San Juan, but so much time has occurred since the movement was decided in that direction and such publicity has been given the enterprise, that the enemy has undoubtedly become apprised of our purpose. While it is advisable to make a demonstration near the harbor of San Juan near Pt. Fajardo, or Pt. Figueroa, I am not decided as to the advisability of landing at either of these places, as we may find them well occupied by strong Spanish forces. If we draw them to that vicinity, we might find it judicious to quickly move to Puerto Guánica, where there is deep water near the shore—4½ fathoms— and good facilities for landing. We can move from Cape San Juan to that point in twelve hours (one night), and it would be impossible for the Spanish to concentrate their forces there before we will be reinforced. I am also informed that there are a large number of strong lighters in the harbors at Ponce and Guánica, as well as several sailing vessels, which would be useful. As it is always advisable not to do what your enemy expects you to do, I think it advisable after going around the northeast corner of Puerto Rico, to go immediately to Guánica and land this force and move on Ponce, which is the largest city in Puerto Rico. After, or before, this is accomplished we will receive large reinforcements, which will enable us to move in any direction or occupy any portion of the island of Puerto Rico.

Your strong vessels can cover our landing and capture any vessels in the harbor of Ponce, Guánica, or the ports on the southern coast; one light vessel can remain at Cape San Juan to notify transports that will arrive where we have landed, and another could scout off the northwest corner of Puerto Rico to interpret others and direct them where to find us.

Very respectfully,
NELSON A. MILES,
Major-General, Commanding United States Army.
Capt. Francis J. Higginson,
Commanding United States Naval Convoy.

The following messages will further explain the circumstances and the final decision to change our course:

[Flag message for Captain Higginson]
Headquarters of the Army,
On Board U.S.S. *Yale*, July 24, 1898.

General Miles·desires, if possible, you send in advance any naval vessels you can spare to the Port Guánica, reported to be without fortifications or torpedoes. If secured, hold, and report quickly to us, Cape San Juan.

It is more important to land at Guánica than at Cape San Juan. If we can land there, he has troops enough to take the harbor of Ponce and let your fleet into that port.

Possibly all of this can be accomplished by going by the south side. Can send Captain Whitney, who was at Ponce in June, to you, if desired. Answer.

[Signal from Massachusetts, July 24, 1898.]

All right. Guánica it is. Shall I send orders to transport at Cape San Juan to join at Guánica?

[Answer sent by General Miles.]

Better be sure we can land at Guánica, then send for the transports. You can notify all vessels accordingly. Do you want Whitney?

[Captain Whitney was sent to report to Captain Higginson on the *Massachusetts*, with his maps and reports.]

[Flag message for Capt. Francis J. Higginson.]
Headquarters of the Army,
On board U.S.S. *Yale*, July 24, 1898.

SIR: I would call your attention to the railroad between Ponce and Yauco, which I was informed passes right by the sea at one point, El Peñon, about 8 miles west of Ponce. A vessel carrying a gun or two dispatched to this point could prevent re-enforcements from being sent by rail from there to Yauco, or detachment of troops, rolling stock supplies, etc., from being brought into Ponce from Yauco.

Very respectfully,

NELSON A. MILES,
Major-General, Commanding.

[Flag message for Capt. Francis J. Higginson.]
Headquarters of the Army,
U.S.S. *Yale*, July 24, 1898.

Railroad from Ponce to Yauco runs close to sea, 6 to 8 miles west Ponce. Shell or destroy this and prevent Spanish troops moving.

NELSON A. MILES,
Major-General, Commanding Army.

Instead of making a demonstration at Pt. Fajardo, it was finally decided to go direct to Guánica. We arrived off that point near daylight on July 25, and the harbor was entered without opposition. The guns of the *Gloucester,* Commander Wainwright, Commanding, fired several shots at some Spanish troops on shore. The landing of the marines, sailors, and our troops immediately commenced, and after a short skirmish the Spanish troops were driven from the place, and the flag of the United States was raised on the island.

In this, and in subsequent movements, I was very ably and cordially assisted by the Navy, which rendered invaluable aid in disembarking troops and supplies from the transports, using their steam launches to tow the lighters loaded with men and animals from the transports to the shore. Ten lighters were captured at Guánica and seventy at Ponce.

In the subsequent military operations in the interior, I found Captain Whitney's knowledge of the country and the information gained by him in his perilous journey through Puerto Rico to be in every respect thoroughly accurate and of great value to me in the conduct of the campaign.

At daylight on the 26th of July, with six companies of the Sixth Massachusetts and one of the Sixth Illinois Volunteer Infantry, under command of Brigadier-General Garretson,[272] an attack was made upon a strong force of Spaniards near Yauco, and after a spirited and decisive engagement the enemy was defeated and driven back, giving us possession of the railroad and highway to the city of Ponce, leaving them open for the march of General Henry's command to that place.

On the 27th of July Major-General Wilson arrived in the harbor of Guánica with General Ernst's brigade. The same day Commander Davis, of the *Dixie,* entered the port of Ponce and found that it was neither fortified nor mined. The next morning the fleet and transports, with General Wilson's command, moved into the harbor of Port Ponce. The troops disembarked and marched to the city of Ponce, a distance of 2 miles, and we took formal possession of the city and adjacent country, the Spanish troops withdrawing on the military road to San Juan, and our troops being pushed well forward in that direction. In the meantime General Henry's command had been directed to proceed to Ponce, where he arrived shortly afterwards, joining General Wilson's command.

Before landing I was aware of the fact that there existed considerable disaffection among the people in the southern portion of the island, and as our force was so much inferior to the Spanish I deemed it advisable, if possible, to encourage this feeling, and also to impress the people of the island with the good intentions of the American forces, and for this and other reasons I issued the following proclamation:

[272]Brig. Gen. George A. Garretson (USMA 1867).

Headquarters of the Army,
Ponce, Puerto Rico, July 28, 1898.
To the inhabitants of Puerto Rico:

In the prosecution of the war against the Kingdom of Spain by the people of the United States in the cause of liberty, justice, and humanity, its military forces have come to occupy the Island of Puerto Rico. They come bearing the banner of freedom inspired by a noble purpose to seek the enemies of our country and yours, and to destroy or capture all who are in armed resistance. They bring you the fostering arm of a nation of free people, whose greatest power is in its justice and humanity to all those living within its fold. Hence, the first effect of this occupation will be the immediate release from your former political relations, and it is hoped a cheerful acceptance of the Government of the United States. The chief object of the American military forces will be to overthrow the armed authority of Spain and to give to the people of your beautiful island the largest measure of liberty consistent with this military occupation. We have not come to make war upon the people of a country that for centuries has been oppressed, but, on the contrary, to bring you protection, not only to yourselves but to your property, to promote your prosperity, and bestow upon you the immunities and blessings of the liberal institutions of our Government. It is not our purpose to interfere with any existing laws and customs that are wholesome and beneficial to your people so long as they conform to the rules or military administration of order and justice. This is not a war of devastation, but one to give to all within the control of its military and naval forces the advantages and blessings of enlightened civilizations.

NELSON A. MILES,
Major-General, Commanding United States Army.

And the following letter of instructions was published for the information and guidance of all concerned:

Headquarters of the Army,
Port Ponce, Puerto Rico, July 29, 1898.
SIR: I have the honor to inform you that the Major-General Commanding the Army of the United States directs me to communicate to you the following instructions, which will govern you or your successor in the discharge of your duties relating to the military government of the territory now occupied, or hereafter to be occupied, by the United States forces under your command:

The effect of the military occupation of the enemy's territory is the severance of the former political relations of the inhabitants, and it becomes their duty to yield obedience to the authority of the United States, the power of the military occupant being absolute and supreme ban immediately operating upon the political conditions of the inhabitants. But generally, as long as they yield obedience to their new condition, security in their person and property and in all other private rights and relations will be duly respected.

The municipal laws, in so far as they affect the private rights of persons and property and provide for the punishment of crime, should be continued in force as far as they are compatible with the new order of things, and should not be suspended unless absolutely necessary to accomplish the objects of the present military occupation. These laws should be administered by the ordinary tribunals substantially as they were before the occupation. For this purpose the judges and other officials connected with the administration of justice may, if they accept the authority of the United States, continue to administer the ordinary laws of the land as between man and man, under the supervision of the commander of the United States forces. Should it, however, become necessary to the maintenance of law and order, you have the power to replace or expel the present officials, in part or altogether, and to substitute others, and to create such new and supplementary tribunals as may be necessary. In this regard you must be guided by your judgment and a high sense of justice.

It is to be understood that under no circumstances shall the criminal courts exercise jurisdiction over any crime or offense committed by any person belonging to the Army of the United States, or any retainer of the Army, or person serving with it or any persons furnishing or transporting supplies for the Army; nor over any crime or offense committed on either of the same by any inhabitant or temporary resident of the occupied territory. In such cases, except when courts-martial have jurisdiction, jurisdiction to try and punish is vested in military commissions and such provost courts as you may find necessary to establish. The native constabulary, or police force, will, so far as may be practicable, be preserved. The freedom of the people to pursue their accustomed occupations will be abridged only when it may be necessary to do so.

All public funds and securities belonging to the Spanish Government in its own right, and all movable property, arms, supplies, etc., of such Government, should be seized and held for such uses as proper authority may direct. And whatever real property the Spanish Government may have held should be taken charge of and administered; the revenues thereof to be collected and reported for such disposition as may be made of the same, under instructions from these headquarters.

All public means of transportation, such as telegraph lines, cables, railways, telephone lines, and boats belonging to the Spanish Government, should be taken possession of and appropriated to such use as may be deemed expedient.

Churches and buildings devoted to religious worship, and all schoolhouses, should be protected.

Private property, whether belonging to individuals or corporations, is to be respected and can be confiscated only as hereafter indicated. Means of transportation, such as telegraph lines, and cables, railways, and boats, may, although they belong to private individuals or corporations, be seized by the military occupant, but unless destroyed under military necessity, are not to be retained.

As a result of military occupation of this country, the taxes and duties payable by the inhabitants to the former government become payable to the military occupant. The money so collected to be used for the purpose of paying the necessary and proper expenses under military government.

Private property will not be taken except upon the order of brigade and division commanders in cases of absolute military necessity, and when so taken for the public use of the Army, will be paid for in cash at a fair valuation.

All ports and places in actual possession of our forces will be opened to the commerce of all neutral nations, as well as our own, in articles not contraband of war, upon payment of the prescribed rates of duty which may be in force at the time of the importation.

A memorandum in respect to the jurisdiction of military commissions and provost courts is herewith inclosed.

Very respectfully,

J.C. GILMORE,
Brigadier-General, US.V.

Maj. Gen. J.H. WILSON, U.S.V.,
Commanding First Division, First Corps, Ponce, Puerto Rico.

Brigadier-General Schwan[273] arrived July 31, and was subsequently instructed to disembark part of the Eleventh Infantry, under Colonel DeRussey,[274] at Guánica, and march to Yauco and thence west with an

---

[273] Brig. Gen. Theodore Schwan, a native of Germany, worked his way up from Private in 1857, awarded the Medal of Honor for Civil War service.
[274] Col. Isaac D. DeRussey, 11th Inf.

additional force of two batteries of artillery and one troop of cavalry. [The letter of instructions addressed to General Schwan followed.]

Major-General Brooke arrived July 31, and was directed to disembark his command at Arroyo, and move thence to Cayey. On August 5 he had a sharp engagement with the Spanish troops at Guayama, which was finally occupied by our forces. An action took place near Guayama on August 8, the Spaniards being driven from their position farther in the direction of Cayey. Arrangements for investing and attacking that place, both directly and in the rear, were promptly made, and were about to be consummated when the order for cessation of hostilities was issued.

On August 9, General Schwan's command advanced from Yauco westward, occupying successively the important towns of Sabana Grande, San Germán, Lajas, Cabo Rojo, and Hormigueros, finally entering the city of Mayagüez, after a sharp engagement on August 10 near Hormigueros, in which a strong force of the enemy was engaged. In this action, in which artillery, infantry, and cavalry were admirably employed, the Spanish forces, although strongly posted on ground of their own selection, and skillfully disposed, and being equal in strength to our own, were routed with severe loss, while our own loss was but one killed and sixteen wounded. The enemy was pursued toward Lares, which town would have been occupied August 13 by our troops had not the order to suspend hostilities been received. Near this place, at the crossing of the Rio Prieto, the advance, under Colonel Burke,[275] overtook the enemy, inflicting upon him a heavy loss in killed, wounded, and drowned.

From August 7-15 General Schwan's troops marched 92 miles, occupied nine towns, made prisoners of war of 162 regulars (including the commander of the military department of Mayagüez), captured and paroled 200 volunteers, captured much valuable material, and cleared the western part of the island of the enemy.

Great credit is due to the troops who composed and the general who commanded the expedition for well-sustained and vigorous action in the face of most trying conditions.

In the meantime General Stone had made a practicable road over what had been considered an impassable trail, by way of Adjuntas and Utuado, through the center of the territory; and General Henry moved his command over that road with the object of intercepting the enemy retreating before General Schwan, and later of effecting a junction with him at Arecibo, his advance troops having already reached the

---

[275] Col. Daniel W. Burke, 17th Inf.

immediate vicinity of that place. This operation would have formed a strong division on the line of retreat of the Spanish troops occupying the western portion of the island.

At Coamo a sharp engagement took place on August 9 between the troops of Major-General Wilson's command, under the personal direction of Brigadier-General Ernst, and the Spanish forces at that place. The United States troops, guided by Lieutenant-Colonel Biddle, of the Engineers, made a skillful flank movement at Coamo, which was admirably executed by the Sixteenth Pennsylvania Regiment Volunteer Infantry, under Colonel Hulings. Passing over a mountain trail, they made a wide detour, coming in rear of the Spanish troops under cover of night, without being discovered, and striking the military road to San Juan, cut off the enemy's retreat. In this engagement the commanding officer of the Spanish troops and the second in command were killed, and 167 prisoners taken.

The road to Aibonito was thus cleared and our troops were advanced and well disposed for the capture of the Spanish forces that had taken positions near that place.

At Asomante, on the 12th of August, the artillery of General Wilson's command began shelling the enemy's position preparatory to an advance in front, while a rear attack was to be made by General Ernst's brigade. This command was under arms and ready to move August 13, when orders were received suspending hostilities.

During the nineteen days of active campaign on the Island of Puerto Rico a large portion of the island was captured by the United States forces and brought under our control. Our forces were in such a position as to make the positions of the Spanish forces, outside of the garrison at San Juan, utterly untenable. The Spaniards had been defeated or captured in the six different engagements which took place, and in every position they had occupied up to that time. The volunteers had deserted their colors, and many of them had surrendered to our forces and taken the oath of allegiance. This had a demoralizing effect upon the regular Spanish troops.

The success of the enterprise was largely due to the skill and good generalship of the officers in command of the different divisions and brigades. Strategy and skillful tactics accomplished what might have occasioned serious loss to achieve in any other way. The loss of the enemy in killed, wounded, and captured was nearly ten times our own, which was only 3 killed and 40 wounded. Thus the island of Puerto Rico became a part of the United States. . .

The artillery was well organized and equipped, under the direction of Brig. Gen. John I. Rodgers, and rendered efficient service wherever used. In my opinion, the siege train should remain as at present organized.

The Bureau of Military Information, under charge of Lieutenant Colonel Wagner, was exceedingly useful, and furnished valuable and important information regarding the nature of the enemy's country and the position of their forces.

The Signal Corps, under Col. James Allen,[276] rendered very excellent service, especially in the use of ocean cables, and the field telegraph and signal detachment under charge of Major Reber[277] rendered most important service. Telegraph and telephone lines were extended hundreds of miles and followed close to the picket and skirmish lines.

While en route to the United States from Puerto Rico, Lieutenant-Colonel Rowan and Lieut. Charles F. Parker made a journey of nearly 2,000 miles through the territory of Cuba, and obtained most valuable information concerning that country and the present condition of its inhabitants, which is both of political and military interest.

I trust that the services of both officers and soldiers in these campaigns may be appreciated by a generous Government and a grateful people. I have recommended a small list of officers who have rendered conspicuous, distinguished, and gallant services for promotion and brevets, and I hope that these recommendations may be favorably considered. I may possibly desire to add a few names to the list already submitted.

It is gratifying to record that during the war not a single defeat has been met, and not a prisoner, color, gun, or rifle has been captured by the enemy. In this respect the war has been most remarkable, and, perhaps, unparalleled. Under all circumstances and in spite of many most trying difficulties the troops have maintained the fortitude of the military forces of the United States.

The experience of the last few months, I trust, will be valuable to the people and Government of the United States. The value of proper defenses for our ports, harbors, and seaport cities, of inestimable wealth, has been demonstrated; and I trust that the system already adopted for coast defenses, the completion of which has been so long delayed, may be carried out without unnecessary delay. I have urged the importance of this in my annual reports for the last thirteen years.

For several years I have urged the importance of the Government's adopting a standard of strength for its military forces that should be commensurate with the interests of the Government in its growth and development, and proportionate to its population and wealth. Spasmodic vibration from a weak and ineffective army to one of gigantic propor-

---

[276]Col. James Allen (USMA 1872).

[277]Maj. Samuel Reber (USMA 1886) who would marry Miles' daughter Cecelia in 1901.

tions does not seem to be best for the welfare and safety of the nation, and I think it more judicious for the Government to fix a certain percentage of trained military men in proportion to the population. The Army would thereby have a more healthy growth as the nation develops. In fact, this system, if once adopted, would be as practicable for one hundred years as for a single decade. The art of war was never so much an exact science as at the present time. The appliances used in modern warfare are constantly changing, and are steadily increasing in effective force; so that it is of the utmost importance that the Government should have the most skilled and efficient forces practicable. I therefore renew my former recommendation that the Government authorize enlistments in the Army at the rate of one soldier to every 1,000 of the population. This would practically continue in service the same number as does the act of Congress, approved April 26, 1898, authorizing the increase of the Regular Army to 62,579 men; but unfortunately there was a provision in that act which required the Army to be reduced to its former peace basis, which was entirely inadequate to the needs and interests of the Government.

I also recommend that Congress authorize an auxiliary force of native troops, to be officered principally by United States Army officers, for service in Puerto Rico, Cuba, and the Philippine Islands, not to exceed two soldiers to every one thousand of the population of those islands. This would give the United States a most valuable auxiliary force. It would pacify the native elements of the islands, and would be in the interests of economy and good government. This force could be used in a way similar to the mounted police in Canada and the British forces in Egypt and India.

I recommend that Congress be requested to take immediate action upon this question of increasing the Army, as I consider it of vital importance. If the system I have suggested is adopted it would give us very nearly an available force of 100,000 men, and would enable the volunteers who enlisted for the war to be returned to their homes without delay.

I desire to make special mention of the officers on my staff, Brig. Gen. J.C. Gilmore, Col. Charles R. Greenleaf, and Lieut. Col. Marion P. Maus, who rendered very important services at Santiago de Cuba and in Puerto Rico, being exposed at the former place to all the dangers of yellow-fever camps; and also Brig. Gen. Roy Stone,[278] Col. James Allen, Lieut. Col. J. W. Clous,[279] Lieut. Col. Arthur L. Wagner,[280] Lieut, Col.

[278] Brig. Gen. Roy Stone, a Brevet Brigadier General in the Civil War, now a volunteer.
[279] Judge Advocate and Brig. Gen. of Volunteers John W. Clous, a native of Germany.
[280] Lt. Col. Arthur L. Wagner (USMA 1875).

William M. Black, Lieut. Col. Francis Michler,[281] Lieut. Col. Andrew Black, Capt. Henry H. Whitney, and Capt. W.S. Scott,[282] who rendered most efficient and valuable services in Puerto Rico.

Accompanying this report are five maps of operations in Cuba and four maps of operations in Puerto Rico.

Very respectfully, your obedient servant,

NELSON A. MILES,
Major-General, Commanding.

The Secretary of War.

ANNUAL REPORT OF THE MAJOR-GENERAL COMMANDING THE ARMY
Headquarters of the Army,
Washington, D.C., October 17, 1899.

. . .At the time of my last annual report the strength of the Army was 9,453 officers and 215,922 men, of which 2,326 officers and 58,310 men belonged to the Regular Army, and 7,127 officers and 157,612 men comprised the Volunteer Army. Subsequent to that time a large number of troops were moved to Cuba, but the majority of them were returned to the United States during the following winter and spring months.

The following statement shows the number of troops present in Cuba on the dates specified:

Date.	Officers.	Men.
August 31, 1898	335	7,342
September 30, 1898	337	7,257
October 31, 1898	364	7,963
November 30, 1898	355	7,945
December 31, 1898	364	7,833
January 31, 1899	1,802	41,357
February 28, 1899	1,858	40,873
March 31, 1899	1,209	25,197
April 30, 1899	647	14,114
May 31, 1899	567	12,424
June 30, 1899	568	12,184

At the present time there are 391 officers and 10,796 men in Cuba. In Puerto Rico there are 108 officers and 3,255 men, which includes a battalion of native troops recently organized and consisting of 400 men.

---

[281]Lt. Col. Francis Michler (USMA 1870).
[282]Capt. William S. Scott (USMA 1880).

On October 1 there were in the Philippine Islands 971 officers and 31,344 men, while there were en route to those islands at that time 546 officers and 16,553 men.

In Alaska there is now a force of 15 officers and 484 men, and in the Hawaiian Islands there are 12 officers and 453 men.

All of the volunteer troops first sent to the Philippine Islands have been returned to the United States and mustered out, or are under orders to return and be mustered out of service. . .

Of the 25 United States volunteer regiments (the Twenty-sixth to the Forty-ninth Infantry, inclusive, and Eleventh Cavalry) some are already in the Philippines, others are en route, and the balance are being rapidly organized for service in those islands.

The demand for troops for foreign service has been unusual, and has been somewhat severe upon them, especially those of the Regular Army. Within the last eighteen months several regiments have been required to leave their stations in the extreme north, move to the islands of the West Indies, there engage in a campaign in summer, return to northern stations in the autumn and winter, and move again to tropical islands in the Pacific and engage in campaigns under the most difficult circumstances. Rarely in any service have troops experienced such unusual changes in climate as those above indicated, yet under all circumstances and at all times the utmost loyalty, fortitude, and faithful performance of duty have been manifested on the part of the troops. In nearly all engagements where the troops have been brought into contact with the enemy they have invariably acted on the offensive, and in not a single instance have they suffered defeat. The intelligence, discipline, and fidelity of both officers and men have been most commendable.

Owing to the additional and extraordinary expense placed upon officers while serving in the Philippine Islands, Cuba, Puerto Rico, and the Hawaiian Islands, it is recommended that they be allowed the same percentage of the increase of pay that is now provided by law for the enlisted men.

It is also recommended that officers of the Army with a creditable record who served during the civil war shall be granted the same consideration concerning rank and pay as has been accorded officers of the Navy by section II, act approved March 3, 1899.

As far as organization is concerned, the Army is in a transition state. From 1874 to 1898 it was confined to a minimum strength of 25,000 men. By the act approved March 8, 1898, two regiments of artillery were added, which increased the enlisted strength of the Army to 26,610. When the war with Spain broke out, Congress, by the act approved April 26, 1898, authorized an increase in the strength of the Army to 62,579 men. Under the act approved March 2, 1899, it was recruited to

65,000 men, which was approximately one soldier to every 1,000 of the population, according to the last census. Under the last-mentioned act authority was also given to organize an auxiliary force of 35,000 volunteers, and under that provision the 25 regiments of volunteers above mentioned have been organized.

It is believed that this force will be ample for the service required of it up to the time authorized, viz, July 1, 1901. It is gratifying to note that the Government has authorized a military force which seems commensurate with its requirements, magnitude, and institutions. . .

During the past few years rapid progress has been made in the equipment of the Atlantic, Pacific, and Gulf coasts with modern defenses, and if the general plan is carried out it is hoped that in a short time our coast will be in proper condition of defense.

Some very important discoveries have been made in relation to ordnance, projectiles, and high explosives, and after careful, thorough, and exhaustive tests appliances have been adopted which will greatly increase the efficiency of our armament.

Very respectfully, your obedient servant,

NELSON A. MILES,
Major-General, Commanding.

The Secretary of War.

ANNUAL REPORT OF THE LIEUTENANT-GENERAL COMMANDING THE ARMY
Headquarters of the Army,
Washington, D.C., October 29, 1900.

. . .Under authority of the act of Congress, approved March 2, 1899, the Army of the United States was increased to approximately 65,000 men; and an auxiliary force of volunteers of 35,000 was organized, making a total military strength of 100,000 men.

At the date of my last annual report there were in the Philippine Islands 971 officers and 31,344 enlisted men; and there were en route for service in those islands 546 officers and 16,553 men—the latter force being principally in California. Since that time an additional force ordered to China was diverted to the Philippine Islands, making a total of 98,668 men sent to the archipelago. Of this number 15,000 volunteers, first sent to that country in 1898, together with the sick and disabled, have been returned to the United States, leaving the present time in the islands, according to last report, 2,367 officers and 69,161 enlisted men. Fifteen hundred men have been left in China to act as a guard for the American legation in that country and for other purposes.

While these changes have been made, the force in Alaska has been increased to 41 officers and 1,088 enlisted men, and the force in Cuba reduced to 260 officers and 5,468 enlisted men, and in Puerto Rico to 98 officers and 2,406 enlisted men, leaving 998 officers and 18,898 enlisted men in the United States (the lowest number since 1861), of which number there are 2,600 recruits under orders to fill regiments stationed without the limits of the United States.

The urgent demand for troops on remote stations has reduced the number in the United States to a much smaller force than has been maintained at any time during the last thirty-nine years. In fact, the number is such much reduced that at the present time there are not one-fourth enough troops to properly care for or man the fortifications which have been erected on the Atlantic, Pacific, and Gulf coasts at an expenditure of nearly $55,000,000.

In addition to the artillery deficiency the present home force is not sufficient to properly occupy the interior garrisons or to protect life and property on the Western frontier, and what is still more serious, the Government is left without the necessary reserve to relieve troops from serving in tropical countries a longer period of time than would seem to be consistent with the preservation of their health and good condition.

The Condition of the Army

Considering the kind and character of the service that has been rendered by the United States Army during the past year in the different campaigns, engagements, and affairs in which it has participated, too much credit can not be given to it for maintaining under the most trying circumstances the same high standard of excellence that it has sustained for more than one hundred years.

This standard of efficiency is due to the training and strict discipline of West Point and to the high sense of honor that has been inculcated at that institution; to the practical and scientific instruction that the officers of the different arms of the service have received at the Artillery School, Fort Monroe, Va., at the Light Artillery and Cavalry School, Fort Riley, Kans., at the Infantry and Cavalry School, Fort Leaven-worth, Kans., and to the valuable instruction and discipline imparted to the troops at every military station and in every military camp in the United States.

While the achievements of the Army and Navy during the Spanish-American war were most creditable to both branches of the service and highly gratifying to the country, yet the war was of such short duration that the Army had not sufficient opportunity to fully demonstrate its capacity and efficiency. Enough, however, was accomplished by the skill and fortitude of the troops to afford great satisfaction, not only to those in the service, but to all interested in the welfare of the Army. For the past three years the Army has been engaged in extensive field service, and has experienced in two hemispheres the many hardships of actual warfare. In the many affairs in which the troops have met an enemy in the field they have on all occasions and under all circumstances exhibited courage and stability, excellent marksmanship, and faithful devotion to duty.

During the past year the following-named gallant officers were either killed in action or died of wounds received in line of duty: Major General Lawton, Colonel Liscum, Majors Howard and Logan, Captains McGrath, Reilly, Mitchell, Warwick, Smith, Godfrey, Murphy, Crenshaw, French, Brown, and Bently, First Lieutenants Cheney, Ledyard, Koehler, Schenck, Galleher, and Evans, and Second Lieutenants Boutelle, Keyes, Way, Cooper, Smith Wagner, and Davis, together with a long list of brave soldiers, besides a large list of officers and soldiers who have died of disease incident to service in tropical countries.

These casualties bear evidence of the severity of the service in which the troops were engaged and of their heroism and fidelity.

During the past year our Army was called upon to perform an additional arduous and trying service, namely, the succor or rescue of the American legation besieged at the capital of the Chinese Empire. When the necessity for a military force in China arose the Ninth Regiment of Infantry was quickly moved from the Philippine Islands to Taku, China, and thence to Tientsin. In the battle of Tientsin the American troops were called upon to occupy and hold a most difficult position, in which they were subjected to a concentrated fire from Mauser rifles and machine guns in the hands of troops who had been instructed in their use, if not commanded at the time, by skilled European officers; and notwithstanding the severity of the fire and the serious loss in killed and wounded the troops maintained their position with the greatest spirit and fortitude. Indeed, it would be difficult to name any occasion on which troops engaged in action were better commanded, were more steady under fire, or where they made the soldier's sacrifice with more unselfish patriotism, or rendered a higher tribute to the honor of their country.

Colonel Liscum,[283] their commander, fell while leading his troops, and it is fitting that especial mention should be made of his and their heroic service. Great reverence should be accorded the memory of Col. E.S. Liscum, commanding the Ninth Infantry, who, up to the time of his death, commanded his force with undaunted courage and marked ability.

[283]Col. Emerson H. Liscum, 9th Inf. was killed while carrying his Regiment's colors in a charge.

After the death of Colonel Liscum the command of the American force engaged in the battle of Teintsin devolved upon Maj. Jesse M. Lee,[284] of the Ninth Regiment of Infantry, who by his sound judgment in the disposition of his command and personal gallantry while directing the firing line in the advance and the successful withdrawal of his command at nightfall sustained the honorable reputation acquired by him during the civil and subsequent wars.

Two battalions of the Fourteenth Infantry, under command of Col. A.S. Daggett,[285] and Battery F, Fifth Artillery, commanded by Captain Reilly,[286] were dispatched from the Philippine Islands July 15, and the Sixth Cavalry was sent from San Francisco, July 3, to follow the advance of the Ninth Infantry; all the forces in China being placed under the command of Major-General Chaffee.

In the advance of Pekin [sic] the American troops were conspicuous for their zeal and courage as well as for their excellent discipline and noble conduct under most trying circumstances. The heroism and fidelity of the American soldier was again demonstrated in the fall of Captain Reilly, of Battery F, who was killed in action at the capture of the Chinese capital. This officer was an ideal soldier, had a distinguished record for his services in the civil war and in Cuba, and, like Colonel Liscum, was without fear and without reproach.

During the past year the men of the volunteer force, authorized and located as previously indicated, have been sent to the Philippine Islands, where, in conjunction with the regular troops, they have rendered good service. Under the act of Congress, however, they will have to be withdrawn and discharged before the 1st of July, 1901. This necessity gives a very short term of service in the archipelago, and in order to meet the condition imposed by law and at the same time bring the volunteers back to the United States by the United States transport steamers—which are the only available means of transportation—it will be necessary to begin their return almost immediately.

Since the date of my last report the artillery school has been re-established at Fort Monroe, under very favorable auspices (as well as the cavalry and light artillery school at Fort Riley); but unfortunately, owing to the large proportion of our military force on foreign stations, it has not been practicable to locate a sufficient number of troops, batteries, and companies at Fort Riley and Fort Leavenworth to fully carry out the purposes for which the cavalry and light artillery school and the infantry and cavalry school have been created.

---

[284]Lt. Col. Jesse M. Lee of Indiana, would be promoted Brigadier General in 1902.

[285]Col. Aaron S. Daggett soon to be promoted Brigadier General.

[286]Gallant Captain Henry Joseph Reilly, a native of Ireland, who enlisted as Private in 1866.

Marked progress has been made in locating heavy batteries for the defense of the Atlantic, Gulf, and Pacific coasts. In this great work approximately $55,000,000 have already been expended, and it will require, to carry out the general plan now under consideration, at least $45,000,000 more. . .

Very great improvement has been made, under the direction of the Board of Ordnance and Fortification, in the development of an explosive invented by Dr. Tuttle, of Tacoma, Wash., which is believed to be superior in effectiveness to all known safe military explosives. It is perfectly safe to transport and handle, and can be used in any service projectile; can be thrown any distance within the capacity of any high-power gun through steel armor plate, and exploded with most destructive effect. Important action has also been taken by the same board in the matter of larger caliber high-power guns, and improvements have been developed in field and mountain artillery, sufficient success having been achieved to indicate that, within the next twelve months, greater advance will be made in seacoast and field artillery than has been accomplished during the last two decades. In fact, the history of recent wars has demonstrated the great advancement, as well as the destructive power of modern artillery, especially in rapid-fire and machine guns.

In future wars both branches of this arm of the service must play a more important part than ever before. The safety of the great harbors of the country, of the commercial ports, where is concentrated a great percentage of the population, as well as a large proportion of the wealth of the nation, depends upon the efficiency and the power of the coast defenses. They not only defend the wealth and treasures of the nation, but they protect the foundries, factories, workshops, savings banks, and the homes of the great masses of our laboring people. The service of modern artillery has now become an intricate science, requiring great study, skill, and efficiency on the part of the officers and of the enlisted men, and the pay of the latter should be increased in proportion to the skill and intelligence required for such service. I may say that those in this branch of the service have manifested great interest and efficiency in their profession.

Although we have not reached the serious consideration of small arms, yet sufficient has been demonstrated during the past few years in the development of automatic and semiautomatic weapons to make it apparent that a change of type and great improvements must be made in the near future. This subject will be brought to your attention during the coming year.

During the last few years great advance has been made in the application of steam and electric power to mobiles, automobiles, and locomobiles, or self-moving vehicles for the transportation of persons and material; and, while considerable progress has been made in utilizing this new military motor-power in European armies, there has been but little development along this line in our Army. In my opinion, it is perfectly practicable to employ this means of transportation in many ways for military purposes. In fact, I do not think it wise to longer delay the practical application of such a well-known power; and I therefore recommend that a liberal appropriation or allotment be given for the purchase of the necessary appliances for use in the different military departments.

I renew my recommendation that authority be granted to the War Department to dispose of, by sale, certain reservations and military posts that have been, or may be, abandoned on account of being no longer of military value; and that the proceeds of such sales may be utilized in purchasing suitable lands that are imperatively required for the immediate use of the garrisons now at the artillery posts and at other points for the better equipment of the service. This plan has been recently adopted by the French Republic with great benefit to their service.

There is needed in the immediate vicinity of the national capital suitable grounds for the encampment of regular troops whenever assembled and for State troops when occasionally required; and I call attention to the necessity for Congress to make the requisite appropriation for putting the ground near the capital, known as Potomac Flats, in suitable condition for such purpose and for such other purposes as may be required. Its condition now is most unsatisfactory, and is a menace to the health of the people living at the national capital.

The events of the past two years and a half have resulted in a condition that the nation must prepare to meet. The need for an efficient and well-organized land force for an indefinite period in the future is most obvious, and the organization of such a force can not wisely be avoided. There are weighty reasons why such a service as is now demanded of the Army can not well be performed by temporary organizations. There is a marked distinction between permanent and temporary organizations. The officers and men of the latter do not sever their connection with their vocations, and a prolonged service makes a demand upon them which should not be required. The especial efficiency of temporary organizations is illustrated in the accomplishment of some specific end, usually requiring a comparatively short time to accomplish.

There is also a highly economic question involved, especially where, as now, the service must be performed on a very remote field. The temporary organizations now serving in the Philippine Islands, although their whole period of service will cover nearly two years, will yet have rendered but little more than one year of service in the field, and the expense of the double transfer adds enormously to the cost of the organization.

Besides these considerations, the need of an increased regular force is urgent, in order to afford a reserve for the relief of regiments that are serving at tropical and subtropical stations. The permanent organization is principally so serving, and some regiments have been more than two years at unhealthy stations and should be relieved.

I have repeatedly advocated a principle, which seems to me to be safe and logical, by which to determine the strength of our regular military establishment. It is based on the population of the United States. Surely one skilled, trained soldier to every thousand of population can not be a menace to the established liberties and free institutions of this great Republic, and such a proportion would give the least force that is commensurate with the necessities, character, and magnitude of the nation. Our Army is a school in which patriotism constitutes the fundamental principle. The act of enlistment is a voluntary and sacred one. Every officer and soldier is a citizen who, of his own accord, chooses to bear arms for a period, either in defense of his country or to prolong peace by enabling the Government to be prepared for war. The highest type of a patriotic citizen is the citizen soldier who, when he enters the service, is prepared, if need be, to give his life for his country.

In supplying the necessary increase in a permanent military establishment, and in effecting its thorough reorganization, I would urgently recommend that appointments of officers be made with a due regard for the principle of seniority, and that each case be passed upon by a board of the highest officers of the Army, as was done in the reorganization following the Civil War.

I will have the honor to submit a draft of a bill embodying my views and recommendations on army reorganization.

Very respectfully,

NELSON A. MILES,
Lieutenant-General.

The Secretary of War.

ANNUAL REPORT OF THE LIEUTENANT-GENERAL COMMANDING THE ARMY
Headquarters of the Army,
Washington, October 1, 1901.

. . .The act of Congress, approved February 2, 1901, authorized an increase in the enlisted strength of the line of the Army to 100,000 men, but owing to the cessation, to a great extent, of hostilities in the

Philippines it was found that that number would not be required, and by an order of the President dated May 8, 1901, the enlisted strength of the line was fixed at 74,504 men, with the addition of 2,783 men in the staff departments, etc. This aggregate does not include the Hospital Corps, which now comprised 4,300 men, or the Puerto Rico Provisional Regiment, whose present strength is 800.

The Army is now recruited to very nearly its full strength, and the following statement shows approximately the disposition of the force, including officers, at the present time:

Country.	Officers.	Enlisted Men.	Total
United States	1,922	31,952	33,874
Philippine Islands	1,111	42,128	43,239
Cuba	166	4,748	4,914
Puerto Rico	51	1,490	1,541
Hawaiian Islands	6	250	256
China	5	157	162
Alaska	17	510	527
Total	3,278	81,235	84,513

The above total includes 4,678 noncombatants, comprising chaplains, officers in the Medical Department, and the men in the Hospital Corps.

In addition to the figures above given, there are 4,973 native scouts, with 73 officers, employed in the Philippines, but their work is not strictly of a military character.

It is expected that the force in Cuba will be very much reduced in the near future and it is hoped that the force in the Philippines can also be very much reduced. It will, however, be necessary to occupy with military and naval forces for an indefinite time certain strategic positions in that archipelago.

The condition of the Indians in the past year has remained practically the same as during the preceding few years, and has been very satisfactory, no disturbances of any importance requiring the use of the troops having occurred. Still, there is no doubt that the presence of military stations within a reasonable distance of their reservations has had a restraining influence upon them. These stations will have to be maintained for some years to come or during the time that they are in a state of transition from a nomadic, uncivilized condition to that of a peaceful, industrious life.

Adequate military garrisons have been maintained adjacent to the Mexican and Canadian boundaries and have been available for assisting our civil authorities in maintaining law and order, thus contributing to the preservation of friendly relations between the governments of these countries and our own. . .

I would call especial attention to the effect of a portion of the army reorganization act pertaining to the artillery branch of the service, which does grave injustice to a large number of artillery officers. Owing to the unfortunate organization of the artillery that existed from 1866 to 1898, by which two first lieutenants were included in a battery instead of one, as in the case of a troop of cavalry and company of infantry, stagnation was caused in the promotions of officers of artillery. That condition of affairs was corrected by the act of Congress of 1898, and although by the recent act of Congress of February 2, 1901, the artillery arm was largely increased, yet a provision of that law suspended full promotion until the enlisted strength had been recruited up to the authorized limit, and most of the officers received their commissions several months after their juniors in the cavalry and infantry had been promoted over them. Thus officers who had rendered longer service were made relatively subordinate to officers who had been their juniors, in many cases by more than ten years, during their whole official lives. I earnestly recommend that this injustice be corrected, and that Congress be asked to authorize that the commissions of artillery officers covering promotions to fill vacancies caused by the said law shall bear date of February 2, 1901. This will give the artillery officers the relative rank to which they were entitled and of which they were inadvertently deprived.

I also call attention to what, in my judgment, is a defective organization of the artillery, namely, an Artillery Corps, which practically establishes another bureau in Washington. Nearly two years ago a bill was introduced in the Senate, not for the purpose of reorganizing the Army, but, as its title indicated, to increase the efficiency of the military establishment of the United States, the principal object being to readjust and improve the staff establishment and to make a necessary increase in the artillery force. As stated by me at the time, the question of organization was subordinate to that of increasing the strength of the artillery, which was then imperatively required. In that bill provision was made for a corps organization. This particular measure I did not consider advisable, but the other features of the bill I regarded as of absolute necessity. I am now more convinced than ever of the inadvisability of a corps organization, and believe that the regimental organization is far more desirable in every respect. The condition of the country, with its 4,000 miles of coast line, requires now an artillery force of 18,862 men, which in the near future may have to be increased. This force should constitute the grant reserve of the Army. A large force is necessary to perform the laborious work of keeping in order and handling the heavy, expensive machinery and ammunition at the artillery forts, yet it is quite unnecessary and inadvisable to keep a large body of troops for that duty alone. If this be all that is required of the artillery, a much smaller force of skilled artillerists with a corps of laborers would meet the requirements.

In my judgment it is highly important that this strong arm of the Government should at all times be maintained in the most effective condition possible, and though the principal duties of the men would be the manning, care, and preservation of the great coast defenses, they should at the same time, being armed with rifles and instructed and drilled in the use of them, be immediately available, in such strength as may be required, for service in case of any emergency that might arise demanding the use of a well-trained, disciplined body of troops. . .

Much has been said concerning the army canteen, which, when first established, was called the "amusement room," and afterwards the "post exchange." It was a place of amusement and recreation for the enlisted men, where they could enjoy reading books and papers, playing games, etc., and could purchase such refreshments, except liquors, as they desired. It was then an eminently successful institution and promoted the contentment and general welfare of the troops. Later, when what was known as the post traders' establishments were abolished, light wines and beers were authorized to be sold in the canteen. The Government has now by act of Congress prohibited the sale of intoxicating beverages in the canteen, and it is believed that no injury has resulted thereby and that the law has in the main been beneficial.

The Army is composed principally of young men who have not formed the habit of using liquor, and although the majority of the enlistments actually occur in large cities, as the recruiting offices are principally located there, a large percentage of the men come from homes in the country and small towns and villages in every part of the United States. The prediction that the change would prevent enlistments and increase desertions has not been fulfilled. Since the law was approved, namely, on February 2, 1901, the recruiting stations have been thronged with men seeking enlistment of the service, 25,944 men having enlisted since that date, and the percentage of desertions is now far less than in former years. Desertions most usually occur during the first six months of enlistment, and a much larger percentage of enlistments have been made during the past six months than heretofore. In many cases the men that have deserted belong to a class whose presence in the service was not desirable under any conditions, but whose real character was not known at the time of enlistment. . .

The discipline and efficiency of commands largely depend upon the commanding officer. An illustration of the excellent discipline, sobriety, and good order that may be maintained in a command is afforded by the fact that in the Fourteenth United States Infantry, under the command of Lieut. Col. William Quinton, while en route from Manila to Fort Snelling, Minn., covering a period of forty days, the men were orderly and soldierly in the extreme, and during the whole time of traveling by transport and rail there was but one case of drunkenness, although the men were subjected to every temptation, having been given three days' liberty while the transport was coaling at Nagasaki, and subsequently four days while the vessel remained at anchor at Yokahama, with permission also, to those who desired, to visit Tokio, [sic] the only condition imposed being that they should at all times respect their uniform, and hold it as sacred as they would the flag of their country. While going from San Francisco to Fort Snelling not a single case of a disciplinary measure was required, the behavior of the soldiers throughout being that of responsible, sober, respectable, self-respecting men. The commanding officer expressed regret, however, that civilian employees traveling on a Government conveyance and discharged soldiers still wearing the United States clothing did bring disgrace upon the service through the uniform which they wore. The above instance, like many others that could be given, illustrates the excellent conduct of the troops when under the command of an efficient, judicious officer.

Probably at no time in the history of the Army have there been so many men serving in their first enlistment as at the present time, and in many of the troops and companies it has been difficult to find experienced soldiers to fill the positions of noncommissioned officers. The Army is composed of men whose average age varies in different companies, in many from only 22 to 26 years, and they are, on the whole, men of fair education, intelligent, and in excellent physical condition. It is hoped and confidently believed that the zeal and loyal devotion to the service that is now being manifested on the part of all officers will in a short time render the Army as near perfection in point of discipline and efficiency as it is possible to attain. . .

During the past year a large number of officers have been appointed to the Army, a great many of whom had previously rendered efficient service with volunteer troops in active campaigning, but all have been required to pass a rigid examination demonstrating their eligibility for the military service.

While but little time has been found available during the past year for purely theoretical instruction, owing to the extra amount of duty, in addition to active service in the field, required of the officers in organizing, disciplining, and instructing the large number of new men in all organizations, yet the attention of department commanders has been called to the importance of a due proportion of theory, taught through the officers' lyceums, and they will carry forward this important branch of military education whenever possible.

War is now more than ever before a most progressive science, and armies require an educated, skilled, disciplined personnel having a thorough knowledge of the use of the most modern and destructive appliances of war, most of which were wholly unknown a generation ago. Four years ago we had a small but most efficient army of only 25,000 men, many of whom, with a majority of the officers, had been schooled in the military profession in the great Civil War, or by years of campaigning on our Western frontiers. Hence at the commencement of the war with Spain our Army, in point of experience, intelligence, efficiency, and physical excellence, was not excelled by any like body of troops in any army of the world. Since that time it has been put to the test over a wider field of duty than any army within my knowledge. From the rigorous climate of northern stations troops have been moved to tropical countries and there opposed to the trained troops of a European army, enduring great hardships and privations and suffering under the depressing and debilitating influence of an unhealthful clime; they have served in the difficult regions of the Philippines; they have borne our flag to the capital of the Chinese Empire; at the same time carrying on extensive explorations in the Arctic regions of Alaska—at all times and places exhibiting the most commendable fortitude and under all circumstances maintaining the honor and high character of the American Army. During this period many of our experienced officers and men have fallen in battle, have become disabled by wounds or disease incident to the service, or, from various causes, have been obliged to retire from active service. Their places have been filled by new men and a large number of new officers, yet I am gratified to say that the same high tone and character prevails in the Army to-day as in former years. By personal inspections of troops that have gone to and are now serving on stations beyond the sea, of those that have returned, and of those that have been added recently to the service, I am prepared to affirm that the personnel of the Army to-day is most satisfactory and creditable to the nation.

Owing to the sending of large military forces beyond the sea it has been necessary to very much reduce the force remaining in the United States; in fact, at times it has been reduced to less than two-thirds the strength of the Army which has been garrisoned in the United States during the last fifty years. The cost of maintaining such a large force at remote stations has been so great that adequate funds have not been afforded to keep the military stations in the United States in a perfect state of preservation, and now that a good portion of the Army has been returned, and more will be returned in the near future, there will be required additional appropriations and allotments to preserve the posts in proper order. . .

The important military stations in this country have been very much neglected, and the public buildings and works pertaining thereto are greatly in need of repair, and unless kept in proper order serious loss will result to the Government. I therefore recommend that liberal appropriations be made by Congress for this purpose, and that the money be allotted to the various departments in proportion to the needs of the troops stationed therein.

Very marked progress has been made in the last three years in equipping the coast defenses with modern high-power guns, and very expensive concrete fortifications, have been built. More than 400 modern guns have been mounted for the protection of our principal harbors, so that safety has been secured to a great extent so far as the fixed armament is concerned, yet the expenditure that has been made of $80,000,000 would be entirely useless unless suitable and ample ammunition is provided with which to destroy hostile fleets. I therefore earnestly recommend that Congress be asked to make appropriations to provide, in addition to the high-power guns, a suitable proportion of small-caliber rapid-fire guns, to constitute auxiliary batteries, and an ample amount of ammunition for the guns of all calibers in order to render them effective.

The Board of Ordnance and Fortification has during the past year made some important tests of war material and has developed the utility of new appliances. I heartily concur in its recommendation as to the importance of providing ammunition for the heavy batteries now established for the defense of our coasts.

While Congress has made ample provision for the management of military affairs in the organization of the Army, whereby the companies, regiments, brigades, divisions, and departments are made the units of administration, and by statute has clothed the officials not only with executive authority but with judicial powers and responsibility, yet the tendency has been to absorb and usurp the entire conduct of the military establishment in the city of Washington and especially in the staff departments. This has been found most injurious in other armies, and is one of the principal defects in our own system. The evil has been increasing during the activities of the wars of the last three years to an extent that, in my judgment, requires serious consideration, and I recommend that decentralization be effected as far as possible, and that all proper and lawful authority be restored to subordinate commanders who are provided with an efficient organization and who can be safely intrusted with responsibility for the efficient and faithful administration of military affairs commensurate with their important commands.

I again renew the recommendations I have made concerning the granting of commissions and discharge to meritorious noncommissioned officers after five years' service who are not eligible for a permanent appointment in the Army by reason of age or other causes, and who shall successfully pass a required examination, as an encouragement and just recognition of their merits and services.

I again call attention to the unhealthful and unsightly condition of the grounds on the west side of the city of Washington, adjacent to the Potomac River, known as the Potomac Flats, and renew the recommendation made in my last annual report. . .

For many years there has been maintained a military garrison at Washington composed of light artillery and infantry or heavy artillery. The advisability of such a measure can not be questioned. Such a force should be within or near the national capital and not separate from it by a river, the crossing of which is liable to be rendered impossible. By a recent order a detachment of the Corps of Engineers has been directed to be stationed at Washington Barracks and all other troops removed. If this is to prevail, then I recommend that a suitable site be secured within a few miles of the city of Washington and on the left bank of the Potomac, either within the district boundaries or in the State of Maryland, where a proper garrison of infantry and artillery can be maintained.

I invite attention to the reference in my last annual report to the heroic conduct of the Ninth United States Infantry at the battle of Tientsin, where the regiment, under its able commanders, sustained severe loss. I recommend that ample recognition be given the officers and men engaged in that battle for their gallant services, especially Maj. Jesse M. Lee (now lieutenant-colonel Sixth Infantry), upon whom the command devolved after the death of Colonel Liscum. Colonel Lee's distinguished gallantry and ability on that occasion have been recognized by foreign officers present in that campaign, and he fully sustained the reputation he had maintained during the Civil War and since.

During the past year attention has been given to the re-establishment and improvement of the service schools at Fort Monroe and Fort Riley, and it is expected that the one at Fort Leavenworth will soon be reestablished.

As a large portion of the Army has been stationed in the western portion of the United States, and over one-half of it is now occupied west of the Pacific Ocean, I recommend that a military school be established on the Pacific coast, preferably in southern California, similar in character to those above mentioned and suitable for the instruction of officers in the duties pertaining to the staff corps and departments, and the engineer, cavalry, artillery, and infantry arm of the service.

I also recommend the establishment of a war college at the seat of government in the city of Washington.

Very respectfully,   NELSON A. MILES,
                                                Lieutenant-General.

The Secretary of War.

ANNUAL REPORT OF THE LIEUTENANT-GENERAL COMMANDING THE ARMY
Headquarters of the Army,
Washington, September 23, 1902.

During the past year there have been no serious engagements, except that of the troops under Gen. Frank D. Baldwin, in Mindanao, P.I., with the Moros. For the number of men engaged this was a very spirited and desperate engagement. Our forces were commanded by one of the most experienced and efficient officers of the Army, whose record has always been of the highest order, and his achievement, together with that of the troops, in this engagement, made another chapter of fortitude, tenacity, and heroic sacrifice in the history of American arms.

In the first paragraph of his report, Major-General Brooke alludes to a subject that has been referred to in several communications, and on which, in my opinion, requires attention and readjustment, namely, the geographical limits of the departments. It will be observed that the Department of the East embraces not only the troops on the entire Atlantic coast and part of the Gulf coast, but also a large number stationed in the interior, as well as those located in Cuba and Puerto Rico while two other departments include principally only the troops located in single States. It must be apparent that this is out of proper proportion and not adapted to the best administration of military affairs.

I concur in the recommendations contained in the reports of Major-Generals Brooke and MacArthur, and invite special attention to the report of Major-General Hughes, wherein he refers to the condition of Fort Rosecrans, Cal., in the following language:

"An entire post for two companies of coast artillery, and the usual buildings for the noncommissioned staff, administration, etc. are required. The batteries located there are in condition for service, and shelter for troops is greatly needed."

Also to his report on the condition of Bonita Point, Cal. (Lime Point Reservation), as to which he uses the following language:

At this place the work of the engineers is approaching completion, and nothing has been done as yet looking to the housing of a garrison. The setting up of the mounts of the high-power guns is going on, and the auxiliary batteries are approaching completion, and it is very desirable that provisions be made for an artillery command in the vicinity to secure proper care and attention for this expensive material.

This subject is especially deserving of early consideration, as the local conditions would render life under canvas on the storm-swept point very objectionable.

These remarks of the department commander simply illustrate the urgent and imperative necessity of having buildings properly constructed to shelter the garrisons when the engineers have completed the fortifications and the Ordnance Department has supplied the guns for these expensive coast defenses.

The same condition exists in the Department of the Columbia, where three companies of artillery are now in tents and some of the officers living in huts not suitable to shelter public animals. Of course, this is discouraging to the troops, injurious to the health of the garrisons, and no doubt is the cause of some desertions; and I would call attention to the fact that hundreds of thousands of dollars are being used, especially for cavalry, while a very small amount is being used to afford shelter to the artillery exposed to the severe climates along the Atlantic, Pacific, and Gulf coasts. These troops are required to be located adjacent to the fortifications, notwithstanding the exposed position of many of them, and I see no reason why buildings should not be properly constructed in time to be occupied, when it is known for years exactly where and when they will be required.

I believe it would be advisable to divide the appropriations made by Congress for military buildings and grounds and for transportation between the geographical departments in proportion to the number of troops in each, the same to be used to construct and keep in order the necessary public buildings under the excellent system that formerly prevailed.

I also call attention to the incomplete condition of the fortifications, especially on the Pacific coast, where millions have been expended in engineering and ordnance work, and yet the commands have not been properly supplied with ammunition, electrical plants, and other appliances essential to the effective use of these fortifications in actual warfare.

The senior officers of the Army composing the board convened by order of the Secretary of War to report upon the retention, location, or abandonment of certain military posts in the United States, gave the subject great care, according to their best judgment and long experience. They took into consideration the strategic advantages of the stations that they recommended retained, and of the additional ones that they recommended to be established, and I recommend that their report be adhered to in the disposition of the different arms of the service.

The withdrawal of the troops from Cuba, the reduction of the garrison in Puerto Rico to the minimum, and the reduction by at least one-half in the number of troops serving in the Philippine Islands, render it necessary to provide additional accomodations for the shelter of troops that are required to be stationed within the United States, and the appropriation for the next year should be largely increased.

The condition of the Indians is quite satisfactory, and there has been no disturbance of importance among them during the last twelve months. This is accounted for principally by three reasons: first, just and humane treatment of the Indians and the judicious management of their affairs; second, their gradual transition from a condition of barbarism to that of a semi-civilized people; and third, the close proximity of the military garrisons, which are always available in case of threatened disturbance.

The experience during the great Civil War, and years of campaigning along our Western frontier, afforded the best schools of practice for our Army in former years. The attention given to calisthenics and gymnastic and military exercises made our small Army a corps of athletes, while the elementary schools established for enlisted men, the post libraries, the post lyceums and officers' schools, the various schools of instruction and practice for officers, as well as the Military Academy, produced an army of such excellence that I was able in my annual report for 1896 to state: "The personnel of the Army was never in better condition."

This was proven to be true by the fortitude, skill, and heroism displayed in every serious campaign on every field of mortal combat wherever the Army has been engaged in any part of the world during the last four years. During that time changes have occurred, and the Army has been very largely increased. The long and varied service of the senior officers, their experience in organizing, disciplining, instructing, and leading their commands, as well as the excellent discipline, instruction, and exemplary conduct of the soldiers of the Army of '98, have been the leaven of the Army of the present time. Evils may creep into any system or great organization. Such as have affected our Army have been or will be eradicated.

The Army has maintained its character for more than a hundred years with great credit to itself and honor to the nation; and the same rules of rigid integrity, of honor, impartial and exact justice to all, and proper recognition of faithful, valuable, and distinguished services that have prevailed in the past are the only ones by which it can be sustained in the future.

As our Government is different in character from any of the great powers of the world, our Army must necessarily be unlike in some respects other great armies.

It has been my endeavor, in general orders and in other ways, to impress upon all that their devotion to the principles of our Government was of the first and highest importance.

Very respectfully,

NELSON A. MILES,
Lieutenant-General.

The Secretary of War.

General Orders, No. 116.
Headquarters of the Army,
Washington, August 5, 1903.

In accordance with the provisions of the act of Congress of June 30, 1882, the undersigned will retire from the active service August 8, 1903.

In relinquishing the command of the Army of the United States, to which he was assigned by the President October 2, 1895, he hereby acknowledges his appreciation of the fidelity manifested by the officers and soldiers during the past eventful years.

To those who were his companions and associates during one of the greatest of all wars he takes pleasure in expressing his gratification that they have lived through the trials and dangers of long service to witness the results of their fortitude, heroism, and unselfish devotion to the welfare of their country. They have also in a most commendable manner exemplified to the younger generation of soldiers those principles of discipline and patriotism which make the Army the protector and defender, and never the menace, of the nation and its liberties.

The time and occasion are considered opportune for expressing to the Army a few thoughts concerning its past and that which may affect its future welfare. It is from the best impressions and influences of the past that the most desirable results may be realized in the future.

Unswerving devotion to our Government and the principles upon which it was established and has been maintained is essential to the efficiency of the national forces, and especially is this so in a democratic government where the individual, in order to be perfect soldier, must first be a true citizen. The boast that every soldier of a great nation carried a marshal's baton in his knapsack is in a higher sense more than equaled in significance by the fact that every American soldier personifies sovereign citizenship and may by his own conduct exemplify impartial justice to those who have never experienced it, and the results of the highest liberty to those who have been strangers to it, thereby aiding to secure for his country a moral influence not otherwise attainable.

During the darkest hour of our history the first commander of the American forces demonstrated the grandeur and nobility of his character by combating the evil influences then pervading the Army and by manifesting the strongest confidence and faith in the ultimate justice and integrity of his government. His words of wisdom uttered at Newburg one hundred and twenty years ago had the effect of inspiring "unexampled patriotism and patient virtue, rising superior to the pressure of the most complicated sufferings." It is one of the glories of our country that the Army has maintained those principles for more than a century.

The commanders of the Army succeeding Washington have by their example, influence, and orders engendered and maintained the highest degree of efficiency, discipline, and patriotism.

Since its organization the Army has been charged with a great variety of responsibilities, all subordinate to defending the country and maintaining the rights of its citizens.

In the discharge of its manifold duties the Army has confronted enemies representing every stage of human development from the highest civilization yet obtained to savagery and barbarism. It has ever been its duty to observe in war those chivalric and humane principles by which inevitable horrors are so greatly mitigated, while by unyielding prosecution of warfare against armed forces its valor has been demonstrated.

All honorable activity and life for the Army must exist within the well-defined lines of patriotism, untarnished honor, sterling integrity, impartial justice, obedience to rightful authority, and incessant warfare against armed enemies. Always to maintain truth, honor, and justice requires the highest moral courage, and is equally as important as fortitude in battle. Drill, discipline, and instruction are but preparatory for the perfection and efficiency of an army.

The events of recent years have placed upon the Army a new obligation and an opportunity for a broader exemplification of its country's principles. The United States Army is now brought into daily communication with millions of people to whom its individual members of every grade are the exponents of American civilization. A serious duty and a great honor are now presented to every officer and soldier—namely, to exemplify to those with whom he comes in contact our country's principles of equal and exact justice, immunity from violence, equality before the law, and the peaceful use and possession of his own.

Marked changes at different times have occurred in the strength and organization of the Army, resulting from diverse influences, and various experiments have been tried. Time has rectified errors in the past, and will do in the future. The Lieutenant-General has faith that under all circumstances the Army will maintain its high character, and that its future will be as honorable and glorious as has been its history in the past. His earnest solicitude and best wishes will ever follow the fortunes of the Army.

NELSON A. MILES,
Lieutenant-General, Commanding.

General Miles delighted in Military Pomp and Ceremony, and participated in such functions well into his eighties. At left, he takes part in the dedication of the Amphitheater at Arlington National Cemetery on May 15, 1920. Below, Miles prepares to lead a Veteran's Day parade on the Elipse in Washington at age 82.
Courtesy, National Archives

Epilogue

If anyone hoped the retired Lieutenant General would be content to "fade away," they were sadly disappointed. Nelson Miles devoted the 22 years remaining to him to the writing of *Serving the Republic* (1911), a book based upon a series of articles he wrote for *Cosmopolitan* magazine titled "My Forty Years of Fighting," and to a number of patriotic and veterans associations. He became a fixture in Washington society, a gray-haired cantankerous old man in dark suit and broad-brimmed western hat who persisted in trotting his thoroughbreds amidst automobiles, though he did own a "horseless carriage" which he drove none too expertly.

Just one year after his retirement the General lost his wife. On August 1, 1904, Mrs. Miles died suddenly at West Point, N.Y., while visiting her son Sherman, a cadet at the Military Academy. For several years she had been plagued with heart trouble, and had been stricken with at least two heart attacks, the first coming as she climbed the steps to an elevated train station in New York City. She was confined to her bed for much of the Spring, but seemed well enough to make the trip to West Point. After services at the Military Academy Chapel her body was taken to Washington and interred in the recently completed Miles mausoleum in Arlington National Cemetery.

By 1906 Miles had recovered sufficiently from his bereavement to ask his recently widowed friend, General Anson Mills, to accompany him on a European vacation. The two old soldiers spent two months touring France, Switzerland, Ireland, Scotland and England. They traveled much of the time in an automobile, chauffered by Miles' brother-in-law Colgate Hoyt, President of the American Automobile Association. In following years Miles made several more trips to Europe.

Miles' dignified fortitude in the face of personal tragedy was strikingly exemplified on February 22, 1912. Alerted by a telephone call that his 85-year-old brother, Daniel, had collapsed from a heart attack while walking through Lafayette Park, the General raced to the scene, only to find that his brother was dead. Rejecting the assistance of his chauffeur and of sympathetic bystanders, Miles lifted his brother's lifeless body from the ground and carried him to the waiting automobile. Several in the crowd were moved to tears at the sight.

In 1912 the General purchased his farmhouse birthplace in Westminster, Mass., and for a time raised dogs and cattle for show at local competitions and fairs. Though most of the work was done by live-in caretakers, Nathan and Celina Howard, Miles made yearly visits until economic considerations forced him to part with the property. The Howards' daughter, Barbara, recalled that the General periodically asked her mother to brew a pot of sage tea—not to drink, but for use as a tonic for his thinning gray hair.[287]

In September 1913 he mounted an unsuccessful campaign for the Republican nomination in the Third Massachusetts Congressional District.

Miles was never entirely removed from military affairs. From June to August 1913 he was one of a group of foreign military observers of the Balkan Wars, and came under fire during the Turkish attack on Sofia, Bulgaria. In 1916 he presided over the Medal of Honor Board, reviewing the merits of past recipients of the nation's highest award. At age 77, still vigorous and itching for a fight, he applied for active duty upon America's entry into World War I. Much to his chagrin, he was rejected. When he learned that a contingent of U.S. troops was being sent to Siberia to aid the White Russian forces in their struggle against the Bolsheviks, he lobbied for command of the expedition. He noted his own extensive experience in winter campaigning on the plains, and his trans-Siberian journey of 1902. Again, he was politely refused.

The retired General spent most of the year in Washington, D.C He had moved from his large home on N Street to an apartment in the Army-Navy Club, and, shortly before his death, to The Rochambeau apartments. Golf became a favorite pastime, and the mustached old gentleman clad in plaid stockings and tam-o-shanter, could often be seen walking the links of local country

---

[287]"Reminiscences of Barbara Howard Morse," Westminster, Mass. Historical Society.

Miles leaving the White House, circa 1924
Courtesy of John M. Carroll

clubs. Whenever military ceremony was the order of the day, as in the celebrations following the end of World War I, or the dedication of the Amphitheater at Arlington Cemetery, General Miles was certain to make an appearance. Without fail, he turned out in the elaborate uniform of General-in-Chief, which seemed to accumulate baubles and braid as he grew older. In the 1919 victory parade he insisted on marching down Pennsylvania Avenue with the Medal of Honor contingent; he collapsed from exhaustion at the foot of Capitol Hill. In 1922 he was named Grand Marshal of the ceremonies attending the dedication of the statue of General Grant. Just prior to the event he was stricken with double pneumonia, but rose from his sickbed, telling a worried aide, "I will lead or bust. Young man, you don't know me. Why, twice I was 'mortally' wounded in the Civil War, yet here I am. You may expect me to be on hand the day of the parade."[288] He was only prevented from attending when worried relatives and friends conspired to hide all his uniforms.

In March 1925, two months before his death, the 85-year-old General had one more moment in the limelight. Testifying before a Congressional Committee investigating the controversial exponent of military aviation, General Billy Mitchell, Miles took a characteristically outspoken stance — in Mitchell's behalf. The elderly veteran of the Civil War made it quite clear that he was a convert to the importance of aviation in military preparedness.

On Friday, May 15, 1925, General Miles accompanied his Reber and Miles grandchildren to the Ringling Brothers, Barnum & Bailey Circus in downtown Washington. With them went Mrs. W.B. Noble, whose daughter had married Sherman Miles. As the band played the National Anthem, the General stood in salute, then fell over backwards nearly into the arms of a local doctor. He was carried from the tent, virtually unnoticed by the crowd, which included the wife of President Coolidge and other notables. He was dead of a massive heart attack before he reached the hospital, three months short of his eighty-sixth birthday. Of all the Union generals of the Civil War only two, John R. Brooke and Adelbert Ames, survived him.

---

[288] *The Evening Star*, Washington, D.C., May 16, 1925.
[289] *The Evening Star*, May 17, 1925.

Eulogized by President Coolidge, and by General John J. Pershing, who said of his old chief, "he was the idol of all who were associated with him,"[289] Miles' funeral was replete with the pomp and ceremony in which he delighted. From St. John's Church, near the White House, a large detachment of soldiers escorted the caisson bearing his remains across Memorial Bridge to Arlington Cemetery. There, clad in the full uniform of Lieutenant General, he was laid to rest beside his wife in the family mausoleum. It stands proudly on a hill crest, as the General stands proudly in the ranks of American soldiers.

Index